MARITIME POWER BUILDING

New 'Mantra' for China's Rise

MARITIME POWER BUILDING

New 'Mantra' for China's Rise

Editors

Kamlesh K Agnihotri
Gurpreet S Khurana

Foreword by

Admiral Sureesh Mehta PVSM, AVSM (Retd.)
Former Chief of the Naval Staff
Former High Commissioner of India to New Zealand
Chairman, National Maritime Foundation

National Maritime Foundation

PENTAGON PRESS

Maritime Power Building: New 'Mantra' for China's Rise
Kamlesh K Agnihotri and Gurpreet S Khurana (Editors)

First Published in 2015

ISBN 978-81-8274-819-4

Published by
PENTAGON PRESS
206, Peacock Lane, Shahpur Jat,
New Delhi-110049
Phones: 011-64706243, 26491568
Telefax: 011-26490600
email: rajan@pentagonpress.in
website: www.pentagonpress.in

Branch:

Flat No.213, Athena-2,
Clover Acropolis,
Viman Nagar,
Pune-411014
Email: pentagonpresspune@gmail.com

Printed at Aegean Offset Printers, Greater Noida

Contents

Foreword *vii*

Preface *xi*

Abbreviations *xiii*

Contributors *xvii*

1. Maritime Power Building: New 'Mantra' for China's Rise 1
Admiral Arun Prakash (Retd.)

2. China as a Maritime Power 10
Rear Admiral Michael McDevitt (Retd.)

3. PLA Navy in 'Military Operations other than War' and Diplomacy Roles 24
Commander Kamlesh K Agnihotri

4. The Evolution of Chinese Maritime Strategy: The Continental Roots of China's Maritime Expansion 35
Dr. Murray Scot Tanner

5. 'String of Pearls' and Beyond: Chinese Influence in South Asian Littoral 47
Commander Raghavendra Mishra

6. Prospects of PLA Navy's Presence in the IOR and Impact on Regional Dynamics 70
Captain Gurpreet S Khurana

7. Maritime Infrastructure-Building: Complementary Endeavours Towards Maritime Powerhood 86
Captain Peter Swartz (Retd.)

8. Chinese Shipbuilding Capabilities 98
Rear Admiral MK Badhwar (Retd.) and Captain Pramod R Kulkarni

9. Polar Security Issues: An American Perspective 114
Captain Mark E. Rosen, JAGC, USN (Retd.)

10. Dynamics of Diplomatic and Security Developments in South China Sea 134
Prof. Chintamani Mahapatra

11. China's Coast Guard: Implications for Maritime Disputes 145
Dr. Gerald Meyerle

12. Geopolitics of Deep-Sea Mining and China 154
Dr. Sunil Kumar Agarwal

Index 173

Foreword

The fast paced economic ascendency of China in the course of a little more than the last two decades plus, has become the highlight of animated discussions and debates at diverse forums internationally. The global strategic community, in the recent past, has also witnessed the veering of such discourse to the new and emerging security challenges in the Indian Ocean Region and its littoral, should the Chinese Comprehensive National Power (CNP) seek to expand its scope of influence in this region. Interestingly, a sub-theme that has been emerging with absolute consistency in all these interactions is the fast-paced modernization of the Chinese Navy; its trajectory towards eventual strategic expansion into the Indian Ocean Region, and the likely implications of such a presence for regional stability. The research community at the National Maritime Foundation (NMF) is, therefore, of the firm viewpoint that maritime security matters, irrespective of the forum or locale, cannot be comprehensively discussed unless China as the proverbial 'elephant in the room', and relevant aspects associated with it, are addressed in a holistic manner. In this context, it would definitely be in order to carry out a brief survey of the entire spectrum of maritime activities that China is currently engaged in.

Since enough literature is available on the modernization efforts of the PLA Navy and consequent expansion of its role, it should suffice to let the issue rest at this point by just quoting one set of statistics. In the year 2013, 17 indigenously built warships comprising new type destroyers, stealth frigates, first line ASW corvettes, replenishment ships, and mine sweepers were inducted into the PLA Navy – four in one North Sea Fleet, six in East Sea Fleet and seven in South Sea Fleet. The year 2013 can also be termed as specifically focused towards maritime matters as one of the most vital reforms, the creation of the Chinese Coast Guard was accomplished by merging four maritime law enforcement agencies of the State. Prior to this restructuring, the PLA Navy, which is primarily meant for tackling the traditional threats and challenges to national sovereignty, was increasingly being drawn into policing, and law and order roles. Moreover, the real foreign policy danger emanated from the act of employing conventional naval capability to resolve low-level security challenges, which had connotations of escalating the situation to a level far in excess of situational demand. The newly formed Coast Guard is now able to offer calibrated responses to various degrees of challenges posed in the maritime domain, while relieving the PLA Navy for a more traditional role of war-fighting.

Concurrently, maritime infrastructure development has been fast-tracked to the extent that it is equated with nation-building. The underlying vision, of course, was that it would ultimately create the necessary wherewithal for wholesome exploitation of the maritime domain. Three of the most important aspects of the maritime infrastructure building process relate to ship-building, port development, and the creation of a deep sea scientific research facility. The ship-building reforms initiated in 1982, which went on to propel China into becoming the leading commercial ship-builder in 2010, have had positive spin-offs in the naval and specialized ship construction too. The resultant accretion in the Chinese maritime assets and platforms, cutting across various functions and roles, is more than evident in the current period. These assets range from oceanographic research vessels, deep-sea manned submersibles, maritime surveillance and patrol ships, ice breakers, ultra-deepwater rigs, submarine rescue ships, diving support vessels, and even an underwater archaeology vessel. Port development in China has been accelerated so as to keep pace with the leap-frogging trade flows. In 2013, seven Chinese ports figured in the global top 10 container ports, in terms of throughput in millions of Tonne Equivalent Units (TEUs). Just to put this achievement in perspective, only one Indian Port figures in global top 50, with JNPT near Mumbai taking up the 32nd spot. A large deep-sea scientific research base is being built near Qingdao. It will act as a centralized national facility for harnessing ocean resources and providing scientific know-how, specialized equipment and vertically skilled manpower for deep sea scientific research.

So what has all this maritime capacity building led to? The increase in Chinese maritime activities all across the globe is more than visible. Incidentally, these all are in addition to the activities of the PLA Navy, which are progressing separately in hyper-drive mode. It may be noted that in one particular time-period in September 2013, there were 17 PLA Navy warships on distant area deployments, in addition to the routine activities being undertaken by the three Chinese Fleets in the vicinity of its coast. Similar deployment pattern was observed in the month of June 2014, which also included four PLA Navy ships' participation in the RIMPAC multinational exercise at Hawaii.

China has been achieving great breakthroughs in deep sea exploration activities in all three Oceans since 2005. In acknowledgement of the Chinese track record in this highly complex field, the International Seabed Authority (ISBA) approved the Chinese bid for under-sea exploration in 10,000 square kilometers in the Southwest Indian Ocean Ridge (SWIR) in 2011. Concurrently, the Chinese 'manned submersible' has set a world record by carrying out the deepest sea dive yet, going down beyond 7000 meters. These two complementary activities, when centrally steered by the specialized deep-sea scientific research base (which has earlier been referred to), will propel China into the top few nations possessing deep sea research capacities, and leveraging the same for appropriate benefits. The Chinese telemetry and satellite tracking ships are continuously deployed in remote locations across the globe to support its robust space vehicles launch programme. With the stated launch rate of more than 100 satellites in the current five-year plan period, these ships are indeed quite busy.

The Chinese Arctic and Antarctic expeditions are progressively becoming more frequent and expanding in scope and content. China has conducted five Arctic research expeditions in recent years, with the last one in 2012, achieving the first sailing through the Arctic Northern Sea Route and back. 28 expeditions to the Antarctic have been launched till date. Four research stations have been set up there, with the latest one being established in the last expedition in 2014. The Chinese maritime survey and patrol fleets, having seen bulk induction of platforms, have been documenting and protecting their expansive maritime claims with renewed vigour. China has, in fact, managed to mount continuous surveillance and offensive patrol with two to three ships around each of the hotly disputed territories and contentious maritime zones like the Senkakus in East China Sea; and the Scarborough and Second Thomas shoals in the South China Seas.

This brief survey of the Chinese maritime activities is not comprehensive by any means and can be considered to be purely indicative at best. Nevertheless, it provides a window for the global community to peep through and get a clear sense of the purpose, directivity and fastidiousness with which the Chinese are proceeding towards holistic interaction with the maritime environment. In fact, one would not be much off the mark in surmising that Beijing, though convinced about its 'national defence forces' being of prime importance for safeguarding its maritime sovereignty, has come around to believe that China cannot become a maritime power by concentrating on this facet alone, to the neglect of the other building blocks. Hence, comprehensive understanding of broad-spectrum maritime environmental elements through patient, painstaking and persistent research, capacity-building and sustainable strategies would be required for that outcome.

This edited volume containing essays by some of the best known professional watchers of Chinese maritime security matters from India and the United States, and delves into most of the issues that have been flagged above in great depth and detail. The contents of this publication will surely facilitate the initiation of a much wider debate on the attendant and complementary issues of great relevance to the global strategic community. It is also hoped that this book will help catalyze a more robust institutional partnership between think tanks in India and the US, predicated on respective understanding and realistic assessment about the above Chinese '*Mantra*' towards great power status.

The next obvious step for the two countries should then be to look for ways and means to engage in synergistic and mutually beneficial cooperation, in addressing the challenges that may arise on account of this holistic Chinese maritime ascendancy, up-front. Evidently, that is what both countries and their maritime agencies must plan for, as prospective long-term partners.

October 30, 2014

Admiral Sureesh Mehta PVSM, AVSM (Retd.)
Former Chief of the Naval Staff
Former High Commissioner of India to New Zealand
Chairman, National Maritime Foundation

Preface

Since the commencement of the new millennium, the increased focus on the modernization of the Chinese Navy, as part of the overall defense forces modernization, has been a much debated subject globally. While the advancements in the capacities and the capabilities of the Chinese Navy are quite visible, obvious, and of vital importance, the strength of the naval forces alone does not and cannot ensure the rise of a nation to a great power status. The sea has to be comprehensively understood, and then explored, as a medium of immense economic, scientific, political, social and military potential, so as to be a contributory factor in the building of a Comprehensive National Power (CNP). However, this requires requisite foundation blocks to be painstakingly placed in position with due diligence, so as to create an appropriate environment for facilitating the nation to 'pull together' towards maritime super power status.

China has, of late, comprehended this maxim in its totality and has initiated activities towards realization of this vision. The former Chinese President, Hu Jintao, during his keynote address at the November 2012 National Party Congress called for 'enhancing the Chinese capacity for exploiting marine resources, resolutely safeguarding China's maritime rights and interests, and building China into a maritime power'. These comments are particularly significant as it is the first time that a leader has clearly enunciated a decisive road map for maritime development in a Party Congress. The public discourse also noted that the total output value of China's marine-based industries was 3.2 trillion Yuan ($508 billion) in 2009, accounting for 9.5 percent of the country's GDP. Hence China's economy relied heavily on marine resources and trouble-free shipping lanes. So, therefore, Beijing needed to build its naval power in order to protect and expand its national maritime rights and interests.

However, seen from a holistic perspective, the modernization of the Chinese Navy forms only a subset for exploiting the greater maritime domain. With its civilian maritime activities being indicative of maritime presence in all the three Oceans, including in the Arctic and the Antarctic, it may well be assumed that

Beijing has understood the '*mantra*' towards achieving great power status. The global community is possibly witness to the implementation of this Chinese path-breaking strategy. Once a certain level of maritime proficiency is achieved, it is posited that the capabilities of the Chinese Navy – the sword arm of the maritime domain – could then be best leveraged in support of the national aims and objectives to consolidate Chinese influences, interests and stakes in the greater maritime domain.

There has thus been an acute and inescapable need felt for investigating various facets of Beijing's maritime endeavours – largely being viewed as vital instruments for facilitating super power status – for some time past. The National Maritime Foundation could localize this important – though not widely studied – aspect of the Chinese growth story through sustained data mining, collection and collation by its 'China Cell', so as to get a broad sense of the direction towards which Beijing was headed. However the proverbial 'straws in the wind' needed to be further probed holistically for arriving at specific conclusions. Accordingly and after much deliberation, NMF decided to address the issue up-front, by embarking on the publication of an edited volume, to bring the Chinese maritime ascendency endeavours to the centre-stage.

The Foundation, however, recognized the fact that this exercise could not yield the desired outcome when attempted in isolation. It was therefore decided to co-opt the Center for Naval Analyses, a Washington-based maritime think tank for sharing in-depth knowledge and gaining synergistic perspective between India and the United States of America (the US). Subject experts of the two think tanks got together to investigate various multi-faceted developments in the larger Chinese maritime environment, generally focusing on the Indo-Pacific, though not limited in any manner to the regional level only. In addition, detailed contributions of the maritime community, strategists, naval professionals and international relations experts of both, the US and India also enabled greater understanding of the challenges which the extended Indo-Pacific region would have to face on account of China's rise as a maritime power.

Their well-researched essays have finally resulted in the compilation of this book, appropriately titled **Maritime Power Building: New 'Mantra' for China's Rise** which contains twelve selected works covering the entire spectrum of the leap-frogging Chinese maritime bandwagon. It is sincerely hoped that the book will be a source of professional guidance to the serious China maritime watchers, and the global public at large.

October 30, 2014

Kamlesh K Agnihotri
Gurpreet S Khurana

Abbreviations

ADIZ	Air Defence Identification Zone
ADMM+	ASEAN Defence Minister's Meeting Plus
ASBM	Anti Ship Ballistic Missile
ASW	Anti Submarine Warfare
CATOBAR	Catapult Assisted take-off but Arrested Recovery
CCAMLR	Commission for the Conservation of Antarctic Marine Living Resources
CCCC	China Communications Construction Company
CCG	Chinese Coast Guard
CCP	Chinese Communist Party
CCPB	Central Committee Political Bureau
CCS	Chinese Communist System
CCZ	Clarion Clipperton Zone
CDSM	China's Defence and Security Ministries
CIMA	China Institute for Maritime Affairs
CLCS	Commission of the Limits of the Continental Shelf
CMC	Chinese Central Military Commission
CMH	China's Maritime Heritage
CMS	China Marine Surveillance
CNP	Comprehensive National Power
CNPC	China National Petroleum Corporation
CNS	China's National Security
COA	Chinese Oceanographic Administration
COMRA	China Ocean Mineral Resources Research and Development Association

COSCO	China Ocean Shipping Company
CR	Cultural Revolution
CRS	Clarkson Research Services
CSIC	China Shipbuilding Industry Corporation
CSSC	China State Shipbuilding Corporation
DDG	Guided Missile Destroyers
DIME	Diplomatic Ideological Military and Economic
DoD	Department of Defence
DWF	Distant Water Fishing
DWP	Defence White Paper
DWT	Dead Weight Tonnage
EEZ	Exclusive Economic Zone
EU	European Union
FAC	Fast Attack Craft
FLEC	Fisheries Law Enforcement Command
GAC	General Administration of Customs
GDP	Gross Domestic Product
GLF	Great Leap Forward
HADR	Humanitarian Assistance and Disaster Relief
HRF	Heavy Rebuild Factory
IDP	Internally Displaced Person
IMO	International Maritime Organisation
IONS	Indian Ocean Naval Symposium
IOR	Indian Ocean Region
IOTE	Indian Ocean Trade and Energy
IRT	International Relations Theory
ISA or ISBA	International Seabed Authority
ISL	International Shipping Lanes
ITLOS	International Tribunal for the Law of the Sea
IUU (Fishing)	Illegal unreported and unregulated (fishing)
JNPT	Jawaharlal Nehru Port Trust
JT	Imperial Japanese Troops
LACM	Land Attack Cruise Missile

LCS	Long Cycle School
LHA	Landing Helicopter Assault
LNG	Liquefied Natural Gas
LPD	Landing Platform Dock
LTC	Legal and Technical Commission
MARIC	Marine Design and Research Institute of China
MDA	Maritime Domain Awareness
MDR	Maritime Diplomacy Route
MDV	Maritime Domain Vision
MET	Maritime Economic Trends
MOOTW	Military Operations Other Than War
MP	Maritime Power
MSA	Maritime Safety Administration
MSR	Maritime Silk Road
NATO	North Atlantic Treaty Organization
NCR	Nationalist Chinese Regime
NDF	National Defence Forces
NDRC	National Development and Reform Commission
NEO	Non Combatant Evacuation Operations
NOAA	National Oceanographic and Atmospheric Administration
NPC	National Party Congress
NRI	Naval Research Institute
NSR	Northern Sea Route
OAD	Offshore Active Defence
ONA	Office of Net Assessment
ONGC	Oil and Natural Gas Corporation
ONI	Office of Naval Intelligence
OPV	Offshore Patrol Vessels
OVL	ONGC Videsh Limited
PAC	Pakistan Aeronautical Complex
PAF	Philippines Armed Forces
PLA	People's Liberation Army
PLAAF	People's Liberation Army Air Force

PoK	Pakistan occupied Kashmir
PPP	Purchasing Power Parity
PRC	People's Republic of China
QIMG	Qingdao Institute of Marine Geology
RCS	Radar Cross Section
SAARC	South Asian Association for Regional Corporation
SAM	Surface to Air Missile
SAR	Specific Absorption Rate
SCSI	South China Sea Islands
SCTW	Standards for Training, Certification and Watch-keeping
SDARI	Ship Design and Research Institute
SLOC	Sea Line of Communications
SMS	Seafloor Massive Sulphides
SOA	State Oceanic Administration
SOLAS	Safety of Life at Sea
SP	Sea Power
SPDC	State Peace and Development Council
SWIR	Southwest Indian Ocean Ridge
SWOT	Strength, Weakness, Opportunities and Threats
SWPRS	Safeguard World Peace and Regional Stability
TEU	Twenty-foot Equivalent Unit
TIV	Trend Indicator Value
TIWTE	Tianjin Institute for Water Transport Engineering
UAV	Unmanned Aerial Vehicles
UNCLOS	United Nation Convention on the Law of the Sea
UNCTAD	United Nations Commission on Trade and Development
UNSC	United Nation Security Council
US	United States of America
USGS	US Geological Survey
UUVs	Unmanned Underwater Vehicles
VSTOL	Vertical or Short Takeoff and Landing
WMD	Weapons of Mass Destruction
WTO	World Trade Organisation

Contributors

Admiral (Retd.) Sureesh Mehta is the Chairman, National Maritime Foundation – an appointment he took over on January 18, 2012. The Admiral served as Chief of the Naval Staff from November 1, 2006 until August 31, 2009, and served concurrently as the Chairman, Chiefs of Staff Committee. After retirement, he was appointed as India's High Commissioner to New Zealand. Admiral Mehta is a naval aviator, has skippered INS Beas, INS Godavari and INS Garuda – the premier Naval Air Station of Indian Navy. His illustrious career saw him command the Western Fleet and the Indian Coast Guard. He also served as the Deputy Chief of the Naval Staff, Chief of Personnel and the Flag Officer Commanding-in-Chief of the Eastern Naval Command.

Admiral (Retd.) Arun Prakash was Chief of the Naval Staff of the Indian Navy from July 31, 2004 until October 2006. He was the first Commander-in-Chief of the newly created United Andaman & Nicobar Command. He specializes in aviation and saw combat over West Pakistan in the 1971 war wherein he was decorated for gallantry. He is a graduate of the US Naval War College. Post retirement, he writes and speaks on strategic and defense-related topics. He has published a compendium of speeches and writings on maritime and other issues entitled, *From the Crow's Nest*. He was instrumental in the creation of the National Maritime Foundation in 2004, and was its second Chairman from September 2008 until January 2012.

Rear Admiral (Retd.) Michael McDevitt, US Navy, is the Vice-President of the Centre for Naval Analyses. During his navy career, he has held four at-sea commands; including that of an Aircraft Carrier battle group. He was the Director of the East Asia Policy office for the Secretary of Defense during the George Bush Administration. He concluded his 34 years naval career as the Commandant of the National War College. He has a Masters Degree in American Diplomatic History from Georgetown University. He is also a graduate of the National War College, Washington DC. His personal expertise is on East Asia, and his most recent research focus has been the maritime dimension of China's national strategy.

Commander Kamlesh K Agnihotri is a qualified Gunnery and Missile specialist, and is presently working at the Indian Navy's Maritime Warfare Centre in the Eastern Naval Command, Visakhapatnam. He commanded a ship at the Andaman and Nicobar Islands. He has also qualified as a Remote Sensing and Photogrammetry expert. He has previously been appointed in the China Desk of the Army Headquarters, New Delhi; and worked as a Research Fellow at the China cell of the National Maritime Foundation, New Delhi. He has authored several articles and commentaries on security issues related to China. He has also presented many papers in India and abroad, including in the US, China and Singapore. He has co-edited two books titled '*Security Challenges Along the Indian Ocean Littoral: Indian and US Perspectives*' (2011) and '*Technological Developments in the Maritime Domain and their Strategic Implications in the Indian Ocean Region*' (2013) He has also contributed a chapter in each book. He has also acquired an Advanced Diploma in Chinese language in order to complement his research work. His email id is *kkumaragni@gmail.com.*

Dr. Murray Scot Tanner is a Senior Research Scientist in the China Studies Division at CNA. He has earlier served as Professor of Political Science at Western Michigan University, as Senior Political Scientist at the RAND Corporation, and as the Co-Chairman's Senior Staff Member for the Congressional-Executive Commission on China. Dr. Tanner received his Ph.D. from the University of Michigan. Some of his books and monographs are *Distracted Antagonists, Wary Partners: China and India Assess their Security Relations*; *China Confronts Afghan Drugs: Law Enforcement Views of the "Golden Crescent"*; *Chinese Economic Coercion against Taiwan: a Tricky Weapon to Use.*

Commander Raghavendra Mishra, a Research Fellow at the National Maritime Foundation, is a specialist in Anti Submarine Warfare besides being an Observer. He holds an M. Phil. in Defence and Strategic Studies and is pursuing his Doctorate from the Jawaharlal Nehru University, New Delhi. He has done a variety of appointments, mostly afloat besides two tenures at Naval Headquarters and a stint as Directing Staff at the Defence Services Staff College. He has commanded the premier frontline Sea King helicopter Squadron INAS 330 (Harpoons) and a mine countermeasure vessel. His research areas include emerging geo-strategic and doctrinal trends in the Indo-Pacific, international security, transformation in international relations and military history.

Captain Gurpreet S Khurana PhD, is a gunnery and missile specialist of the Indian Navy. Among his various staff and operational appointments, he has held the command of two warships, including the commissioning command of a Fast Attack Craft in the Andaman & Nicobar Islands (2002). During his Research Fellowship at IDSA from 2003 to 2008, he specialized in maritime security and China's maritime strategy, and authored a book titled '*Maritime Forces in Pursuit of National Security*' (2008). From 2009 to 2013, he served at the Navy's Maritime Doctrine & Concept Centre (MDCC). He was awarded the Navy Chief's Commendation for co-authoring the *Indian Maritime Doctrine*, 2009. At MDCC, he authored several documents on maritime strategy, naval operational concepts and the Navy's first ever handbook on 'Law of Maritime Operations'. He is presently the Executive Director of NMF.

Captain (Retd.) Peter Swartz is a Senior Strategic Analyst at CNA, specializing in the study and analysis of maritime strategy and naval operations. He has completed a study on the evolution of US maritime strategy since 1970, changes in global US fleet deployment policies since 1775, and reorganization of the staff of the US Navy Chief of Naval Operations. His service in the US Navy includes two tenures as a naval advisor to the Vietnamese Navy during the Vietnam War. He was Special Assistant to General Colin Powell, Chairman of the US Joint Chiefs of Staff, during the First Gulf War. He holds a BA from Brown University and advanced degrees from The Johns Hopkins School of International Studies and Columbia University.

Rear Admiral (Retd.) M.K. Badhwar is one of the most qualified shipbuilding professionals in the country with multifarious qualifications. He served in the Indian Navy for almost four decades before retiring in 2009 as Director General of Naval Designs. While in the Navy, he dealt with the whole spectrum of warship acquisition and upkeep issues, including design, overseeing construction, processing of financial sanctions, and management of shipbuilding budgets. He was also involved in the preparation of the 'Warship Building Procedure', an integral part of the Defence Procurement Procedure (DPP), from its very inception. Post retirement, he was the Chief Operating Officer, Strategic Business with Pipavav Defence & Offshore Engineering Company Ltd, India's largest private shipyard.

Captain P.R. Kulkarni belongs to the Corps of Naval Constructors of the Indian Navy and presently heads the Naval Construction Wing, Department of Applied Mechanics at Indian Institute of Technology, Delhi. He is a post graduate in Naval Architecture from University College London, and holds a PhD from IIT Delhi and MMS from Osmania University, Hyderabad. He has served onboard Indian naval ships, Naval Dockyards, Warship Overseeing Team, Mumbai and Directorate of Naval Design. His fields of interest include Warship Design, Ship Hydrodynamics, Ship Dynamics, Ship Aerodynamics and Computational Fluid Dynamics. He has authored over 20 publications in reputed International Journals and presented technical papers at Conferences. He is also teaching and researching the subject of Warship Design at IIT Delhi.

Mr. Mark E. Rosen is a retired Navy Captain (JAGC) and an international and national security lawyer. He is presently the VP and Deputy General Counsel at CNA Corporation, wherein he provides corporate law support to CNA on a variety of ethics, government contracts, intellectual property and regulatory matters including export compliance. He has authored numerous international and operational law studies for various clients including the US Navy, the National Reconnaissance Organization, the State Department and the National Academy of Sciences. His particular expertise is in the maritime field including boundary and maritime disputes, piracy, law enforcement and maritime confidence building measures. He has recently authored analyses of the East China Sea for CSIS, conflicting claims in the Arctic (Stanford University-Hoover Institute), the Bay of Bengal, the Turkish Straits and the South China Sea (CNA).

Prof. Chintamani Mahapatra is currently Chairperson, Centre for Canadian, US & Latin American Studies at the School of International Studies of JNU. Recently, he was Tagore Chair Professor at Yunnan University of China. He has conducted research in several US Presidential Libraries and US National Archives; British Public Record Office in London. He has authored four books, one edited volume, and has contributed chapters to above 30 edited books. He has published above 70 research articles in reputed journals. He has been awarded a number of international fellowships, such as Fulbright Fellowship, Commonwealth Fellowship, and Visiting Fellowships to undertake research in the US, UK, Austria and Australia. He has been a visiting faculty in several UGC-run Academic Staff Colleges, the Foreign Service Institute of the Ministry of External Affairs, National Defense College, Army War College, Naval War College and the College of Air Warfare.

Dr. Gerald Meyerle is a Senior Research Scientist at CNA's Center for Strategic Studies. He has served as an advisor for military commands in Afghanistan at all levels and on policy reviews in Washington dealing with Pakistan and Afghanistan. He has published numerous reports and articles on these issues. He is currently working on nuclear weapons policy and US carrier strike group operations. In 2003-04, he was a David L. Boren Graduate Fellow in India. He has a PhD in political science and South Asian Studies from the University of Virginia.

Dr. Sunil Kumar Agarwal was an Associate Fellow at the National Maritime Foundation, New Delhi, wherein he was working on the issues related to the law of the sea. He has done his PhD in International Law from Jawaharlal Nehru University. He is also an alumni of the Hague Academy, Rhodes Academy and Xiamen Academy. He was a Nippon Fellow at the International Tribunal for the Law of the Sea (ITLOS) at Hamburg during 2009-10. He was also a Visiting Fellow at the British Institute for International and Comparative Law, London and Max Planck Institute for International, Law Heidelberg in 2009.

1

Maritime Power Building: New 'Mantra' for China's Rise

Admiral Arun Prakash (Retd.)

The Maritime Silk Road

The Chinese President, Xi Jinping, while speaking to the Indonesian Parliament in October 2013, had mooted a proposal for the establishment of a 'maritime silk road' which calls for China to work with ASEAN partners to develop maritime infrastructure, especially ports. The issue was brought into focus once again in Beijing in February 2014, during the Sri Lankan Foreign Minister's visit, and the bigger picture began to emerge.

A few years ago, a US firm of consultants, M/S Booz Allen Hamilton, coined the phrase 'String of pearls' which became a much-used cliché to describe Chinese investment in Indian Ocean ports as part of a larger, coherent strategy. By acquiring maritime footholds in Pakistan, Seychelles, Sri Lanka, Myanmar and Bangladesh, China was seen as creating a supporting network of facilities along its vulnerable sea-lanes of communication. China neither acknowledged the 'string of pearls' nor ever used this term. However, it seems to have gone a step further now by employing the historically evocative phrase 'maritime silk route' to push an even more ambitious maritime agenda of creating a linkage between China's interests in the Indian and Pacific Oceans.

It is obvious that domestic economic imperatives continue to focus attention of China's leadership on the security of sea-lanes that carry its trade and energy. However, even if the 'maritime silk road' is an exclusively economic strategy, it would have important strategic implications. A string of friendly ports in the Pacific would help it overcome the handicap posed by the first and second island chains. The commercial connotations of the 'silk road' would also help camouflage the hidden military agenda it may have in the disputed maritime regions of the East and South China Sea as well as the larger Indo-Pacific region.

This topic has been broached right at the start because it seems to carry a clear signal of intent from the highest levels of China's hierarchy. Doctrinally speaking, the Chinese are adhering to Admiral Mahan's prescription, which emphasizes that the importance of sea power lies in its ability to control sea lanes, as well as the critical geographical nodes that can facilitate or impede the flow of commercial and naval shipping. Mahan also saw the Indian and Pacific Oceans as the 'hinges of geo-political destiny', for they would allow a maritime nation to project power and affect political developments anywhere on the Eurasian landmass. This is obviously an end sought by China's leadership.

International Relations Theory

Whatever is true for China, is in some ways, true for India. A fellow Asian nation, India, is also rising economically and militarily; albeit on a much lower trajectory, and is trying to secure its maritime interests. In which case, is it appropriate for New Delhi to speculate, nervously, about Beijing's maritime plans and policies? The answer to this question is neither simple nor straightforward, and requires the attention to be drawn towards some facets of the International Relations theory.

First of all, the concept of neo-realism needs to be paid heed to. This conveys a clear warning that in an international system governed by anarchy, a State acts in pursuit of its self-interest, with the primary goal of ensuring its own security and survival. Obsession with security often makes States aggressive, and induces them to amass resources and power. Territorial expansion is only constrained by opposing power. Thus, security can become a zero-sum game in which relations between states are determined by their military, economic, and political capabilities.

Secondly, there is a general correlation between a State's hegemony – both political and economic – and its standing as either a *status quo* or a revisionist State. A *status quo* power will be satisfied with the existing international system, and seek to work within it, without challenging the current order. A revisionist state, on the other hand, would be primarily concerned with its own power and prestige above all other considerations, seeking to remodel the international system and order for its own benefit and in its own interests. The question uppermost in all minds is whether China is a *status quo* or a revisionist power. If a *status quo* power, and generally content with its place in the world order, China can be expected to rise peacefully and be a stabilizing influence. However, if China is revisionist, it will seek to change, if not overturn, the regional and world order; shaping it according to its vision. In this process, it could attempt to push its influence in the region, grab territory, rewrite the rules of international conduct, and arm-twist existing institutions to suit its own interests.

Against this backdrop, as an immediate neighbour of China, with a number of unresolved bilateral issues, India has more to worry about than others. The inexorable rise of China's economic and military power remains a dominant concern for India. Its seaward push on both of India's flanks (through Pakistan as well Myanmar), its quest for resources, and its paranoia about trade and energy transit through choke points, are seen as precursors of muscular Chinese maritime presence in the Indo-Pacific.

The Rhyme of History

For these reasons, China's maritime rise has been attracting special attention of analysts who struggle to decipher its significance. While evaluating chances of conflict in the Indo-Pacific, they often take recourse to history; and the precedent quoted most often is that of Imperial Germany. Just as Germany was a continental power which aspired to match British naval mastery in the early 20th century, China is seen as a maritime novice seeking to challenge US supremacy in Pacific waters. With the 100th anniversary of World War I falling this year (2014), the urge to draw parallels with the contemporary scenario, has triggered an active discourse.

In a recent essay titled 'The Rhyme of History: Lessons of the Great War,' Canadian historian Margaret MacMillan argues that there are strong similarities between today's geopolitical landscape, and the Europe of 1914. The same structural forces that led to the Great War a century ago will, according to her, be in action in 2014. The past, therefore, offers a multitude of lessons from which one may pick and choose as appropriate. According to Prof. MacMillan, the foremost lesson of World War I and a cause for concern today, is the fact that the assassination of Archduke Ferdinand was not the actual *casus belli* for World War I, as one would commonly assume. Therefore till today, the world does not know why Europe and Russia actually embarked on this great sanguinary conflict. Was it the overweening ambitions of the reigning monarchs, or competing ideologies and national rivalries, or just the sheer unstoppable momentum of militarism? Therefore, her suggestion that 'arms races can lead to aggressive war-plans that can turn into self-fulfilling prophecies' need to be heeded.

Further, *globalization* is generally thought of as a modern phenomenon, created by the spread of international investment, growth of the Internet and widespread migration of people. MacMillan says that all of this existed a hundred years ago too. Remote parts of the world were being linked by steamship, rail, telegraph and wireless; leading to a huge expansion in trade and investment. Then, as happens now, immigrants in large numbers sought distant shores. All this had lulled Europe into imagining that due to economic inter-dependence and high cost of a conflict, mankind had moved into a realm beyond the savagery of war. On the contrary, globalization has heightened rivalries. Quick communications have made it easy to spread radical philosophies and inflame popular sentiment. All these have led to a world of today, fraught with perils. In addition to the quasi-civil war in the Ukraine and high drama on the Crimean peninsula, there are ongoing or incipient civil wars in Syria, Thailand, Venezuela, South Sudan, Egypt, Iraq, and Afghanistan. So, one needs to question the current sense of complacency based on globalization, symbolized by the somewhat naïve 'MacDonalds syndrome' which rules out conflict between countries hosting franchises of the MacDonald's fast-food chain!

The dynamics of Sino-American relations also follow much the same pattern. Huge growth of trade and investment between China and the US has not allayed mutual distrust. China has readily translated economic strength into military power and has declared its intention of becoming a peer competitor of the US in the power-game.

The Rise of China

China's historical past indicates three dominant factors that underpin its present postures. A brief review of these would be of help if borne in mind, while formulating responses to the phenomenon of China's rise. Firstly, China has an imperial tradition going back many centuries, in which a well-defined heartland overwhelmingly populated by ethnic *Hans* exercised military dominance over the surrounding peripheral states. Thus, China has historically had a 'great-power' self-image, underpinned by the abundance of resources, economic self-sufficiency and vastness of the imperial state and its population. Secondly, in tandem with the cultivation of a great power persona, the Chinese people have also nurtured a deep-seated 'victim mentality' as a result of China's defeat, subjugation and humiliation by foreign powers. China's inability to resist Western military pressures led to the 19th century 'Opium Wars' and signing of the 'Unequal Treaties' that granted extra-territorial rights to foreigners. In 1900, China suffered the humiliation of an invasion by Western coalitions to put down the 'Boxer rebellion'. The 1937 Japanese invasion and an intense eight-year war resulted in 20-million Chinese casualties and many atrocities at the hands of Imperial Japanese troops. Thirdly, this 'victim syndrome' has served to intensify a strong urge to emphasize foreign threats and justify the creation of a powerful Chinese nation, which not only commands international deference, but can redress past wrongs.

Having barely emerged from the devastation of World War II, China became engulfed in turmoil by a sanguinary civil war. Chairman Mao, who came to power in 1949, believed that the country must be kept in a continuous state of revolution to achieve the goals of Communism. To this end, he organized the *Great Leap Forward* in 1958, and the Cultural Revolution in 1966; each lasting for a decade. Both movements caused untold misery and hardship and led to deaths by the million due to imprisonments and starvation. They have left a legacy of deep divisions and discontent in Chinese society that persists. Mao died, leaving his revolution unfinished, and the Chinese economy did not start firing until the late 1970s, when Deng Xiaoping opened it to the world. As far as the PLA was concerned, it remained a 'paper tiger' till the 1990s, when China mounted a concerted effort to replace and upgrade its military hardware, and started devoting considerable attention to the acquisition of maritime, cyber and space-warfare capabilities. Analysts who had argued that the PLA was at least 2-3 decades behind the US in terms of defense capabilities, have had to revise their estimates after observing China's ability to innovate, borrow or reverse-engineer advanced defence technologies, and effectively incorporate these in next-generation weapons systems.

Current Imperatives

So much for history; but what are the current imperatives propelling China's leadership on their chosen path? For one, ethnic tensions simmer just below the surface in non-Han majority areas like Tibet, Xinjiang, Mongolia and Manchuria, incorporated into China in the last Century. Frequent outbreaks of ethnic violence represent a source of insecurity for the state. Secondly, maintenance of internal order and domestic well-being are considered to be the foundation of China's national security. Today, the Communist system, still repressive and corrupt, exists alongside a market economy; and the Chinese people often question the compatibility of the two. There is a growing demand for the political and social systems to change in consonance with the economy. These two factors create enormous pressure on the Communist regime to sustain high levels of economic growth, in order to cope with emerging economic disparities between the industrialized coastal provinces and the agrarian hinterland.

The party leadership is convinced that it is just a matter of few years before China attains the economic and military attributes of a great power. However, this can happen only if China's external geo-political environment remains stable, and social and ethnic tensions can be kept under control internally. Till very recently, China's strategy to accomplish these objectives was a pragmatic combination of market-led economic growth, and maintenance of amicable relations with neighbours as well as major powers. While focusing on expansion of military capabilities, restraint was exercised in the use of force. It is now becoming increasingly clear that China no longer considers it prudent or necessary to project the image of a benign and peaceful power. Having achieved its self-assigned indices of 'comprehensive national power', China's internal dynamics are possibly compelling it to assume aggressive postures while staking territorial claims. This has startled the neighbourhood as well as the international community, and has set alarm-bells ringing.

In order to underwrite a full range of political and strategic objectives, China has made the development of military capabilities an integral part of its overall growth strategy, and in this paradigm, maritime power occupies centre-stage.

China's Maritime Heritage

The Chinese stake claim to an ancient maritime tradition, going back to the 1st millennium BCE, which gave rise to important navigational and shipbuilding innovations, and saw the opening of many trading routes to Asia and Africa. Early 15th century narratives of the Ming Dynasty describe Admiral Zheng He's remarkable fleet of huge junks carrying troops, treasure, merchandise and victuals; which made seven epic voyages to India, the Middle East and Africa. That era of impressive Chinese naval power lasted a mere 30 years, as a combination of fiscal and political compulsions led the Ming Emperor to impose a ban on further voyages, and order the destruction of Zheng's 'treasure fleet.' Over the next few centuries, protracted threats from China's north and west, ensured that its naval power remained at a low ebb, and therefore, incapable of repelling Europeans who came by sea in the 18th and 19th centuries. This inability to resist Western commercial and military pressures led to the 'Opium Wars' and signing of the 'Unequal Treaties', as mentioned before.

The PLA Navy (PLAN), on its official founding in May 1950, was equipped with warships and submarines supplied by the Soviets, who also helped establish training and maintenance infrastructure. The Sino-Soviet split of 1960, followed by the decade long Cultural Revolution, were both major setbacks for the PLA Navy and hindered its technological development.

China's Maritime Perspective

China's early maritime outlook was shaped by the Soviet naval advisers positioned at staff, command, and unit levels to disseminate Communist dogma along with Soviet naval doctrine. This doctrine emphasized coastal defense against amphibious assault by capitalist navies using small craft and submarines to wage 'guerrilla war' at sea. Even as the Soviet Navy underwent a dramatic change after the Cuban missile crisis, the PLAN clung to its coastal defense and peoples' war doctrines through the Cultural Revolution.

It was a combination of Deng Xiaoping's economic reforms, induction of nuclear submarines, and the appointment of General Liu Huaqing as Navy commander in 1982, that triggered the process of its transformation. The PLAN began to change from a relatively inconsequential coastal force to a substantive blue-water navy. Liu had a strong technological background, and as a Vice Chairman of the CMC, he pushed through a strategy to propel the PLAN from a 'coastal defense' to 'offshore defense' role. He then split the term 'offshore' into different maritime zones, to be brought under China's influence in three phases.

In Phase I, to be attained by 2000; the PLAN was to establish itself in the area delineated by the 'first island chain', which is defined by a line running through the Kurile Islands, Japan, Taiwan, the Philippines, Borneo, and the northern tip of Indonesia. Phase II of Liu's strategy envisaged control of the 'second island chain', marked by a line running through Japan, 2000 miles south to the Mariannas, and Caroline islands in the Central Pacific by the year 2020. The IIIrd and final phase envisaged the PLAN becoming a global force by 2050.

The non-attainment of Phase I weighs heavily on the consciousness of PLAN strategists, because the first island chain is seen as a geographical barrier obstructing China's access to the high seas. In the Chinese perception, it also constitutes a 'blockade' which could enable interdiction of PLAN forces. In this context, Taiwan is perceived as the single most critical asset which, if restored to China, would break the constricting barrier and enable the creation of a major maritime base for offense and defence in the Pacific.

Till this objective is achieved, the PLAN will deploy its 'anti-access and area denial' or A2AD strategy, that is based on the Dong Feng-21 D anti-ship ballistic missile and a layered defence of cruise-missiles, submarines, shore-based aircraft and minefields. Experts are of the belief that the Chinese maritime strategy looks well beyond the restoration of Taiwan, and that a much more expansive role is visualized for the PLAN over a longer timeframe.

If maritime power is the 'mantra' for China's rise, the PLAN is definitely on song. It has a rapidly growing fleet of diesel submarines, destroyers and frigates, and its force of homebuilt nuclear submarines is now ready for operational deployment. China's first aircraft carrier is at sea, and more are probably on the way. The extended anti-piracy deployments off the Horn of Africa have helped hone its skills for deployment in distant waters.

Indo-Pacific Tensions

As China progressively extends its maritime reach and capability to control, first its near seas and then the larger Pacific, it is bound to challenge the existing order in the Asia-Pacific. How the US manages this power transition will be of great interest to India, because it will decide how and when the PLAN heads for waters of the Indian Ocean. The US decision to stay 'hands-off' in territorial disputes between China and its neighbours has conveyed an impression of ambivalence and caused concern amongst some of its allies. There is also an emerging view that China, because of its economic heft, may be acquiring more salience in US strategic perspectives; and that despite its 'pivot' to Asia, the US may hesitate to adopt an overtly negative stance *vis-a-vis* China.

While these fears may or may not have substance, the reality is that China's recent conduct represents a distinct challenge to countries of the Indo-Pacific, and India as a proximate neighbour has the most to worry about.

India's Concerns

As the contours of a Chinese grand-strategy, based on the acquisition of substantive maritime power, emerge, India needs to worry about overlapping interests leading to conflict. While China's neurosis about its Indian Ocean trade and energy lifelines receives much attention, less well-known are the rapidly growing Indian interests in the Pacific. Almost 55% of India's trade with the greater Asia Pacific area transits through the South China Sea. An Indian oil company, ONGC Videsh Ltd (OVL), pumping 50,000 barrels a day from its Sakhalin project, ships it, via tankers, to a refinery on India's west coast. The same oil company has been awarded offshore drilling rights in Vietnam's Phu Khanh Basin, but work has been suspended due to Chinese claim over the Vietnamese EEZ.

Given its need for unfettered economic access to the region, India launched an energetic 'Look East' policy in the early 1990s, which has resulted in a strategic ASEAN-India partnership. A new factor in the regional equation is the budding Indo-Japanese rapport, which is being driven substantially by a shared sense of apprehension about China's intentions; especially after China's vociferous claims on both Indian and Japanese territory.

An area of emerging strategic focus for China is its newly-acquired sea-bed exploration venture in the South-west Indian Ocean. Obtained on lease from the International Seabed Authority in 2011, the seriousness of China's purpose is revealed by the fact that its manned submersible vehicle recently broke the world record by diving to a depth of 7000 meters. The Chinese deep sea exploration program has the potential for bestowing upon China access to huge quantities of strategic seabed minerals.

Last, but not the least, is the fact that the Sino-Indian military equation along the Himalayan borders is heavily tilted in China's favour, given the relative military balance and state of communications on the Tibetan Plateau. In case of conflict, the best that the Indian forces can hope to achieve is a precarious stalemate. It is against this setting that New Delhi needs to look seawards and examine what the maritime domain has to offer. Analyst Robert Kaplan provided a clue, when he referred to India's Andaman & Nicobar Islands as a '*metal chain to lock shut the western entrance of the Malacca Straits*'. President Hu Jintao too, had echoed similar sentiments when he spoke of China's 'Malacca dilemma'.

Conclusion

In conclusion, it would be worthwhile to revisit the Chinese proposal of a 'maritime silk road'. It must be borne in mind that this proposal originates in a troubled arena, where China's overbearing sovereignty claims have embroiled it in strife with many countries. While invocation of 'historic rights' and declaration of 'core interests' by China is unlikely to stand legal scrutiny, they have already triggered a precautionary arms race in the region. The question uppermost in everyone's mind is: how far will China reach out to extend hegemony, and what levels of coercion would it use in the process?

As the global community speculates about the contours of China's strategy, it must be remembered that the Chinese leadership draws upon its distinct cultural roots. The Chinese version of chess is called *Weiqi* and is played with 180 pieces instead of 32. Whereas chess is about manoeuvre, direct attack and total victory by checkmate, *Weiqi* players plot a protracted campaign seeking relative advantage through occupation of vacant spaces and strategic encirclement of the adversary.

The crux of the matter therefore, lies in the knowledge that '*whereas most nations pursue war through direct conflict, the Chinese way is to wear down the opponent and gain psychological advantage.*'

2

China as a Maritime Power

Rear Admiral Michael McDevitt (Retd.)

Introduction: A New Element in the Maritime Competition Equation

A new factor has emerged in the maritime landscape of Asia-China's determination to become a maritime power. Since late 2012, this has become an explicit Chinese objective. In his swan-song work report to the 18th Party Congress, then President Hu Jintao urged that China 'should enhance our capacity for exploiting marine resources, develop the marine economy, protect the marine ecological environment, resolutely safeguard China's maritime rights and interests, *and build China into a maritime power.*'[1] Hu's work report also called for building strong national defense and powerful armed forces that are *commensurate with China's international standing* and meet the needs of its security and development interests.[2]

These two points were repeated in the 2012 PRC Defence White Paper, which was not released until April 2013, after Xi Jinping had assumed Party and national leadership, giving him 'ownership' of the document. According to the White Paper:

> *China is a major maritime as well as land country. The seas and oceans provide immense space and abundant resources for China's sustainable development, and thus are of vital importance to the people's wellbeing and China's future. It is an essential national development strategy to exploit, utilize and protect the seas and oceans, and build China into a maritime power. It is an important duty for the PLA to resolutely safeguard China's maritime rights and interests.*[3]

What Does Becoming a Maritime Power Mean?

By making *becoming a maritime power* a national objective, without much elaboration of what is meant or intended, the Chinese leadership has added more uncertainty to those who live in its shadow, and are carefully watching its growth in power. The goal of being a maritime power seems likely to raise the anxiety of countries that do not share a common frontier with China and see the ocean as a security buffer. China's hard-nosed approach to the sovereignty disputes in the East and South China seas has already raised issues about what sort of a power China will be when it has 'fully risen', i.e. when Xi Jinping's 'China's Dream' is finally realized.[4] Becoming a recognized maritime power will be a major addition to what China calls its comprehensive national power, and will be one more step toward becoming the undisputed power in Asia.

As Professor Geoffrey Till has written in his well-regarded work *Sea Power,* definitions of *maritime power* and *sea power* are often vaguely defined.[5] Even Admiral Alfred Thayer Mahan, who coined the term *sea power*, did not define it, but it was clear in his seminal work that he equated *sea power* with success in major naval battles.[6] *Maritime power* on the other hand, is a more commonly employed term in the current military doctrine, and its use emphasizes the connection to the broader civil maritime sector. It is an inherently broad concept embracing all uses of the sea, including both civil and military. In its widest sense, it can be defined as military, political, and economic power or influence exerted through an ability to use the sea. The maritime power of a state reflects sea-based military capabilities, such as ships and submarines, and also a range of military land-based assets and space-based systems that may or may not be operated by the navy. It also includes civilian capabilities, such as a coast guard, port infrastructure, merchant shipping, fishing, or shipbuilding.[7] This is what Beijing may mean when it speaks about sea power.

Elements of China's Maritime Power

The PLA Navy

China is at a distinctive crossroad in its naval development. The PLA Navy actually has to operate as two types of navies. It needs to be a regional force that is equipped, organized and trained for the defence of security and economic interests in China's 'near seas'. At the same time, it needs to be a navy that can engage in long-distance operations in 'far seas' to support China's increasingly global political and economic interests.[8]

First, the one most directly relevant to US interests and its allies in East Asia has to do with its 'near sea' – capabilities those associated with extending China's defence perimeter hundreds of miles to seas, to the area between the so-called first- and second-island chains. These capabilities are intended to provide China with what it terms as *counter intervention*. The Pentagon has called this 'anti access and area denial' (A2/AD). This concept is aimed at preventing an attack from the sea on China proper, and its offshore island claims. The PLA Navy plays an important role in this concept, but it is not simply a navy show. Land based aircraft belonging to the PLA Air Force and PLA Naval Air Force play an important role, as does the PLA Second Artillery (the PLA missile force). PLA Navy's submarine arm has a very important role in 'counter intervention' mission. This is why China's growing (and modernizing) conventionally powered submarine force is strategically very important.

The second category of PLA Navy's role has to do with peacetime operations, which include sea lane defence (which implicitly is also a wartime mission), and power projection operations against other Asian countries. This mission set primarily involves the PLAN's burgeoning 'far seas' or 'blue water' capabilities, represented by its surface ships, including its aircraft carrier force(s). This category is of particular interest to India, since these ships and nuclear powered submarines are the PLA Navy forces most likely to operate in the Indian Ocean. Unlike the submarine force, PLA Navy surface ships would probably play a limited role in a 'counter intervention' campaign against the US, because once out from under China's land-based air cover, which, at best, is around 300 NM from China's coast, these ships would be vulnerable to either US attack submarines or carrier-based aircraft. This means that in any major conflict most PLA Navy surface ships would probably limit operations to the East China Sea or the northern portion of the South China Sea. However, in operations short of a major conflict involving the United States, these ships play an important role in advancing China's regional and global interests in the Indian and Pacific Oceans.

There are very strong pressures on China to develop a navy that is capable of conducting more than just regional operations. Nevertheless, as yet, there is no evidence to suggest that the Chinese are building a global navy which is intended to challenge the United States beyond East Asia. This may change in the future, but at present, the major drivers that are pushing Beijing to develop such 'far seas' capabilities as multi-product replenishment ships, and modern guided-missile destroyers – capable of providing escorts for China fledging sea-based tactical aviation capability – are aimed at protecting China's overseas economic interests and dealing with peacetime threats to its sea lanes, such as piracy.

In short, China's emergence as a global actor created a 'demand signal' for a PLA Navy that can support UN-sanctioned missions, protect China interests abroad, respond to situations where China citizens are in jeopardy or require evacuation, protect sea lines of communication, respond to natural disasters, and by implication, demonstrate China's resolve in support of embattled friends in Africa, and along the South Asian littoral. In other words, this is the typical mission set that traditional naval powers have practiced for centuries.

The global 'demand signal' created a new PLA Navy operational concept, termed *yuanhai* in Chinese, translated as 'far seas'.[9] This term is not a substitute for 'offshore active defense', which is still used to frame wartime doctrinal development and potential operations in regional waters near China, but rather, it is a parallel concept.[10] In other words, these new missions were additive; they did not supplant the mission to defend the maritime approaches to China.

The 2012 PRC Defence White Paper also defined specific 'far seas' operations for the PLA Navy. These included Humanitarian Assistance and Disaster Relief (HADR), escort operations, non-combatants evacuation operations (NEO), and joint exercises with foreign partners. In analyzing the white paper, the first one to be issued with a thematic focus, US experts judge that it has an 'expeditionary' flavour. The White Paper provides justification for why the PLA is deploying for 'diversified missions' that support China's international standing, and its security and developmental interests.

As a result, the PLA Navy has been introducing more 'far seas' capabilities, such as logistics support ships, amphibious ships with helicopter facilities, more destroyers with better endurance, helicopter hangers, and facilities and longer range air defences. Far seas missions have almost certainly created the basic rationale behind PLA Navy's decision to build a modest aircraft carrier force.[11] The 'experimental' aircraft carrier *Liaoning* (CV-16) was commissioned on September 25, 2012; and since that time has been engaged in a methodical process of training and qualifying PLA Navy Air Force pilots on carrier borne operations, and learning how to operate jet aircraft at sea. By early in the next decade, it is forecast that the PLA Navy will have two operating aircraft carriers, and for the first time will have the capability to operate in far seas with the knowledge that it is not totally bereft of friendly air cover. Whether the Carrier will be able to use its J-15 air wing for strike missions against a littoral country is not certain at this time, given the payload penalties that ski-jump launches impose. As a working assumption however, it is prudent to assume that the PLA Navy will determine a way to overcome this limitation over the next decade; if not in an improved aircraft, then through commissioning of a carrier that will utilize catapults to launch its jets.

The backbone of these *far seas* forces will be the multi-mission *Luyang* II/III (type 052C and 052D) class destroyers. These ships have phased-array radars and a long range Surface to Air Missile (SAM) system which provides the PLA Navy with its first credible area air-defence capability. As a result, additional flexibility including the possibility of loading Land Attack Cruise Missiles (LACM) will be incorporated because the Type 052Ds have a multi-purpose 64 cell vertical launch system. The PLA Navy will have around 20 of these modern guided missile destroyers available for *far seas* missions in the early 2020s, either as independent task groups, or, as escorts for PLA aircraft carriers/modern amphibious ships.

Other significant *far seas* capable ships include the *Jiangkai* II class (type 054A) frigates. These 3900 ton ships, which began entering active service in 2008, have become the workhorses of the PLA Navy's counter piracy operations in the Gulf of Aden. Forecasts indicate that the PLA Navy will have around 48 modern frigates in its inventory. In total therefore, the PLA Navy of 2022 will be able to call on close to 70 modern surface combatants that are capable of far seas operations throughout the Indian Ocean, and potentially in the Eastern Mediterranean. [The China Ocean Shipping Company (COSCO), a government owned shipping and logistics services group, has a substantial investment in Piraeus, Greece, the largest port in the Eastern Mediterranean.][12]

PLA Navy has mastered the logistics of sustaining small task groups on distant stations. The advantage of a state owned enterprise like the COSCO, which is in the logistics services business worldwide, means that there is built-in shore based support structure available at virtually all the major ports along the Pacific and Indian Ocean littoral. When combined with multi-product replenishment ships, this has become a successful model that the PLA Navy has followed in more than five years worth of counter-piracy operations.[13]

The PLA Navy commenced its counter-piracy patrols with only two modern multi-product replenishment ships in commission. As a result, for the first two and half years of counter piracy patrols, these two ships operated on an unsustainable *port and starboard* rotation. The PLA Navy has learned how important these ships are in sustaining far seas deployments. They presently have four *Fuchi* class replenishment ships. Forecasts indicate that the PLA Navy will soon have a total of 12 multi-product replenishments ships to support the growth in *far seas* surface combatants.

Improving the inventory of these ships in such a dramatic fashion is the clearest indicator possible that the PLA Navy intends to develop the capability to sustain as many as three small task groups on distant stations indefinitely. The two *Fuchi* class ships currently in commission have demonstrated through repeated counter-piracy deployments that they can support at least two and periodically three PLA Navy surface combatants. Arguably, they are the 'long pole in the tent' when it comes to forecasting the viability of sustained PLA Navy *far sea* operations.

For a number of years, the role of the PLA Navy amphibious ships has focused around the ability of PLA to invade Taiwan. While that remains a contingency that requires continued attention, the fact is that the PLA Navy is in the process of putting together an impressive *far seas* expeditionary capability. In the summer of 2010, *Kunlunshan* LPD was included in the Sixth Counter-Piracy Task Group. This 20,000 ton 'amphib' can carry between 800-1000 PLA marines or soldiers, four high speed air cushion landing craft, and several helicopters. Forecasts suggest that a total of five Landing Platform Docks (LPDs) and two larger 40,000 ton amphibious ships, similar to US Navy amphibious assault [Landing Helicopter Assault (LHA)] ships that could carry both helicopters and Vertical or Short Takeoff and Landing (VSTOL) jets, will be in PLA Navy inventory over the next ten years. If realised, these seven large state of the art amphibious ships will constitute the second largest modern amphibious capability in the world (after the US Navy), and could potentially embark between 5,500 and 6,500 marines. When combined with modern destroyers, and potentially an aircraft carrier to provide air defence, China, for the first time since Admiral Zheng He in 1405, will have a capability for *far seas* power projection.[14]

It is important to emphasize that more than five years of uninterrupted anti-piracy operations in the Arabian Sea have been most useful in educating the PLA Navy in how to conduct distant sea operations. One reason they have learned so quickly is because the anti-piracy patrols are a real time 'battle-laboratory' for the PLA Navy, providing it an opportunity to observe the day-to-day operations of most of the world's great navies and absorb best practices for its own use.[15]

Maritime Constabulary Forces – the Chinese Coast Guard

For years, China's five largest civil maritime agencies were controlled by different parent organizations, earning them the moniker 'five dragons contending for the sea.' In March 2013, Beijing announced that it intended to merge four of these agencies (as shown below) under the State Oceanic Administration (SOA) into a single Chinese Coast Guard:

- China Marine Surveillance (CMS) [already under SOA]
- Border Control Department (BCD) [formerly under the Ministry of Public Security]

- Fisheries Law Enforcement Command (FLEC) [under the Ministry of Agriculture]
- General Administration of Customs [under the State Council]

The fifth dragon, the Maritime Safety Administration (MSA), under the jurisdiction of the Ministry of Transport, is not included in the merger. In remarks delivered in conjunction with the National People's Congress, State Councilor Ma Kai said that China needed to remedy the fact that the country's five separate maritime law enforcement bodies were insufficient to fulfill China's law enforcement needs, protect its sovereignty, and safeguard its maritime rights and interests, including a maritime economy that could account for 10 per cent of national economic output by 2015.[16]

This author attended a conference in Beijing in July 2013 that focused on the safety at sea. During see event, the Chinese explained that MSA was not included in the initial merger because of its responsibilities. These were so closely intertwined with the smooth running of Chinese ports that officials were concerned that including it in what was already going to be a bureaucratically complex merger would have an adverse impact on sea port efficiency, and hence, on trade. This could, in turn, have an adverse impact on the economy.[17] According to Chinese interlocutors at that conference, the Chinese Coast Guard decided to emulate the model of the US Coast Guard. They were impressed by how the US Coast Guard, between the years 1900 and 1941, successfully absorbed several different maritime agencies to become the US Coast Guard of today.[18]

Although the jury remains out on the ultimate impact of China's decision to form a Chinese Coast Guard, years of thought and operational experience behind today's ongoing reforms suggest that they have strong political support and enjoy a good chance of succeeding in materially enhancing China's maritime law enforcement capabilities.[19]

China's Shipbuilding Industry – Already World Class

In contrast to Japan and South Korea, both of which have used shipbuilding to rebuild industrial capacity by building ships for export, the China classifies shipbuilding as a strategic sector, and the impressive capacity it has developed was aimed primarily at enabling China to be self-sufficient in sea trade. From Beijing's perspective, the supply of raw materials for its economy, meeting the food needs of its people, and transporting its exports should, to the extent possible, be undertaken by Chinese-built ships; in other words, a strong shipbuilding industry is a central pillar in China's maritime development.[20] That goal was expanded to include building ships for export when the global demand for ships made it possible for China to successfully compete internationally because of low labour costs and a greatly improved quality.

As a result, by 2008, China grew into the world's leading shipbuilder, as hundreds of private yards opened to compete with state-run companies. Starting with the 2008 global economic crisis, all Asian shipbuilders, especially the Chinese, were hit by the sharp decline in the demand for new ships. Not only did new orders dry up; many existing orders were cancelled. During the heady days before the turndown, the number of shipyards in China had swollen to 1,647.[21] This growth was a major contributor to a global shipbuilding capacity glut – particularly in the area of low technology dry-bulk and container vessels (Dry-bulk ships carry raw materials such as iron ore and are much less complex than tankers or LNG carriers).

According to *The Economist*, 'Many Chinese firms have focused on making ships that are bigger, especially giant container vessels. In contrast, South Korean and Japanese yards have invested in new technologies and advanced engines to make ships of all sorts cleaner and more efficient. Such firms are not only growing, but also fetching premium prices'.[22] China is well aware of this trend and has already begun to focus on quality above quantity. According to the Director of China Shipbuilding Industry Research Center, China wants to '...move from a shipbuilding country to shipbuilding power'.[23]

To that end, China will have to reduce capacity by around 30 per cent to remain competitive.[24] That said, in 2013, China has again leapt to the front of the pack. Yards in China won orders to make 47 per cent of new global contracts in the first seven months of 2013. State-backed builders won almost three-quarters of those deals, helping China to gain a 7.8-million-ton lead over South Korea, the second largest builder. Chinese shipyards and related companies employed about 671,564 people in 2012.[25]

China's quest to become a maritime power will be furthered by its emphasis on shipbuilding. China is already a global leader in shipbuilding and has its sights set on moving into the niche market for technically complex vessels. It has already demonstrated the ability to build world-class warships like the Type 052 C and D class Guided Missile Destroyers (DDG)[26] and has the modern facilities needed to build additional warships. Notable among these facilities is the world's largest shipyard, the historic Jiangnan, located on Changxing Island near Shanghai.[27]

China's Merchant Marine

China's merchant marine has been able to grow and develop because of two central decisions; first, because shipbuilding was classified as a strategic sector in the economy, and second, because China wanted to be as self-sufficient as possible while importing strategic raw materials central to its economic growth. As a result, a modern and large Chinese merchant marine has emerged in a relatively short time. China's merchant marine has transformed itself from a modest and elderly fleet predominantly employed in domestic trading into a group of the best-equipped internationally trading shipping companies.[28] As a result, based on current trends, Lloyds of London forecasts that China will own more than a third of the world's merchant tonnage by 2030.[29]

Based on 2010 data, China has about 2,030 registered merchant vessels. According to the 2010 CIA *World Fact Book*, another 1,559 ships are Chinese owned but registered abroad, largely in various 'flag of convenience' states such as Panama and Liberia, which rank one and two in total ships registered.[30] China's total ownership of 3589 merchant vessels places it third in the world behind Germany (3,847) and Japan (3806).[31]

Expansion of the maritime workforce has also been a crucial part of the fleet's growth. China now runs some of the world's biggest maritime training colleges. There are seven maritime universities/colleges, such as the Dalian Maritime University and the Shanghai Maritime University's Merchant Marine College. China also has 18 high- and middle-school level vocational colleges dedicated to training seafarers. These institutions graduate about 5,000 students a year, which is considered adequate to replace attrition in the 60,000 seafarers that man the Chinese flagged merchant vessels.[32]

China's Fishing Industry – Another Global Leader

The first impression one gathers when assessing China's fishing industry is that the numbers are staggering. China's consumption and capacity to catch fish is massive. In 2010, China consumed about 50 per cent of global fisheries production (fishing and fish farming). By comparison, India, which was number two on the list, consumed about 10 per cent. In 2010, China had more than 675,000 registered motorized fishing vessels.[33] Of these, about 1900 are designed for Distant Water Fishing (DWF). Although this is a small percentage of China's total fishing fleet, it is also the world's largest DWF fleet and is scheduled to grow to around 2,300 vessels by 2015. By comparison, the US operates around 200 DWF vessels.[34]

Distant waters refer to major fishing areas that are not adjacent to the fishing country, such as in the exclusive economic zone (EEZ) of another host country or on the high seas. Article 62 of the UN Convention on the Law of the Sea (UNCLOS) stipulates that when a coastal State does not have the capacity to harvest the entire allowable catch, it shall, through agreements or other arrangements, give other States access to the surplus of the allowable catch. This provision has led to the development of numerous fisheries access agreements to allow a State's DWF fleets to fish in the EEZs of other host countries.

A major issue associated with China's fishing industry is that its humongous appetite for fish and the size of its DWF fishing fleet, is having an adverse impact on the world's fisheries, which are already depleted. Although China has done a reasonable job of regulating its domestic fishing industry, it has not been good on important indicators for international fishing – measures of illegal, unreported, and unregulated (IUU) fishing.[35]

Concluding Thoughts

This overview of the various aspects of China's maritime capability indicates that China is already a major maritime power in terms of its merchant marine, shipbuilding and fishing industries. Yet, despite this reality, Xi Jinping is calling for China to become a maritime power. An open question is the shortfalls Xi thinks that China has to redress. This is not been spelled out to this author's knowledge, but based on this cursory review, the answer seems clear – the PLA Navy and Coast Guard are the maritime capabilities of China that are not yet world class, although in the case of the PLA Navy, if the projections discussed above are realised within a decade, the PLA Navy will likely be the second most powerful navy in the world.

Implications

- **The focus of the maritime competition will remain in East Asia and be between the United States and its East Asian allies; primarily Japan, and China.** It is unlikely that China will halt development of what it considers necessary for its defences. It is also clear that the US does not intend to sit by idly and permit the introduction of military capabilities that could deny it access to East Asia in a time of conflict, and in peacetime undermine its credibility as a capable ally. Thus, it seems likely that for the foreseeable future the region will witness a 'military capabilities competition' in which China will introduces capabilities that could deny access, while the US military, especially the Navy and Air Force, would introduce capabilities that will assure access. It will be a period of competing strategic concepts – assured access versus denied access, manifested by the introduction of military capabilities by both sides to accomplish these ends.

- **China is putting together an impressive 'far seas' capability that within the decade is likely to be on a par with India, and second only to the United States.** For the PLA Navy, this will go a long way toward satisfying the high level direction to build a Chinese military that is 'commensurate with China's international standing'. This is likely to have long term implications for how China is perceived (feared) along the Indo-Pacific littoral, and is likely to place added pressure on the US to demonstrate – through present and forward operations – that it still has the ability to gain sea control when and where it chooses. Even if China has no intention of deviating from its 'peaceful development' narrative, the cumulative impact of a modern *far seas* naval capability will make countries that live in the shadow of China more wary; and for those that can financially afford it, spur the acquisition of access denial capabilities aimed at defending their maritime approaches. This is already going on in Vietnam and India, and to a lesser degree in Japan.
- **The Far Sea mission set – The importance of Sea Line of Communications (SLOC) protection.** China's anti-piracy patrols represent peacetime SLOC protection against a non-traditional security threat. However, as Chinese commentators have pointed out, sustaining China's maritime commerce is directly related to China's survival and development, which also makes SLOC protection a wartime task. Protecting China's merchant ships is an 'important strategic task'. This suggests that China could possibly conclude that the only way to really protect its SLOCs from India, Japan or the US would be to build a *far seas* navy that is large enough and capable enough to incorporate sea control into its SLOC protection concept.
- **Is China building a 'Far Seas' sea control navy?** There is no credible information to suggest that the growing importance of 'far seas' operations is the first step in constructing a navy that would slug it out with the US Navy in a battle for sea control. In other words, there is nothing to suggest the PLA Navy is on a path toward becoming a Chinese version of the Japanese Imperial Navy. That said, the capabilities that China is fielding, can in no way, foreclose that option, and could be the first steps towards such a capability.
- **No one knows for certain how China will employ its 'far seas' Navy. New capabilities are likely to present new options to China's leadership.** When the PLA Navy introduces LACM to its surface combatants and/or

nuclear powered submarines that are deployed on far seas missions, it will provide China with an immediate off-shore coercive capability. US Navy operations against Libya, and the discussions in 2013 about coercive operations against Syria that would depend on LACMs from ships and submarines without a US carrier in the immediate vicinity, provide a contemporary example of how Beijing might choose to employ its far seas forces at some point in the future. The possibility of intermingled PLA Navy and US Navy ships off the coast of a South Asian or African littoral State when Washington and Beijing have different interests cannot be ignored. Instructive examples from the Cold War in the Eastern Mediterranean suggest that US freedom of action could be negatively impacted.

- **A central implication of China's naval development is that within the decade, the PLA Navy will become the predominate regional naval force, and will be in a position to have more modern high-end naval capability in East Asia than the US Seventh Fleet, if the United States does nothing beyond announced plans.** This does not mean that China could push the US Navy out of the Western Pacific; for the simple reason that in peacetime, it simply cannot be done. Short of a war that drives the US out, the US Seventh Fleet will remain a fixture in the region as long as Japan is willing to host it, and the US is willing to remain militarily engaged in East Asia. However, if China becomes confident that its 'counter-intervention' capabilities (what the US calls A2/AD) will work well enough to keep the US Navy beyond effective strike range of China, then its 'far seas' capabilities, operating in 'near seas' might be judged good enough to deal with the US 7th Fleet and Japanese Maritime Self Defense Force.

NOTES

1. Full text of Hu Jintao's Report at the 18th Party Congress, as reported by Xinhua on November 17, 2012 is available at http://news.xinhuanet.com/english/special/18cpcnc/2012-11/17/c_131981259.htm.
2. Hu Jintao's Report at the 18th Party Congress ibid.
3. State Council Information Office, 'The Diversified Employment of China's Armed Forces', (hereafter, referred to as China's 2012 Defense White Paper) April 2013, Beijing, The official English translation is available at http://news.xinhuanet.com/english/china/2013-04/16/c_132312681.htm Also see Chen Zhou, ed., *Strategic Review 2011* (Center for National Defense Policy, Academy of Military Science, Beijing, April 2012).
4. In 2013, the Communist Party (CPC) General SecretaryXi Jinping began promoting the phrase as a slogan, leading to its widespread use in the Chinese media. Xi has described the dream as 'national rejuvenation, improvement of people's livelihoods, prosperity, construction of a better society and military strengthening.' According to the party's theoretical journal *Qiushi*, the 'Chinese Dream' is about Chinese prosperity, collective effort, socialism, and national glory.

5. Geoffrey Till, *Seapower: A Guide for the Twenty-first Century* (3rd edition), (Routledge, New York, 2013).
6. Geoffrey Till, *Seapower* ibid, p. 24.
7. The definition of 'maritime power' is drawn from Dr. Ian Speller, *Understanding Naval Warfare,* (Routledge, London, 2014), p. 5.
8. The dichotomy was first explored by Michael McDevitt and Frederic Vellucci, Jr., in 'The Evolution of the Peoples Liberation Army Navy: The Twin Missions of area denial and peacetime operations,' in Geoffrey Till and Patrick C. Bratton, eds., *Sea Power and the Asia-Pacific: the Triumph of Neptune? The Cass Series: Naval Policy and History* (Routledge, Milton Park, Abingdon, UK, 2012).
9. The term *yuanhai* can also be translated as 'open seas' or 'distant oceans'. Some English sources translate the term as 'blue water'. However, current usage of the term indicates that the Chinese are using the term to differentiate between 'near seas' operations, i.e., those in defense of China proper and its offshore possessions, including Taiwan, and those which take place beyond the 'near seas'. It is important to keep in mind that 'near seas' and 'far seas' are not conceptually limited by 'island chain' boundaries. It would be incorrect to suggest that near seas are bounded by the first island chain. Clearly China 'counter intervention' (A2/AD) operations will reach almost to the second island chain.
10. The 2008 Defence White Paper states that China continues to develop its ability to conduct offshoreoperations while gradually building its ability to conduct operations in distant seas. *China's NationalDefense in 2008* (Beijing: Information Office of the State Council, 2009).
11. Nan Li and Christopher Weuve, 'China's Aircraft Carrier Ambitions: An Update,' *Naval War College Review*, Winter (2010), p. 15, www.usnwc.edu/publications/Naval-War-College-Review/2010 – Winter.aspx.
12. Harry Papachristau, 'Piraeus investment deal eases privatisation prospects,' *Reuters*, September 2, 2013, http://uk.reuters.com/article/2013/09/02/us-greece-china-piraeus-*idUKBRE98109Q20130902.*
13. Michael McDevitt, 'PLA Naval Exercises with International Partners,' in *Learning by Doing: The PLA trains at Home and Abroad,* Roy Kamphausen, Davis Lai, Travis Tanner eds. (Army War College Strategic Studies Institute Carlisle, PA, November 2012), p. 109.
14. For the most accurate account of Zheng He's 'power projection' voyages, see Edward Dreyer, *Zheng He: China and the Oceans in the Early Ming Dynasty, 1405-1433*, Pearson, 2006.
15. Michael McDevitt, 'PLA Naval exercises with International Partners,' ibid, p 102.
16. 'China Plans to Regroup Oceanic Administration for Maritime Law Enforcement,' *Xinhua*, March 10, 2013.
17. Discussion at the Northeast Asia Maritime Safety Cooperation Project Workshop, July 16-17, 2013, Beijing, China, co-sponsored by the China Institute of International Studies (CIIS) and the University of California at San Diego Institute on Global Conflict and Cooperation.
18. Discussion at the Northeast Asia Maritime Safety Cooperation Project Workshop, ibid.
19. Andrew Ericson and Gabe Collins, 'New Fleet on the Block: China's Coast Guard Comes Together' *Asia Wall Street Journal, Japan,* March 12, 2013, http://blogs.wsj.com/japanrealtime/2013/03/12/new-fleet-on-the-block-chinas-coast-guard-comes-together.
20. Yin-Chung Tsai, 'The shipbuilding industry in China,' *OCED Journal*-General Papers-Volume 2010/3, 2011, OECD Report http://www.keepeek.com/Digital-Asset-Management/oecd/economics/the-shipbuilding-industry-in-china_gen_papers-2010-5kg6z7tg5w5l#page1.
21. Jasmine Wang & Kyunghee Park, 'China Poised to Gain Control as Shipyard Shakeout Looms,' Aug 12, 2013. http://www.bloomberg.com/news/2013-08-11/china-poised-to-gain-control-as-shipyard-shakeout-looms-freight.html

22. 'Too sick to sail: Ailing shipbuilders test China's commitment to reform,' *The Economist,* July 13, 2013, http://www.economist.com/news/business/21581753-ailing-shipbuilders-test-chinas-commitment-reform-too-sick-sail
23. Pradeep Rajan, 'China's shipbuilding sector must consolidate to stay competitive: official,' *Platts,* November 7, 2013. http://www.platts.com/latest-news/shipping/ningbo-zhejiang/chinas-shipbuilding-sector-must-consolidate-to-27604700.
24. Pradeep Rajan ibid.
25. Pradeep Rajan ibid.
26. Michael McDevitt, 'Arming the PLAN Surface Fleet (Destroyers),' unpublished paper for the China Maritime Studies Institute conference: *China's Evolving Surface Fleet*, May 1-2, 2013, Naval War *College*, Newport, RI.
27. http://china-defense.blogspot.com/2010/01/photos-of-jiangnan-changxing-shipyard.html
28. https://www.bimco.org/en/Education/Seascapes/Maritime_Matters/2006_11_06_Chinas_Merchant_Marine.aspx
29. Global Marine Trends Report 2030, by QinetiQ, Lloyd's Register, and the University of Strathclyde, Glasglow. http://www.lr.org/sectors/marine/GTC/gmt2030.aspx
30. CIA World Fact Book, November 2013, https://www.cia.gov/library/publications/the-world-factbook/geos/ch.html
31. All data taken from CIA World Fact Book ibid.
32. Report of the Second Regional Forum on Maritime Manpower Planning, 2005, http://www.unescap.org/ttdw/ Publications/ TFS_pubs/Pub_2335/pub_2335_China.pdf
33. Chuin-Wei Yap and Sameer Mohindru 'China's Hunger for Fish Upsets Seas: Reach of Massive Fleet Cuts into Stock, Tests Ties on Opposite Side of the World,' Dec. 27, 2012, http://online.wsj.com/news/articles/ SB10001424127887324669104578205041179985354.
34. Tabitha Grace Mallory, 'Testimony before the U.S.-China Economic Review Commission', January 26, 2012, http://transparentsea.co/images/c/ca/12_1_26_mallory_testimony.pdf
35. Tabitha Grace Mallory, 'China's distant water fishing industry: Evolving policies and implications,' *Marine Policy* 38, (2013) pp. 99-108. www.elsevier.com/locate/marpol

3

PLA Navy in 'Military Operations other than War' and Diplomacy Roles

*Commander Kamlesh K Agnihotri**

Introduction

International discourse in maritime security domain over the last decade plus has invariably veered around the rapid pace of the Chinese naval modernization, and abundant literature has been generated, largely expressing concern at this development. While potential traditional role of the PLA Navy which is becoming increasingly capable with time, and the methodologies of addressing this emerging challenge has been at the forefront of discussions, another important facet of the PLA Navy, that of engaging in Military Operations other than War, is also paying equal, if not more dividends, in furtherance of Beijing's maritime diplomacy.

In that context, this paper seeks to expound on the various non-traditional activities of the PLA Navy and their main areas of operation. The Chinese propensity to grab or create such opportunities for non-traditional naval tasks has also been investigated. Finally, the intentions behind its increasing maritime focus in the long-term have also been assessed.

Expanding Maritime Domain Vision

The then Chinese President Hu Jintao, during his final keynote address at the 18th National Party Congress in Beijing on November 8, 2012, called for 'enhancing

---

*The views expressed are solely of the author and do not reflect the official policy or position of the Indian Navy or National Maritime Foundation. The author can be reached at *kkumaragni@gmail.com*

the Chinese capacity for exploiting marine resources, resolutely safeguarding China's maritime rights and interests, and building China into a maritime power'.[1] President Xi Jinping, the present incumbent has lent full support to this vision as can be amply discerned from his comments to the effect that "...China will depend on the ocean to prosper and will steadily promote the building of its maritime power ...",[2] made during a discussion with members of the CPC Central Committee Political Bureau on July 30, 2013. These comments are particularly significant as it is for the first time that the Chinese leadership has clearly enunciated a decisive road map for expanding the scope of maritime development, in no uncertain terms.

PLA Navy's Strategy

The doctrine, tactics and procedures of the PLA Navy all, emanate from a combined PLA's military strategy of 'active defence', which has in due course, been duly adjusted to reflect the demands of the contemporary 'local wars under modern high-tech conditions' strategy. However, specific rules for conducting military operations are not spelt out in the 'active defence' concept. This matter has been addressed by formulation of 'a military strategic guideline of active defence for the new period'. The guideline strives to increase PLA's capabilities to maintain maritime, space and electromagnetic space security in order to be able to accomplish tasks, such as counter-terrorism, stability maintenance, emergency rescue, and international peacekeeping.[3]

'Offshore defence' strategy is the naval component of the 'active defence' strategic guidelines, wherein the PLA Navy has been endeavouring to enhance its capabilities of integrated operations, strategic deterrence, conducting operations in distant waters, and counter non-traditional security threats.[4] Owing to an increasing focus on the need to operate in distant waters, this strategy has also come to be known as the 'far seas strategy'. However, in acknowledgement of the emerging security challenges in the current maritime domain, particularly of non-traditional nature, Military Operations Other Than War (MOOTW) have been finding greater mention since 2008,[5] in the diversified roles that the PLA Navy is expected to perform.

PLA Navy's Tasks

As per the latest Chinese Defence White paper of April 2013, the tasks of the PLA Navy have been broadly divided into traditional and non-traditional groups. The traditional role involves maintaining combat readiness for Taiwan scenario, national defence and coastal security; and the non-traditional one envisages *supporting economic & social development.*[6] This second role involves the under mentioned tasks:

- The all important role of safeguarding maritime rights and interests
- Protection of overseas interests
- Safeguarding world peace and regional stability

The authority for this last task though, seems to have been largely self-mandated, and appears to derive strength from the Chinese ruling elite's new found confidence in taking leadership roles in global affairs.

Strategic Direction for MOOTW Activities

The statement of the Chinese President Xi Jinping as regards '*China having heavy responsibilities to assume, and also possessing the capability for discharging the same*',[7] while meeting with the UN Secretary General, Ban Ki Moon, on June 19, 2013, indeed provides the apex direction to the PLA Navy also, in the context of MOOTW. In consonance with the above policy stance adopted by the top leadership, the Chinese Central Military Commission (CMC) has promulgated a 'Military Operations Other than War Capacity Building Plan' in 2011. This document provides the guidelines and prescribes measures for the PLA to accomplish diverse non-traditional tasks.

Situating MOOTW in the Four 'W's Framework

In common naval parlance, a contact report at sea is transmitted in terms of four elements of '*what*', '*where*', '*whither*' (purpose) and '*when*'. Applying these yardsticks to the current context, China appears to have surmised the 'what' component of MOOTW model for its Navy. After revisiting the 'what' component, this paper covers the PLA Navy's MOOTW and maritime diplomacy activities, in the Pacific Ocean first, and then in the Indian Ocean. The 'whither' (purpose) and 'when' components are subsequently addressed.

'What'

The 'what' component of this model comprises the all important role of 'safeguarding maritime rights and interests'. The protection of overseas interests has interestingly been explained as the security of Sea Line of Communications (SLOCs) and evacuation and emergency rescue of its overseas nationals and legal persons. Anti-piracy escort missions, engagement in peaceful diplomacy, and disaster relief activities have been clubbed under the banner of safeguarding world peace and regional stability. Introduction of legal persons in the white paper, and the need for their rescue and evacuation, should be open to interesting interpretations, with regard to their roles in the first place.

'Where'

The where component mainly covers the PLA Navy's MOOTW and maritime diplomacy activities in the Pacific Ocean first, followed by those in the Indian Ocean.

Naval Diplomacy in the Pacific and Beyond

In early July 2013, seven ships from China's North and South Sea Fleet and 12 vessels from Russia's Pacific Fleet took part in the week-long exercise off Vladivostok. In September 2013, three PLA Navy ships visited Hawaii, conducted joint maritime exercises with the US Navy, and thereafter sailed across the Pacific to join international navies in Sydney for naval celebrations to mark the 100th anniversary of the Royal Australian Navy's warships entering the Sydney Harbour. Prior to entering harbour, the PLA Navy ship *Qingdao* participated in the first maritime security exercises of ADMM-PLUS with 25 warships from different countries, including India. Subsequently, the same group proceeded toward Auckland in New Zealand.

Coinciding with this PLA Navy task group sailing on Hawaii-Australia route, yet another 3 ship group was on a trans-Pacific mission to show Flag in Latin American countries.[8] This extended voyage, which concluded on December 11, 2013, saw the PLA Navy ships calling at ports in Chile (Valparaiso), rounding the cape horn through the Magellan Strait, entering Rio De Janeiro harbour, carrying out joint Air Defence exercises with the Brazilian Navy, going on to visit Buenos Aires in Argentina, and returning via the Panama Canal; thus circumscribing the whole of the South American Continent in the process. Special note may be taken of these voyages so far from China, mainly on account of reach and sustenance exhibited by the PLA Navy while undertaking these tasks.

The *Peace Ark* hospital ship and *Zheng He* training ship have concurrently been making their own contribution to the Chinese maritime diplomacy. The hospital ship successfully undertook a three month long medical mission tour of Cuba and the Caribbean islands in 2011, thereby crossing the entire Pacific Ocean non-stop, and entering the Atlantic through the Panama Canal. The hospital ship, along with additional medical teams from China, and accompanied by one LPD from the PLA Navy, participated in the multilateral Humanitarian Assistance and Disaster Relief (HADR) and military medicine exercise at Brunei, under the aegis of the ASEAN Defence Minister's Meeting Plus (ADMM+) mechanism in June 2013.

The ship was deputed to the typhoon-ravaged Tacloban region in the Philippines for humanitarian medical assistance from November 21 to December 15, 2013, though a little late in the day, after Beijing was subjected to quite a bit of international flak for its insensitivity and indifference in the face of this humanitarian crisis.

MOOTW in Indian Ocean

The PLA Navy, at present level of evolution, would decidedly be in a disadvantageous position in the Indian Ocean Region (IOR) – mainly on account of non-availability of integral air-defence capability. The situation may, however, decisively change within a decade or so, by which time the gap between the Chinese intent of '*...conducting operations in distant waters...*' and its 'power projection' capabilities would have substantially narrowed down to manageable levels. This intervening time-frame would also have enabled Beijing to gain relevant technical expertise in carrier construction and aircraft manufacture, learn the highly specialized art of carrier air-operations, and acquire enough influence over its regions of interest to support such a force at extended ranges. In the meanwhile, increasingly modernizing PLA Navy is being appropriately utilized for 'military operations other than war', which project the benign face of the State. And the IOR has provided numerous opportunities for the PLA Navy to engage in these activities.

The most important and highly visible facet has been the PLA Navy's anti-piracy escort mission which has now been in progress for more than 5 years, with the 16th task force presently deployed. It has undertaken many maritime and diplomatic activities which are either associated with, or complement its presence in the Gulf of Aden. Chinese ships participated in the Pakistan initiated multilateral maritime exercise *Aman* 2013, as they have been doing since 2007. *Zheng He* training ship's transit through IOR, followed by Atlantic crossing as part of its global voyage in 2012, is common knowledge. (Table 3.1)

The US and PLA Navy ships conducted a counter-piracy exercise in the Gulf of Aden on August 25, 2013. The PLA Navy ships are projecting the benign face of China by displaying the intent of sharing international responsibilities for global good. In the Middle-eastern context, a PLA Navy frigate *Yancheng* has been diverted from the Gulf of Aden since January 2014, and is temporarily operating from Cyprus for escorting ships which are transferring Syria's chemical weapons for destruction in the Mediterranean Sea.

Table 3.1: Zheng He Training Ship's Global Voyage April – September 2012

S. No.	*Date/Month/Year*	*Country*	*Place/Port*
1.	23-25 April 2012	Vietnam	Saigon Port
2.	29 April–3 May 2012	Malaysia	Port Klang
3.	9 May–13 May 2012	India	Kochi
4.	20-21 May 2012	Republic of Djibouti	Djibouti
4A.	27 May 2012	Egypt	Crossed Suez Canal
5.	31 May–6 June 2012	Italy	Taranto
6.	9-14 June 2012	Spain	Cadiz
7.	25-27 June 2012	Canada	Halifax
8.	13-18 July 2012	Ecuador	Guayaquil
9.	6-10 August 2012	French Polynesia	Papeete
10.	11-14 August 2012	Tonga	Nuku'alofa
11.	22-24 August 2012	Australia	Cairns
12.	3-7 September 2012	Indonesia	Surabaya
13.	11-14 September 2012	Brunei	Muara

The medical tour of Asia by *Peace Ark* hospital ship between July to September 2013 is the second such mission in IOR, after the first one in 2010. The ship's medical teams provided free health services, diagnostics, and treatment to the local public and military personnel, conducted medical cooperation with local hospitals, primary schools, orphanages, nursing homes, and the poor communities. Some Chinese analysts, in fact, linked this Asian mission with Beijing's growing status on the global stage; by asserting that '*as the world's second-largest economy, China has the responsibility and the capability to provide humanitarian services to people across the world.*'[9] The author though, had presented his views on this mission by describing it as an attempt at 'First Aid Diplomacy', in a related article at that time.[10] Notwithstanding, the fact remains that these voyages have achieved much more international mileage for China as well as the PLA Navy, than what mere words on White Papers and rhetorical statements from various platforms can do.

PLA Navy Ship Visits Post Gulf of Aden Anti-Piracy Deployment

Finally, one must take an objective look at the PLA Navy's post anti-piracy deployment arena. This has progressively expanded, as its escort mission has endured with time. Ships of the 11th task force, in fact, ventured into the Black Sea for the first time ever, making maiden visits to Ukrainian, Bulgarian, and Romanian ports. They subsequently docked at Istanbul, and the Israeli port of Haifa, thus remaining in a potentially volatile area for close to a month in July-August 2012. The 13th task force ships went all the way into the Atlantic, via the Mediterranean, visiting ports in Portugal, France, and Morocco. The ships of the last i.e. 15th task force routed themselves home via Mombasa, Dar-e-Salaam and Trincomallee in Sri Lanka. The emergent pattern, even on perfunctory analysis, resembles a wheel, with the hub at the Gulf of Aden and the spokes fanning out in all corners of the region and beyond.

'Whither'

Having discussed the 'What' and 'Where' parameters of PLA Navy's MOOTW endeavours, the 'Whither' component of this framework has been investigated in this section. This loosely translates into intent; and the global community has been asking this question for some time now, with regard to the PLA Naval modernization. At a macro-level, the answer to this question may be seen to stem from two distinct imperatives. The first relates to the securing of its ever expanding maritime interests and endeavours, broadly translating to security of its SLOCs, on which its growing economy is so dependent. The second relates to the need for a growing power to find increasingly larger operating space, and strive for presence in all global hotspots, so as to be able to influence events in favour of its own national interest. The above imperatives possibly obligate China to harbour different intents for the two main maritime areas of its focus i.e. the Pacific, and the Indian Ocean regions. An intent assessment for these two Regions has been attempted in the succeeding paragraphs.

PLA Navy's Intent in the Pacific Ocean

Consecutive Congressional Research Service (CRS) reports for the US Congress, since 2011,[11] have been highlighting the increasing Chinese maritime focus, including fast-paced PLA Navy modernization, and its expanding activities. In their assessment, it mainly aims at:

- Asserting sovereignty over territorial claims and control over the associated maritime zones in the South and East China Seas
- Forcing others to acknowledge that it intends to regulate foreign military activities in its EEZ
- Progressively challenging the US naval hegemony in the pacific
- Ultimately, displacing the US influence in the Pacific region
- Eventually asserting its status as a major world power

These objectives definitely have a hard ring to them. However, Beijing is trying to present them in velvet gloves as long as it can do so, through the MOOTW and the Maritime Diplomacy route. All this while, its forces continue to be operationally active and get well trained and equipped in the process. Thus, the US must continue to carefully watch all expansive Chinese maritime efforts with a view to assess their exact intentions.

PLA Navy's Intent in the Indian Ocean

There is an idea taking root in the Chinese discourse that China should increase its efforts at influence building in the Indian Ocean littoral, under the so called 'march west' paradigm.[12] In the maritime domain, this could possibly mean expanding the PLA Navy activities, like the anti-piracy patrols into permanent presence. The Chinese leadership, of late, has been stressing the need for protecting the resources and energy interests either located or transiting through this region. It is therefore argued that they are likely to address the greater Middle-east sub-region first, in this endeavour. Some pointers to this pattern are already visible, with Beijing indicating its willingness for participatory role in the Israel-Palestine peace process.[13] Similar efforts were also visible in its mediation efforts between North and South Sudan.

Increased frequency of PLA Navy ships going to or transiting through the Mediterranean, particularly during the current state of instability along its Asian and African coastal states, lends credence to the belief that it seeks to be able to leverage its presence in this area of simmering disquiet, should an opportunity for maritime diplomacy arise. The Chinese influence being brought to bear on various so-called 'pearls' in the IOR with a future objective of upgrading one or two of them into naval bases, is always a possibility. Such influence building in the South Asian neighbourhood may, in their assessment, compel the Indian security establishment to largely remain engaged in addressing the capacity accretion in these countries, and their consequent aspirations, itself. For instance, its maritime engagement with the Pakistani military establishment through sale of ships and submarines, training, development of port infrastructure etc., would possibly cause enough concerns for India to be on constant watch. Above all, this presence, in times to come could be seen in terms of preparing for another front, should the boundary question across the Himalayas assume precarious proportions.

'When'

It is evident that in the context of the current world order, the occasions and opportunities for using Navies in their conventional role as instruments of coercive diplomacy are few and far in between. However there are numerous opportunities for these navies to engage in non-traditional activities. Both oceans of their interest are presenting sufficient opportunities of this kind. Beijing recognizes this unique opportunity and is accordingly building dual nature capabilities in its Navy, so as to leverage them to its advantage. Accordingly, there is accretion in the number of LPDs, landing craft, troop carriers, replenishment ships, air-cushion vehicles, submarine rescue and diving support ships, alongside the destroyers and frigates.

The new aircraft carrier, though quite limited in operational capabilities, can prove to be an ideal platform for HADR and post-calamity support roles in the western Pacific and beyond. Deployment pattern of PLA Navy ships and auxiliaries, particularly in last six months, seems to suggest that China wants to be within reasonable reach of most areas of its interest. China is grabbing the all chances for multilateral cooperation, and is also not shy of creating such opportunities for unilateral participation. So it can be argued that the bottom-line as regards the 'When' component is: *anytime and every time that the opportunity presents itself.* There is whoever, exceptions to this a caveat to this, as was evident during the intentional delayed response to the post-Typhoon crisis in the Philippines.

Conclusion

Non- traditional activities project the benign face of the State while keeping the force well trained, equipped, and operationally active,. These non-traditional tasks also help in justifying the capacity building, infrastructure upgrade and greater financial outlay to a certain extent. China has thus found a near justifiable way of modernizing its Defence Forces, particularly its Navy, by emphasising the importance of MOOTW. The international community, in such a situation, has to grudgingly accept these justifications, and feels a little awkward in questioning the 'real motive' for such a grand force expansion. Thus, there are vital lessons to be learnt from the Chinese approach of naval capacity building by highlighting the relevance of non-traditional role of this service.

However, there is nothing new or extraordinary in what the PLA Navy is doing, which other navies have not done before, or are not doing now. However, the Chinese are projecting their achievements to the world in an organized and relentless manner under the broad rubric of 'Three Warfares' – media, legal and psychological – so as to lend credence to their 'peaceful development' formulation. Needless to say, the investment of so much of national effort, resources and 'international relations' capital can really be considered to stand China in good stead in the long run This is quite evident in that the PLA Navy and its personnel have developed strong sea legs in a multinational environment, gained vital lessons in jointmanship and inter-operability, and above all, a reasonably acceptable presence in global maritime matters. It can thus be inferred that China considers this course of action as a win-win situation – one of *continuing modernization, but with a benign pretence.*

In light of this conclusion, it will indeed be apt to close this paper by citing the statement of Rear Admiral Qiu Yanpeng, Commander-in-charge of the PLA Navy's 'Mission Harmony 2011' to the Caribbean islands, wherein he stated:

> "*The current mission was of great significance in publicising the ideas of 'Harmonious World' and 'Harmonious Ocean', demonstrate China's friendly relations between the Latin American countries, and highlight the PLA's image as a peaceful and a civilized force.*"[14]

These words need to be read between the lines by the world at large; and whether or not the international community is convinced about these words, does remain a moot question.

NOTES

1. 'Hu calls for efforts to build China into maritime power', *Xinhua*, November 8, 2012, http://news. xinhuanet.com/english/special/18cpcnc/2012-11/08/c_131959403.htm (accessed April 15, 2014).
2. 'Xi advocates efforts to boost China's maritime power', *Xinhua*, July 31, 2013, http://news.xinhuanet.com/english/china/ 2013-07/31/c_132591246.htm (accessed April 25, 2014).
3. White Paper on 'China's National Defense in 2008, Section II - National Defence Policy', http://www.china.org.cn/ government/central_government/2009-1/20/content _17155577_4.htm (accessed April 22, 2014).
4. 'Chinese navy to stick to defensive strategy', *Xinhua*, April 23, 2009, http://news.xinhuanet.com/english/2009-04/23/content_11239423.htm (accessed April 22, 2014).
5. White Paper on 'China's National Defense in 2008, ibid.
6. Chinese Defense White Paper on 'Diversified Employment of China's Armed Forces', April 16, 2013, sections III and IV, http://www.china.org.cn/government/whitepaper/ node_7181425.htm (accessed April 22, 2014).
7. 'Chinese president meets UN chief', *Xinhuanet*, June 19, 2013, http://news.xinhuanet.com/english/ china/2013-6/19/c_ 132468995.htm (accessed April 22, 2014).
8. Kamlesh K Agnihotri, 'China's Continental Strategy Expands into Maritime Domain', India-China Chronicle of the India-China Economic and Cultural Council, November 2013, pp. 14-16, http:// www.icec-council.org/india-china/index.php?param=news/379251/80.
9. 'Peace Ark: From China with love and care', *China Daily*, June 19, 2013, http://english.peopledaily.com.cn/ 90786/ 8290054.html (accessed April 22, 2014).
10. Kamlesh Kumar Agnihotri, 'China's 'Peace Ark': The Navy and Band-Aid Diplomacy', Institute of Peace and Conflict Studies Article No. #4026, July 9, 2013, http://www.ipcs.org/article/military/chinas-peace-ark-the-navy-and-band-aid-diplomacy-4026.html (accessed April 22, 2014).
11. Ronald O'Rourke, CRS Report for Congress, '*China Naval Modernization: Implications for U.S. Navy Capabilities – Background and Issues for Congress*', June 8, 2011, p. 5, http://www.fas.org/ sgp/crs/row/RL33153.pdf (accessed April 22, 2014). All subsequent reports at rough quarterly periodicity by the Author till the report of September 5, (2013), reiterate much the same point.

12. Wang Jisi, 'Marching Westwards: The Rebalancing of China's Geo-strategy' Center for International and Strategic Studies, Peking University Report No. 73, October 7, (2012).
13. Xinhua, 'Chinese president meets Israeli PM, pledges efforts for peace in Middle East', May 10, 2013, http:// news.xinhuanet.com/english/china/2013-05/09/c_132370959.htm (accessed April 22, 2014).
14. China Military Online, 'Peace Ark hospital ship to write new chapter of harmony', September 20, 2011, http:// eng.chinamil.com.cn/news-channels/china-military-news/2011-09/20/content_4680673.htm (accessed April 22, 2014).

4

The Evolution of Chinese Maritime Strategy: The Continental Roots of China's Maritime Expansion

Dr. Murray Scot Tanner

Introduction

Among many security analysts, China's growing maritime interests have raised the question of whether it should be regarded as transforming from a primarily 'continentalist' power into a primarily 'maritime' power. This chapter examines the evolution of China's maritime strategy, and the relationship between its land-based or continental security concerns, and its expanding maritime security concerns. It focuses on the array of forces that are driving a shift in the relative importance of land-based and maritime interests in China's perceptions of its national security interests. It, however, also argues that China's land-based internal security concerns remain Chinese Communist Party's most prominent and pressing sources of anxiety. Moreover, many of China's maritime security interests and concerns in many cases derive their importance from their potential impact on China's land-based security concerns – most notably their impact on China's internal security and domestic security. It is, therefore, at best premature to re-label China as a 'maritime' rather than a 'continentalist' power.

Beyond these issues, this chapter also focuses on the 'so what' question for the Indian and US maritime security specialists – what the implications are of China's

---

The views and ideas put forward in this paper are entirely those of the author. They do not necessarily represent the views of CNA Corporation, its corporate officers, or of any of its sponsors.

land-based and maritime security concerns for the Indian and the American ability to deal effectively, and engage with China, as an increasingly active maritime power, especially in distant seas regions such as the IOR?

Land-based and Maritime Concerns in China's National Security

For just over 25 years, maritime issues have grown increasingly important to China's pursuit of its critical national security interests – labelled 'core' interests, since about 2003. Successive waves of new interests have deepened the importance of the maritime dimension of China's security concerns over the past 10-15 years. These include its efforts to assert near seas territorial and resource rights and interests; its 'going out' investment strategy, growing expatriate population and overseas investments; its reliance on imported mineral resources from 'distant sea' areas, especially the IOR; and the gradual shift in the direction of China's external trade, from East Asia and the US to the IOR, Africa, Europe, and Latin America. A review of key leadership speeches and central policy documents indicates that the Chinese Communist Party's leadership increasingly recognizes that many of the front lines in its struggle for national security have moved more towards the maritime domain.

Impact of maritime concerns on China's core national security interests varies between its offshore (*jinhai*) regions and distant seas (*yuanhai*); and these different packages of core interests drive the important differences in China's maritime security strategies toward these regions.[1] China's offshore regions are the locus of all of its remaining disputes over territorial sovereignty and national unity, as well as several increasingly tense energy and other resource disputes. As per China's assessment, it a most likely to face a military threat to its east and south-eastern coastal regions, which therefore, are the focus of Beijing's efforts to enhance its strategic depth.

Portions of the distant sea regions immediately beyond China's offshore areas are also a focus of Chinese efforts to expand strategic depth. Most notably, this includes the region between the so-called 'first-' and 'second-island' chains, and the Strait of Malacca. Security of China's growing expatriate population in distant sea areas is also becoming perhaps the greatest non-economic security challenge in the distant seas, especially since the PLA's participation in the 2011 Libyan evacuation. However, China has no territorial claims beyond its offshore regions. Thus, its national security concerns in distant sea regions relate primarily to Beijing's core interest in sustained rapid economic growth through protection of its existing energy and non-energy trade routes – especially in the IOR, and the establishment of access to new trade routes and resources, as in the Arctic. The greater security import of China's offshore regions is especially clear in the intensity of nationalist sentiment surrounding the territorial disputes in the East and South China Seas.

Still, despite growing attention that foreign analysts have paid to China's intensifying maritime concerns, land-based security issues will remain major focus of China's national security strategy. At the root of this, the nature of the Chinese state – and the security challenges on which it places the greatest emphasis – reinforces the importance of land-based security concerns for the regime, and intertwines its land-oriented and maritime-oriented security challenges. To a great extent, Chinese Communist Party's land-based interests in state security, social stability, and ethno-national unity are the forces that imbue its growing maritime security interests in sovereignty, national unity, economic growth, and the safety of Chinese abroad, with their underlying security importance for the regime.

There are at least three major reasons why China's land-based security concerns remain robust, and are, to a great degree, intertwined with China's growing maritime concerns. These reasons include:

- China continues to confront a distinct set of land-based national security issues on which it cannot turn its back, and which will continue to demand significant investment of military and paramilitary resources, as well as leadership and diplomatic attention. These include national unity challenges in Xinjiang and Tibet, domestic security challenges broadly defined, and border security concerns with very large and difficult set of neighbours in the northeast, west and southwest – notably North Korea, Afghanistan, and Pakistan. These concerns have taken on a far greater intensity in just the past year (2013) since Xi Jinping's accession to power as the new General Secretary. He has focused his personal attention on responding to a string of protests, attacks and even terrorist incidents in China's Muslim regions – or reportedly involving members of China's Muslim community.
- China's land-based security concerns, and success in pursing them, remain a critical 'enabler' and a critical backstop for China's pursuit of its maritime security concerns. In the late 1980s-early 1990s, one of the key factors in China's security shift to the east and its maritime regions was the decline in perceived security threats to its northern and western land borders. Xi Jinping's activism in reinvigorating China's 'peripheral diplomacy' in 2013 quietly reaffirmed the importance of China having good ties with Russia and Central Asia at a time when both land-based and maritime peripheral relations to China's east and southeast were growing increasingly stressed. Any future intensification of new and emerging security challenges from China's interior border regions would at least partially re-adjust Beijing's

balance of land-based and maritime concerns. Also, China seems to be geopolitically uncomfortable with relying too heavily for its energy security on either offshore and sea-borne sources of crude oil and gas, or on land-based sources from Central Asia and Russia.

- China's maritime security concerns, to a great extent, have their roots in China's internal security concerns. For the sake of encouraging argument and discussion, the author takes a fairly fundamentalist line in contending that, basically, it is the Chinese Communist Party's ultimate national security issue – regime security and domestic stability – that continues to drive its growing maritime security concerns. The manner in which China approaches two or three of its other 'core' national security interests is rooted in its desire to maintain regime security and internal stability. Specifically, Beijing is concerned that there are likely to be serious domestic security consequences if it does not show continued strong performance in maintaining rapid economic growth: protecting China's growing overseas personnel and interests, and assuaging nationalist feeling by asserting and protecting its maritime stakes in national unity, sovereignty, territorial and resources rights. One also wonders how China's regime security concerns shape its perceptions of the long-term strategic intentions of several democratic regimes with which it will have to cooperate to protect its maritime security interests – especially the US, India, Japan and Australia in the distant sea regions. Further, how these concerns will affect China's willingness to protect its distant seas maritime security through cooperation with these partners, rather than through pursuit of autonomous power or dominance.

Growing Maritime Dimension of China's National Security Interests and Strategy

The balance of the importance China has placed on land-based and maritime forces in its national security strategy has evolved significantly over the past 25 years – largely, but not linearly, in the direction of greater emphasis on maritime interests. A critical milestone that both enabled and required China to rebalance attention toward its coastal and maritime regions began during the mid-1980s and culminated in 1993, when the Chinese leadership – apparently the Central Military Commission – officially determined that China should adopt a new 'main strategic direction' (*zhuyao zhanlue fangxiang*). China's main strategic direction is a contingency-based official judgment of Party and military leaders concerning where the main body of Chinese forces are most likely to be engaged in during a major conflict. It reflects a judgment about the direction from which China's most pressing threat is likely to come – a judgment so fundamental that the main strategic direction has only been changed a handful of times since 1949; and these judgments have historically coincided with the tectonic shifts in Chinese security strategy and diplomacy.[2]

In 1993, China's leadership felt able to shift its main strategic direction away from a focus on China's north-eastern, northern and north-western borders where, for more than two decades, it had perceived a potentially existential and overwhelming land-based and missile-based threat from the recently dissolved Soviet Union. It declared the new 'main strategic direction' was oriented toward Taiwan and China's south-east coastal region.

In addition to the decline in the land-based threat facing China, a mix of factors drove this strategic shift toward China's coast. The exact mix remains unclear to the author, but very likely could have included the following:

- Concerns about the growing quest in Taiwan for independence under President Lee Teng-hui
- Dramatic high-technology military victory of the US in the first Gulf War
- China's attendant need – set forth in a key 1993 speech by Jiang Zemin – to develop the capability to fight and win a high tech limited war (which implied expanding China's coastal strategic depth)
- Enormous importance of maritime trade and investment to China's economy, especially along its southern coastal regions

This shift may not have been driven by another critical turning point that occurred in 1993 – China's shift from a net oil exporter to an importer, but China's 20 years of anxieties about the risk that its energy imports via Malacca and the IOR might be cut off, has certainly reinforced its rebalance from land-based toward a maritime strategic focus in the decades since.

Sometime in the early-mid 2000s, however, China undertook a partial recalibration of its strategic directions back toward land-based concerns in its west and south-west. China's maritime east and south-east, in particular Taiwan, remain its main strategic direction. However, to its west and south-west, China saw growing concerns about: (1) the increasing power of India (the time link between this decision and India's 1998 nuclear test remains obscure); (2) the presence of NATO/US forces in Afghanistan and Pakistan after 2001; (3) ethnic unrest in Tibet and Xinjiang (and links between the latter and Pakistan and Afghanistan); (4) China's growing importance of energy imports from Russia and Central Asia; (5) the regime threat of the so-called 'colour revolutions' between 2000 and 2004; and (6) rising illegal drug imports to China from Central Asia. In a set of speeches in 2009, Defence

Minister Liang Guanglie told national defence committees in western China that their land borders to the west and south-west were an 'important strategic direction' for China – in Chinese parlance, an important source of threat and direction of defence, but one still clearly secondary to the 'main strategic direction' of Taiwan, and the south-east coastal regions.[3]

Over the past decade, China's top leaders have signalled increasing importance of China's security interests in maritime regions through an unprecedented series of public statements from the period of Hu Jintao's leadership to the period of the new leadership under Xi Jinping and Li Keqiang. Several important strategic themes have been evident in these and other speeches. Chinese leaders have promoted what we might call a 'defensive expansion' of China's maritime security presence and activity by arguing that China's important maritime security interests face increasing challenge from both traditional sources (e.g., other states) and non-traditional sources. Consequently, China has a right and a need to develop a wide range of means for asserting and protecting its interests in both offshore and distant sea regions – including political, diplomatic, economic, military, and other means. Finally, under Xi Jinping and Li Keqiang, Chinese maritime policy statements have, at times, stressed the importance of the inter-relationship between its maritime and land-based interests. Some of the articulations of Chinese leadership in this regard are mentioned below in chronological order:

- 2003: Hu Jintao contended that China's energy security was at risk because 80 per cent of its rapidly rising petroleum imports had to transit the Malacca Strait – a speech which led to the coining of the phrase *China's Malacca Dilemma.*[4]
- 2004: As part of his PLA's 'new historical missions' speech, Hu told senior PLA officers that China's maritime interests were expanding beyond its immediate coasts, and that other nations were scrambling to assert their competing maritime territorial and resource claims at China's expense. Hu contended that the PLA had a mission to assert and protect these interests.[5]
- 2009: In a meeting with the Singapore Prime Minister Lee Hsien Loong, Hu proposed that their two countries should cooperate in maintaining security in the Malacca Strait.[6]
- November 2012: In his final speech as CCP General Secretary, Hu set forth a vision of establishing China's global reach as a maritime power. This included improved ability to develop its marine economy, exploit marine resources, protect marine ecology, and resolutely safeguard China's maritime rights and interests.[7] Hu also called for China to strengthen its

military, diplomatic, and other means of protecting China's legitimate rights and interests overseas.[8]

- July 2013: In a Politburo study session, Xi Jinping delivered the first major public address by a CCP leader devoted entirely to maritime affairs and building China into a maritime power. On the conciliatory side, Xi said China would pursue 'converging interests' with other countries, would 'use peaceful means and negotiations to settle disputes and strive to safeguard peace and stability,' and would adhere to the policy of 'shelving disputes and carrying out joint development for areas over which China owns sovereign rights.' At the same time, Xi insisted that China would 'in no way...abandon its legitimate rights and interests, nor...give up its core national interests.'[9]
- March 2014: Prime Minister Li Keqiang, in his annual Government Work Report before the National People's Congress, made more references to the importance of China's maritime 'rights and interests', and the need to protect them than any Prime Minister since at least 1996; and probably in PRC history. A particularly noteworthy recurrent theme in Li's speech was the importance of better linking China's land and maritime interests both through the construction of port facilities at home, and building overseas links to South and South-east Asia such as the 'maritime silk road' and the Yunnan-Burma-Bangladesh-India and China-Pakistan corridors.[10] Li's strategy also underscores China's concern that its increasing maritime economic links to the south and west help contribute to the economic development of its ethnically restive interior regions.

In October 2013, Xi Jinping emphasised the need to strengthen China's peripheral diplomacy to both its maritime and land neighbors in a major speech at a national conference on peripheral diplomacy. While the summary of Xi's remarks did not contain an explicit criticism of China's failures in maritime security diplomacy with its neighbours, that criticism reportedly occurred at the meeting. Also, while Xi's published remarks said little about China's Central Asian neighbours and Russia, Xi's powerful emphasis on the importance of a secure periphery for China underscored, again, how critical China's continued good relations with its western land neighbors were, for enabling its maritime security strategy.[11]

Implications for China's Offshore and Distant Seas Maritime Security Strategies

Offshore Regions

In its offshore regions, China's more immediate nationalist pressures, and political and security interests, have led it to a much more conflicted strategy than in distant seas regions. Chinese security analysts underscore that Beijing's stakes in these regions are much heavier, and in the words of one, much more tightly tied to the core interests on which the Chinese Communist Party has staked its political legitimacy.[12]

These stakes in recent years seem to have propelled a conflict with the 'low-tension, long-term security' strategy which China had pursued with some success during the late 1990s-early 2000s, in its relations with East and South China Sea neighbours. Prior to about 2009, China had tried to emphasize more of a positive sum (win-win) engagement, and actions consistent with a long-term strategy of building strong bilateral economic ties that maximized its leverage, discouraged multilateral regional resistance, and deferred serious negotiations on territorial issues, presumably until a day when China could negotiate from a position of dominance. This period also saw more low-key, persistent mixture of efforts to assert China's territorial claims in the East/South China Sea, while working to challenge or erode the basis of competing nations' claims, and develop the capabilities to deter or dominate escalating tensions over these claims.

Since 2009, however, China's increasing maritime assertiveness, coupled with challenges from Philippines and Japan, has ratcheted up the nationalist pressure on Beijing to assert and protect these claims. The author would not go so far as to assert that authorities in Beijing are little more than a slave to the nationalist forces they called into being, although Chinese interlocutors often try to portray their hands as being tied by such forces. The historical record of China's handling of domestic protests against Japan, in 2005, 2010, 2012, and 2013, however, shows that China is playing a far more challenging and unpredictable game. At times, China has had difficulty in containing this protest, and at other times – such as in the first quarter of 2014, when Japanese actions would certainly foretell unrest in China – anti-Japanese protest has been surprisingly minimal. Whether or not this was because China felt compelled to head off domestic pressures by more assertive diplomacy and security actions – such as the Air Defence Identification Zone (ADIZ) declaration or the persistent air and sea patrolling of the Senkakus – remains a challenging analytical question.

Distant Seas

Since Hu Jintao's new historic missions speeches in 2004, Hu and the Communist Party's leadership have collectively given their assent to a critical update in the PLA Navy's official strategy that takes account of the growing importance of China's distant seas interests to China's security and economic development, and the PLA Navy's increasing strategic missions to help protect China's critical sea lanes, maritime transport, overseas interests, and the security of China's growing numbers of expatriate citizens abroad. China amended its longstanding strategy of 'offshore defence' (*jinhaifangyu*), and added a second objective – 'distant seas protection' (*yuanhaifangwei*).[13] In distant sea regions, especially the IOR, China has demonstrated an increasing commitment to expand its naval presence and activities, and its overall strategic influence. The defensive expansion elements of China's approach reflect its growing belief that the Indian Ocean broadly conceived – including all of Africa and the Middle East littoral – is increasingly important to China's economic growth, protection of its expatriate workers, and by extension, its domestic stability.

China's strategy in these distant seas regions is also driven by its assessment – reflected in the writings of its military and non-military analysts – that China's interests, especially in the IOR, are increasingly vulnerable.[14] China sees this vulnerability arising, in part, from non-traditional security threats – mostly piracy, but also political instability in the region, such as the 'Arab Spring.' China also sees this vulnerability arising from traditional security threats. In the IOR, this includes India's increasing naval capabilities – especially in its Eastern Fleet and Andaman Joint Command – as well as the US rebalance to Asia, and both countries' increasing maritime cooperation with Japan, Australia, and other regional powers.

The largely economic nature of China's distant seas interests permits it greater flexibility and probably a longer time frame in its strategic approach to these regions than it feels it can follow in its offshore regions. For example, as some Chinese and many foreign specialists have noted, China appears to have a conscious and strategic element of opportunism to the expansion of its distant seas presence, activities, and cooperation.[15] China has taken opportunities when the needs of the international community or regional countries required additional naval assistance, or when China's own interests were so indisputably at stake that little objection was raised to its expanded presence. Examples include China's participation in the Gulf of Aden anti-piracy mission, its agreement to assist Seychelles with its piracy problems, a PLA Navy frigate's participation in the Libyan evacuation, the Peace Ark hospital ship's tour of East Africa, China's recent Arctic rescue attempts, and China's exercises with other regional and extra-regional navies in the IOR.

China's strategy in distant seas has also reflected greater public emphasis on these regions as a 'global commons' in contrast to the more zero-sum orientation of territorial and resource disputes in China's offshore regions. In both the Arctic and Indian Ocean region, China has emphasized that despite being an extra-regional power, it, as also and other countries, have increasing rights and interests, as important stakeholders. This position, Beijing contends, entitles them to a 'seat at the table' in established and emerging regional economic and security organizations, notably the Arctic Council, Indian Ocean Naval Symposium (IONS) and South Asian Association for Regional Corporation (SAARC). China has also used these grounds to criticize what it portrays as efforts by leading maritime powers in these distant seas – notably India and the US – to maintain maritime 'hegemony' at China's expense.

Over the longer term, China has used this expanding presence and activity to acclimate countries of these 'distant sea' regions to its naval presence, and to legitimise its role as an extra-regional protector of security and stability. China has gradually expanded the range of activities and vessels in these regions – notably the recently reported first visit to the IOR by a PLA Navy nuclear-attack submarine.[16] A key aspect of this strategy has, of course, been the long-term development of a wide network of ports and support facilities, at which Chinese Gulf of Aden task forces and other PLA Navy ships can call.

A critical long-term concern for the US and Indian maritime security specialists should be whether, and how much, would China be willing to pursue its security interest in the IOR and other distant seas through primarily cooperative means. Conversely will the Chinese leadership's concerns about the long term trustworthiness and intentions of these democratic naval powers encourage China to seek more autonomous means of guaranteeing its security, as its naval capabilities in these regions increases?

NOTES

1. Chinese military sources define China's offshore regions as including the Yellow, East China, and South China Seas, in addition to an undefined maritime region east of Taiwan. Distant seas regions are defined simply as the regions beyond the offshore areas.
2. The path-breaking scholar of China's concept of a main strategic direction is Dr. David M. Finkelstein 'China's National Military Strategy: An Overview of the 'Military Strategic Guidelines' in Roy Kamphausen and Andrew Scobell, eds, *Rightsizing the People's Liberation Army: Exploring the Contours of China's Military* (Carlisle, Pennsylvania, U.S. Army War College Strategic Studies Institute, 2007) pp. 69-140. There is still not much known about the implications of the main strategic direction as a military planning device, or its impact on diplomacy, intelligence, or weapons procurement, or its possible interrelationship to internal security affairs.
3. For a report on one of these speeches, see 'Liang Guanglie: to boost innovative development of national defense mobilization construction,' *China Military Online*, August 18, 2009, http://eng.chinamil.com.cn/news-channels/china-military-news/2009-08/18/content_4024262.htm (accessed September 7, 2014). Liang told this audience that 'Northwest China is China's important strategic direction and involves heavy military struggle preparation task,' and he emphasized the threat from terrorism, ethnic separatism, and religious extremism – what Beijing calls the 'three evil forces'.
4. Hu's November 2003 Speech to the National Financial and Economic Work Conference is

discussed in Shi Hongtao, 'Energy Security Encounters the 'Malacca Predicament.' Can China, Japan and South Korea Join Hands?' *China Youth Daily*, reported in Renmin Wang (no date), www.people.com.cn/GP/jingji/1037/2571366.html (accessed September 13, 2012).

5. For his help with understanding Hu's speech and its implications, the author is especially indebted to his CNA colleague Dan Hartnett, the first US scholar to seriously analyze Hu's speech and its importance. See Hu Jintao, 'Understand the New Historic Missions of our Military in the New Period of the New Century' (*renqing xinshiji xinjieduan wojun lishi shiming*; 人情新世纪新阶段我军历史使命), December 24, 2004, speech to an expanded meeting of the Central Military Commission, published on the National Defense Education website of Jiangxi Province, http://gfjy.jiangxi.gov.cn/yl.asp?idid=11349.htm, (accessed by this author in September 2012. This link is apparently no longer accessible).
6. 'Hu Jintao Meets with Singaporean Prime Minister Lee Hsien Loong,' November 12, 2009, People's Republic of China Foreign Ministry website, www.fmcoprc.gov.hk/eng//zgwjsw/t627433.htm (accessed September 7, 2014).
7. Hu Jintao, 'Full Text' of Report to the 18th Chinese Communist Party National Congress, November 8, 2012, Beijing, *Xinhua News Service*, in English, November 17, 2012, http://www.china.org.cn/ china/18th_cpc_congress/2012-11/16/content_27137540.htm (accessed September 7, 2014).
8. Hu Jintao, Report to the 18th Chinese Communist Party National Congress. Hu said that 'We should attach great importance to maritime, space and cyberspace security…' and 'We will take solid steps to promote public diplomacy as well as people-to-people and cultural exchanges, and protect China's legitimate rights and interests overseas.'
9. 'Xi advocates efforts to boost China's maritime power,' *Xinhua News Service*, July 31, 2013, at http://news.xinhuanet.com/english/china/2013-07/31/c_132591246.htm (accessed September 7, 2014).
10. Full Text of Li Keqiang's Government Work Report at 2nd Session of 12th NPC, March 5, 2014, Beijing CCTV-1 in Mandarin, March 5, 2014.Among Li's remarks are: 'We have firmly safeguarded national territorial sovereignty and maritime rights and interests. China's influence abroad has been further enhanced;' and 'We will step up the planning and construction of the Silk Road economic belt and the 21st century maritime Silk Road, and promote the construction of Bangladesh-China-India-Burma and China-Pakistan economic corridors.' Also 'The Ocean is our precious blue national territory. We must adhere to land-sea coordination, comprehensively carry out marine strategy, develop a marine economy, protect marine environment, resolutely safeguard national maritime rights and interests, and vigorously build maritime power.'
11. 'Xi Jinping: China to further friendly relations with neighboring countries,' *Xinhua News Agency in English*, October 26, 2013, http://news.xinhuanet.com/english/china/2013-10/26/c_125601680.htm (accessed September 7, 2014).
12. A Chinese security analyst's conversation with the author, 2012.
13. Translation of the amended strategy – *jinhai fangyu, yuanhai fangwei* – into english is difficult, because the meanings of the terms *fangyu* and *fangwei* overlap, and both could most reasonably be translated as 'defense'. The author has not located an official Chinese government translation of this strategy. The author's understanding of these terms, however, is that *fangyu* implies a somewhat more active, assertive, and possibly aggressive defense than *fangwei*, which has more the flavor of protecting or safeguarding. On the amendment of the strategy, see: Liu Fei, 'China's Maritime Strategic Thought During Reform and Opening to the Outside', (Gaige Kaifangyilai Zhongguo de Haiyang Zhanlue Sixiang), *Social Sciences Review*, No. 4 (April), (2012), pp. 40-41; Zhang Yong and Su Xiaodong, 'From a Higher Point, Promote the Better, Faster Development of the PLA Navy's Construction', (ZaiGeng gao Qidian Shang, Tuidong Renmin Haijun JiansheYouhaoYoukuai Fazhan), *Research on Military History*, No. 4, (2012); Gao Ning,

'Construction of a System of Modern Military Power with Chinese Characteristics', (LunGoujian Zhongguo Tese Xiandai Junshi Liliang Tixi), *Journal of the Naval Institute of Engineering*, No. 12, (2013), p. 39; Peng Kehui, 'Discussing the Historical Evolution of the New China's Maritime Strategy', (Luelun Xin Zhongguo Haiyang Zhanlue de Lishi Yanjin)*Shehui Kexue Luntan*, No. 10, (2012), p. 235.

14. On the vulnerability of Chinese maritime interests, see, for example, Liang Fang, On Maritime Strategic Access (Haishang Zhanlue Tongdao Lun), (Beijing, Shishi Chubanshe, September 2011); Liu Zhen, 'Strategic Analysis of India's Maritime Military Expansion' (Yindu hai shang junshi kuozhang de zhanlue fenxi), Modern Navy, July 2011; Guan Dai, 'The Effect of the Indian Navy and Its Sea Control Strategy upon China' (Yindu haijun he haiquan zhanlue dui hua yingxiang), NAAS and Inertial Technology, No. 97, January (2011).
15. Author's conversations with Chinese security analysts, 2012. Other characterisations of opportunism in China's strategy are relatively easy to locate. See, for example, *Safeguarding Prosperity in the Indian Ocean: Exploring India-US Cooperation*, Observer Research Foundation, Delhi, 2012, esp. pg. 9; Cdr. Gurpreet S. Khurana, 'China's Maritime Strategy and India: Consonance and Discord, Maritime Affairs' (Delhi, National Maritime Foundation) Vol. 7, No. 2 Winter (2011), esp. pp. 52-53.
16. In the US Defense Intelligence Agency's February 11, 2014, 'Annual Threat Assessment' report, submitted to Congress, DIA Director Lt. Gen. Michael T. Flynn noted that 'The PLA navy is developing the Jin-class nuclear-powered ballistic missile submarine and JL-2submarine-launched ballistic missile. We expect the navy will make their first nuclear deterrence patrols in 2014. It has also recently deployed for the first time a nuclear-powered attack submarine to the Indian Ocean.' The report is available at http://www.dia.mil/Portals/27/ Documents/News/2014_DIA_SFR_SASC_ATA_FINAL.pdf (accessed September 7, 2014).

5

'String of Pearls' and Beyond: Chinese Influence in South Asian Littoral

Commander Raghavendra Mishra

World on the Cusp of a Systemic Change

In the contemporary context, there exists a need to examine the 'String of Pearls' logic through a wider scope – in content as well as intent – to frame the Chinese geo-strategic posture. The first issue that needs emphasis is the prevailing strategic environment that portends an era of uncertainty and flux, characteristic of an impending systemic change in the international order. 'Long cycle school' theorists have devised a loose sixteen-point logic[1] in this regard. While there is no consensus on universal application of all the determinants, a fair degree of correspondence, however, does exist that a radical transformation in global architecture is invariable preceded by definite signs. Major indicators, amongst other things, include instability and changes in international hierarchy, dominance of *realpolitik* syndrome in strategic discourse, serial crises in a region(s), multiple strategic and commercial rivalries at various levels, shifting economic hubs, destabilising innovations (Kondratieff Waves), and changes in energy use patterns, besides weakening of Kantian Peace dynamics. Economic downturn, political churn, and changing balance of military power has resulted in emerging Indo-Pacific maritime stakeholders – both resident and non-resident –adopting a posture of 'strategic hedging'. This hedging policy has resulted in the nations attempting to design a delicate, and somewhat difficult, balance among the competing economic, politico-diplomatic, and security imperatives. In certain cases, while strategic choices have been made, alternate options to complement or supplement them are being explored and implemented for the proverbial 'rainy day'.[2]

South Asian Littoral – A Region in Political Transition

As part of analytical framework, trend mapping has been attempted for four countries in this paper, namely, Myanmar, Bangladesh, Pakistan, and Sri Lanka, for the period 2000 onwards. These countries have been chosen as they are contiguous maritime neighbours of India with reportedly significant Chinese influence at various levels of national decision-making. A further reason for choosing these countries is their mention in almost all analyses dealing with 'String of Pearls' discourse since the time it came to be used in strategic parlance. Taking global systemic change as a point of reference, it could also be argued that the south Asian littoral is also in the midst of transition of sorts. China, by itself, has undergone a power transition with the new government in place under the stewardship of President Xi Jinping since March 2013. Myanmar seems to be on a road of democratic change after a prolonged period of military rule with the next elections due in 2015. Sri Lanka is gradually emerging from the shadows of a long-drawn bloody ethnic strife with terrorist overtones that ended in 2009. The elections in Pakistan were held in May 2013, marking the first ever government transition through democratic means – where the new dispensation, at least on the surface, seems to seek better relations with India. While the legality of the Bangladeshi general elections of January 2014 could be considered valid, their legitimacy has been questioned in some quarters considering the opposition boycott. The elections in India during April-May 2014 have ushered in a new coalition with overwhelming mandate for promises of inclusive development, better governance and speedier reforms. Thus, it would not be amiss to aver that South Asia is in the midst of political restructuring.

The 'String of Pearls' Strategy: Changing Contours and Scope of the Narrative

The 'String of Pearls' phraseology to describe the expanding Chinese geo-strategic influence was first used in 2004 by the US Consulting firm Booz Allen Hamilton in a report submitted to the Office of Net Assessment (ONA) of the US Department of Defence (DoD).[3] This report made a case that China was developing '*strategic relationships along the sea-lanes from the Middle East to the South China Sea in ways that suggest defensive and offensive positioning, not only to protect its energy interests, but also to serve broader security objectives*'.[4] In this instance, energy and geo-strategy were considered as the driving factors for Chinese influence building in the region. Based on other developments from then onwards, primarily driven by a more assertive and maritime-military centric Chinese posture, 'string of pearls' logic was further expanded in a 2006 US Army War College monograph.[5] At this stage, these 'pearls' extended westwards from Hainan Island immediately offshore across the South and South-East Asian littorals, till the Middle East. In a more recent analysis, the viability of some of the earlier pearls was contested, and a new formulation based on the Chinese geo-economic and military security factors was devised.[6] In this case, it was argued that China, instead of 'bases', would be far more interested in access to 'places' to replenish commercially available logistics, like fuel and other consumables, in a manner similar to that carried out by the international shipping and other navies. The author was also of the view that these places as replenishment 'pit stops' may not be available to China, or for that matter to the maritime forces of other countries, as the host nation(s) may be unwilling to take sides so as to avoid unnecessary entanglements. From a well-researched Indian viewpoint, Chinese interests in the Indian Ocean have been linked to its larger geo-economic and security anxieties.[7] To add to the existing discourse from a purely maritime economic perspective, it has also been propounded that there is a worldwide network of ports that have a significant Chinese stake and these could be considered as another set of 'pearls' in their own right.[8] An aggregated depiction of these 'pearls' as they have evolved as part of strategic discourse in political,

Figure 5.1: An Aggregated Chinese 'String of Pearls'

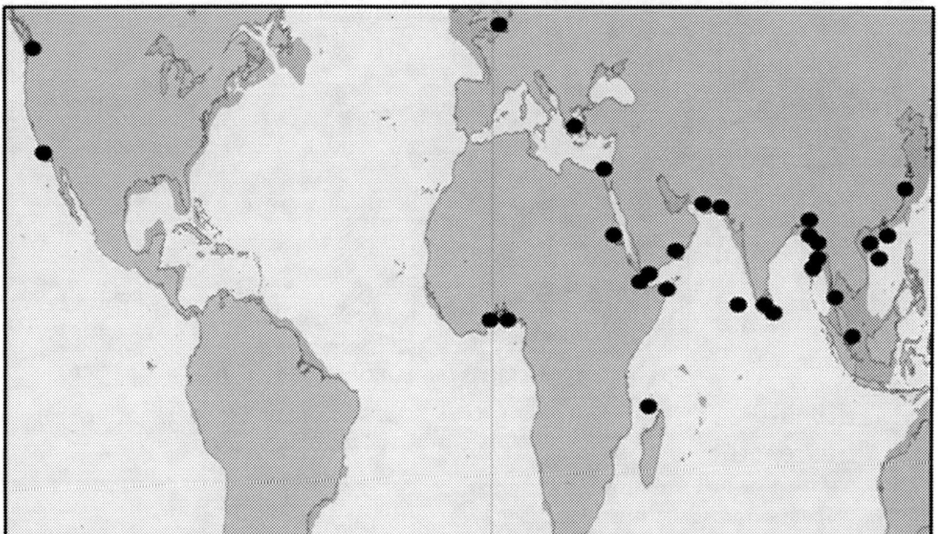

Source: Author's Compilation.

economic, and military sense, is shown in Figure 5.1. While the validity of this 'String of Pearls' narrative, based on strategic-cum-security perceptions, remains a matter of conjecture and ongoing debate, an important issue worth emphasis is the concentration of these 'pearls' in and around India's maritime periphery.

Changing Face of Global Maritime Economics

Global maritime economics have undergone a transformation since 2000, with greater acceleration since 2009. The United Nations Commission on Trade and Development's (UNCTAD) 'maritime economic trends' annual report of 2013 brings out that 50 per cent of global exports (in tonnage terms) were loaded within the Indo-Pacific and the region was the import destination for 58 per cent of global goods (Figure 5.2). This trend was first mentioned in the 2007 edition and has remained virtually unchanged, with Asia and Oceania – loosely conforming to Indo-pacific construct – emerging as the locus of global maritime commerce. In the contemporary scenario, besides the resource rich character, the region is also contributing to an ever-greater share of white and finished products as well as high technology, capital-intensive goods. The region is also improving on the *Tofflerian* scale characterised by a strong services sector.[9]

Figure 5.2: Regional Distribution of Goods Loaded and Unloaded by Volume

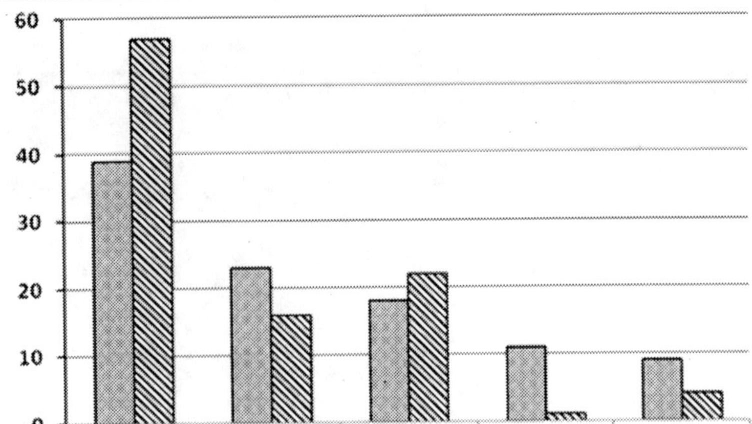

	ASIA	AMERICAS	EUROPE	OCEANIA	AFRICA
LOADED	39	23	18	11	9
UNLOADED	57	16	22	1	4

(Gross Tonnes expressed as percentage share of World Total)
Source: UNCTAD, Review of Maritime Transport, 2013 Edition, p. 9.

Rise of China and Its Emergence as the Maritime Mercantile State

Since the 1978 liberalization reforms initiated under the leadership of Deng Xiaoping, China has emerged as the second largest economy in a short span of about 35 years. During this period, it has left some of the traditional powerhouses, such as Germany, Japan, UK, and France in its wake. This hierarchy of international economic order with the US as leading economic power, and China as the second largest economy, remains valid, irrespective of the scale adopted, be it the Purchasing Power Parity (PPP), Nominal GDP, Real Term (Nominal GDP adjusted for deflators) or in current US Dollar Terms (Figure 5.3). China has been able to maintain this impressive growth trajectory, despite the global economy suffering two major shocks in 1998-99 and 2008. While it is poised to post a high but single digit growth rate of around 7.5 per cent in 2013-14, the growing differential between the economic heft of China *vis-a-vis* other large economies needs special emphasis.

Figure 5.3: GDP of Select Countries 1980 – 2012 [In Current Dollar Terms] (Trillion USD)

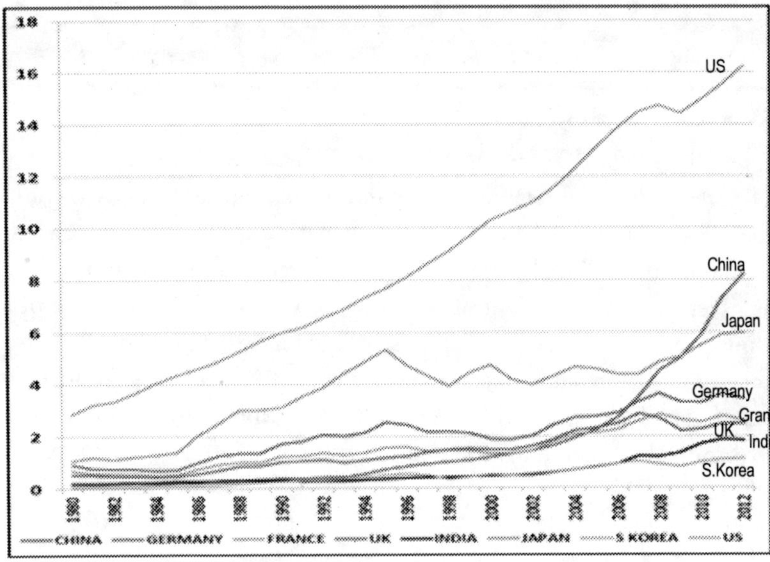

Source: World Bank Database, Author's Compilation.

In 2012, despite a slowdown due to the 2008 shock, the share of exports and imports, as a component of China's GDP, have grown from mere 21.6 per cent in 1980 to 51.7 per cent in 2012. Similarly, share of merchandise trade – primarily carried by maritime means – has grown from 20.1 per cent to an impressive 47 per cent during the same period (Figure 5.4).

Figure 5.4: Share of Exports, Imports and Merchandise Trade in Chinese GDP (1980-2012)

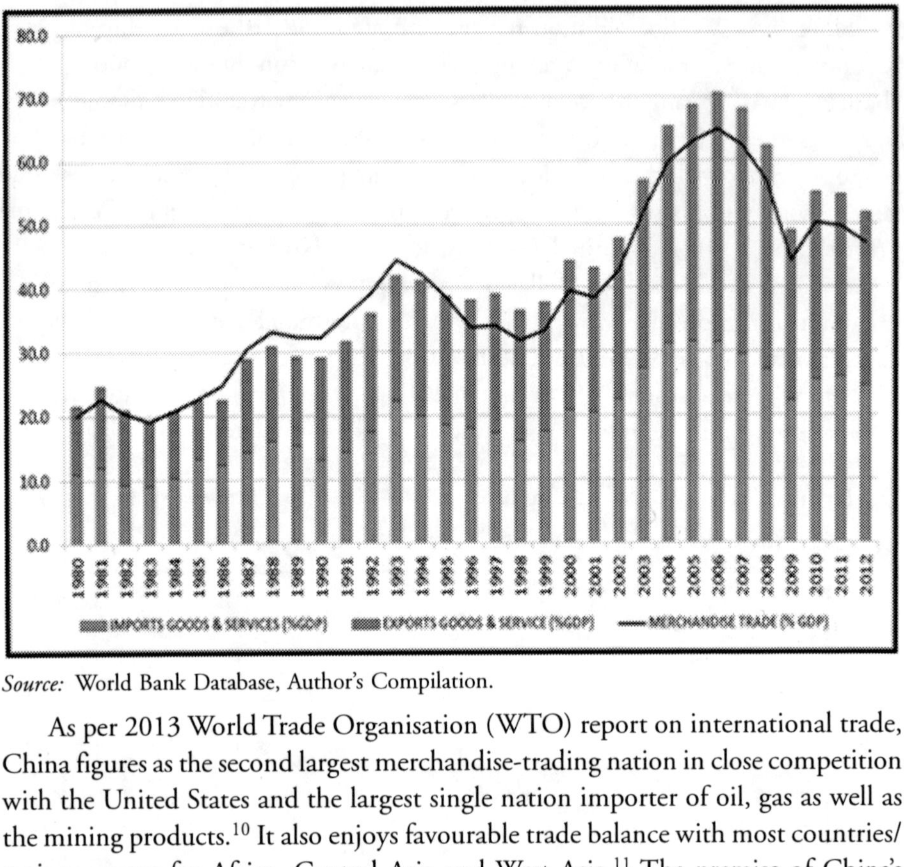

Source: World Bank Database, Author's Compilation.

As per 2013 World Trade Organisation (WTO) report on international trade, China figures as the second largest merchandise-trading nation in close competition with the United States and the largest single nation importer of oil, gas as well as the mining products.[10] It also enjoys favourable trade balance with most countries/regions except for Africa, Central Asia and West Asia.[11] The premise of China's increasing dependence on areas rich in strategic resources for sustaining its growth trajectory has been explained as a reorientation in its geo-strategic focus towards 'Region of the Four Seas', with one analyst describing this tendency of a great power to control critical maritime nodes for strategic influence as 'proto-maritime colonialism'.[12]

Salient Global Maritime Trends with Relevance to China

A comprehensive examination of Chinese maritime capability accretion, besides its widely discussed naval modernization in areas such as deep-sea exploration and drilling technology has already been undertaken by an Indian scholar[13] wherein he surmises that these facets represent a more holistic appreciation of expanding and deepening Chinese maritime interests in areas of oceanic relevance. The following trends across a spectrum of multi-faceted economic and commercial aspects further highlight the growing relevance of maritime domain to China:[14]

- In 2012, China, Republic of Korea, and Japan together built 92 per cent of the world's new ships (in Gross Tonnage terms), with China alone accounting for more than 40 per cent share [China's position - No. 1].
- Among the top 35 ship-owning economies, 17 are in Asia [China's position - No. 2], 14 in Europe, and four in the Americas.
- National concentration of fleet ownership among five countries – in order of decreasing tonnage, Greece, Japan, China, Germany and the Republic of Korea – together accounts for 53 per cent of the world tonnage.
- Estimates for January 2013 (Clarkson Research Services) suggest that the Japanese-owned fleet currently reaches the highest value, amounting to almost $100 billion, followed by the United States ($92 billion), Greece ($72 billion), China ($61 billion) [China's position - No. 4] and Germany ($60 billion); equalling almost 48 per cent of the world fleet value.
- Sixteen out of top 20 ports in Twenty-foot Equivalent Unit (TEU) throughput terms are located in the Indo-Pacific [China leads with nine such ports].
- Chinese port throughput (in TEU terms) comprised 28.4 per cent (2010), 29 per cent (2011), and 29.2 per cent (2012) [China's position - No. 1].
- 98.18 per cent [highest in the world] of Chinese shipping capacity in Dead Weight Tonnage (DWT) terms is nationally owned and registered.[15]

Growing Spread of Chinese Military Hardware

The global spread of Chinese origin military hardware is another noteworthy indicator of its improving defence-industrial capabilities. China's arms exports were estimated at US$ 300 Million in 2000. In 2012, this figure stood at US$ 1783 Million – a six-fold increase over a span of just 12 years. Further, China was ranked as the third largest exporter of military equipment in 2012, after US and Russia, well ahead of traditional strong military-industrial countries such as UK, France, Netherlands, and Israel. It would thus be evident that China is fast emerging as major arms supplier of global stature.[16] A list of 42 countries that imported military equipment from China during 2000-2012 is mentioned in Table 5.1.

It is evident from the table 5.1 that the majority of arms imports instances from China were from Asia, especially, Bangladesh, Indonesia, Iran, Myanmar, Kuwait, Pakistan, and Sri Lanka. Pakistan with 32, Bangladesh with 19, followed by Myanmar with 16 instances, were the leading three countries. Asia, with 68 per cent share (US$ 6.9 Billion) of the total Chinese defence exports during this period,

Table 5.1: Arms Importing Countries From China During 2000-12

Sl.	*Name*	*Sl.*	*Name*	*Sl.*	*Name*
1.	**Algeria (05)**	2.	**Iran (14)**	3.	Peru (02)
4.	Argentina (01)	5.	Iraq (01)	6.	Rwanda (02)
7.	**Bangladesh (19)**	8.	Jordan (01)	9.	Saudi Arabia (01)
10.	Benin (01)	11.	Kenya (03)	12.	**Sudan (07)**
13.	Bolivia (02)	14.	**Kuwait (08)**	15.	Syria (01)
16.	Cambodia (03)	17.	Laos (02)	18.	**Tanzania (06)**
19.	Chad (02)	20.	Malaysia (01)	21.	Thailand (04)
22.	DRC (02)	23.	Mali (01)	24.	Timor-Leste (01)
25.	Ecuador (03)	26.	Mauritania (02)	27.	Turkey (02)
28.	Egypt (03)	29.	**Namibia (05)**	30.	Turkey (01)
31.	Equatorial Guinea (01)	32.	Nepal (01)	33.	Uganda (01)
34.	**Gabon (05)**	35.	Niger (02)	36.	**Venezuela (05)**
37.	Ghana (03)	38.	Nigeria (02)	39.	Guyana (01)
40.	**Indonesia (07)**	41.	Oman (02)	42.	**Pakistan (32)**

Notes: 1. The figures in brackets adjacent to the names of countries indicate the number of instances of arms transfer from China during this period.

2. Countries with five or more instances of arms transfer from China are in bold letters.

Source: SIPRI Trade Transfer Database, February 27, 2014, Author's Compilation.

has also emerged as the most important hub in Beijing's arms transfer calculus (Figure 5.5).

Figure 5.5: Regional Breakdown of Chinese Military Exports (2000-2012) (Million USD in Constant 2011 Dollar Terms)

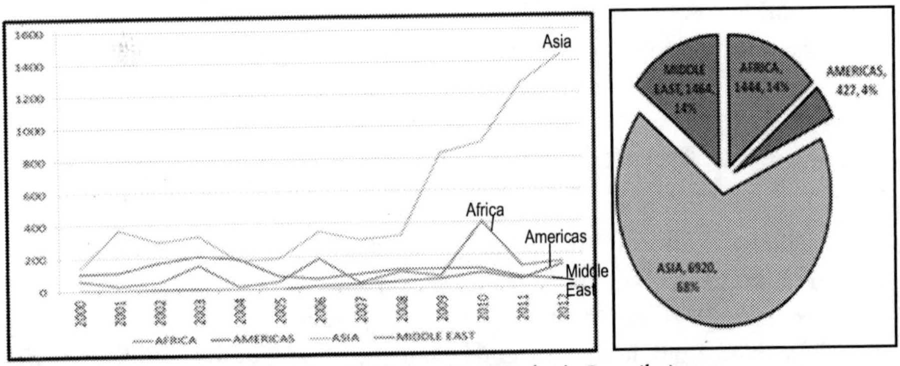

Source: SIPRI Trend Indicator Value (TIV) Database, Author's Compilation.

Chinese Influence in the South Asian Littoral

Myanmar

Myanmar was the first non-communist country to recognize China in 1949. Their bilateral relations had soured in the 1960s due to ethnic riots, but had stabilized in the 1970s with a change in the Chinese leadership. The establishment of State Peace and Development Council (SPDC) regime in 1988 ushered an invigorated phase of Sino-Myanmar relations. Chinese influence predominantly prevails at the political and economic levels and the assistance is primarily predicated towards maritime, rail and land infrastructure development, besides significant involvement in the energy sector. The initial operationalization of a gas pipeline in July 2013, with an under-construction oil pipeline planned to run in parallel, connecting the offshore Shwe Field to Kunming (Yunnan province), and further on to Nanning (Guangxi Zhuang Province) in China is a recent example (Figure 5.6). These pipelines, when complete, are expected to bring 12 Million Tonnes of crude oil and 12 Billion cubic feet of gas on an annual basis.[17]

Figure 5.6: Trans Myanmar – China Oil and Gas Pipeline

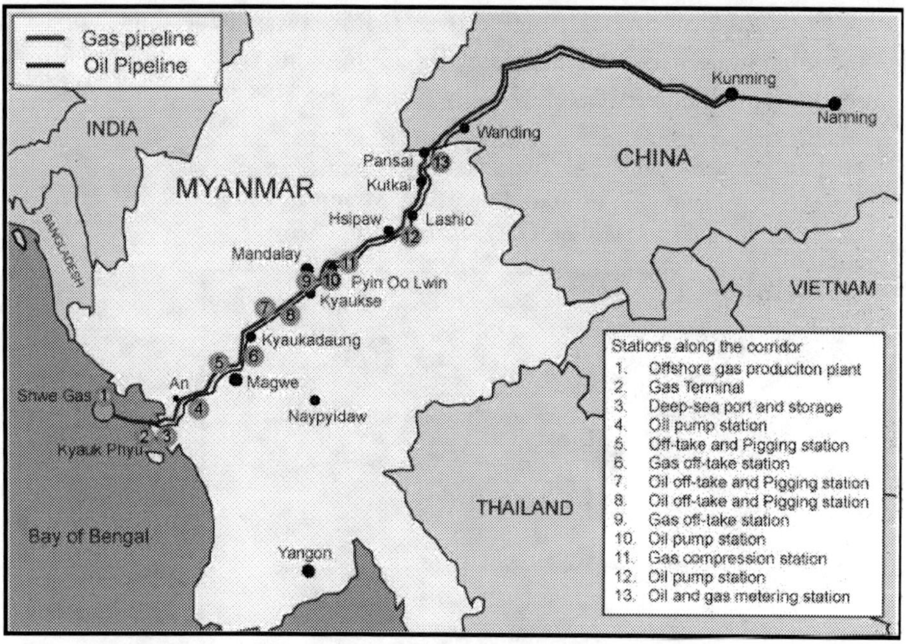

Source: Indo-Pacific Review Website, for additional details refer Note 17.

Some analysts estimate that this pipeline could also serve as an alternate offloading point for oil and gas from Middle East and Africa. However, it is for consideration that pipelines as a mode of resource movement, in almost all cases, are single commodity specific. Further, oil, and for that matter gas pipelines, are generally designed to handle a very narrow range of chemical grades. The practicality of this proposition, to a large extent, would depend on the compatibility of different fossil fuel grades at two cardinal stages – the first being the ability of transportation mode (pipeline) to handle the commodity (oil/gas) of different chemical grades; and the second being the refining ability to process these. It would be obvious that both these requirements entail substantial capital outlay.[18] Whether this is possible in this case, would require a separate study and could form a subject of further research.

As per SIPRI trade register, Myanmar was the third largest importer of Chinese military hardware, after Iran and Pakistan, during 1980-1990. A diversification in defence hardware acquisition is visible since late 1990s through Russia, Serbia, and Ukraine, with India and Italy emerging as alternate, though minor, sources. It is, however, difficult to undertake a comprehensive trend analysis for Myanmar due to scanty information available as the country was virtually closed to the international world till 2010. Myanmar's defence expenditure was estimated by SIPRI as 1343 billion Kyat in 2011 (equivalent to 3.4 per cent of GDP) and 1856 billion Kyat in 2012 (4.2 per cent of GDP) respectively.[19] Russia was the leading supplier of military hardware with 51.2 per cent of share by value (US$ 1 billion) of total imports during 2000-2012, followed by China with US$ 809 million (41.3 per cent) (Figure 5.7).

Figure 5.7: Military Imports by Myanmar: 2000-2012 (Million USD, constant 2011 terms)

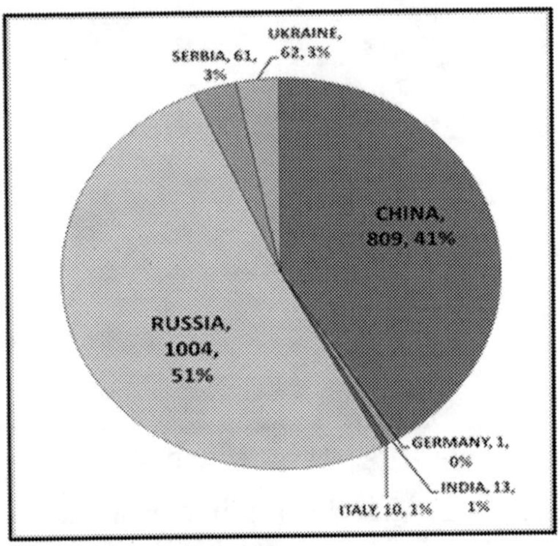

Source: SIPRI TIV Database, Author's Compilation.

During this period, major projects involving China in the maritime sector were the transfer of two refurbished Type 053H1(Jianghu Class) guided missile Frigates (FFGM) in 2012. China was also actively involved in providing the technical and design assistance for the construction of two Aung Zeya Class FFGM (2011-2012), 03 Anawrahta Class Corvettes (2001-2005) as well as ten Type 491 Series guided missile Fast Attack Craft [FAC (M)] in two batches (2004 and 2008-2012). China has also supplied C802/802A and HY 2 anti-ship missiles (AShMs), besides Medium/Short Range (MR/SR) Gunnery Systems for these platforms.[20]

Bangladesh

At the time of its formation in 1971, Sino-Bangladesh bilateral relations were difficult, but they improved with the exchange of diplomatic missions in February 1975, and the grant of mutual recognition in January 1977. The cornerstone of Sino-Bangladesh defence linkages is the 2002 Agreement on Defence Cooperation.[21] This strategic connect was strengthened through the 2010 'Closer Comprehensive Partnership' agreement. As with Myanmar, the Chinese focus areas are infrastructure and energy sectors. The most visible signs are the 'friendship bridges', and the ongoing Chittagong port development project, from where the proposed 'energy corridor' to China would start. However, this energy corridor would have to pass through either India or Myanmar, or even both these countries for achieving connectivity with the southern provinces of China. One media report after the December 2013 first joint working group meeting of BCIM (Bangladesh China India and Myanmar) sub-regional economic cooperative framework suggests that the connectivity is likely to be achieved along the route of Kolkata to Kunming (K2K) Car Rally which was held in February 2013. This route traverses through India's North-East, and Myanmar.[22] Another issue related to pipeline that does not receive adequate recognition is the advantage of maritime medium for transporting large volumes over long distance. One analysis brings out that the cost of transporting oil by pipelines is about five times more expensive as compared to the maritime mode, and about 44 times more expensive, if transported by railroad.[23]

Bangladesh allocated between 13 to 15 per cent of its annual budget since 2000 towards defence expenditure, which translates to an average 1.2 per cent in GDP terms. China was the largest supplier of military equipment to Bangladesh during 2000-2012 with total imports valued at US$ 743 Million with an overall share of 53 per cent (Figure 5.8).

Figure 5.8: Military Imports by Bangladesh: 2000-12 (Mn USD, constant 2011 terms)

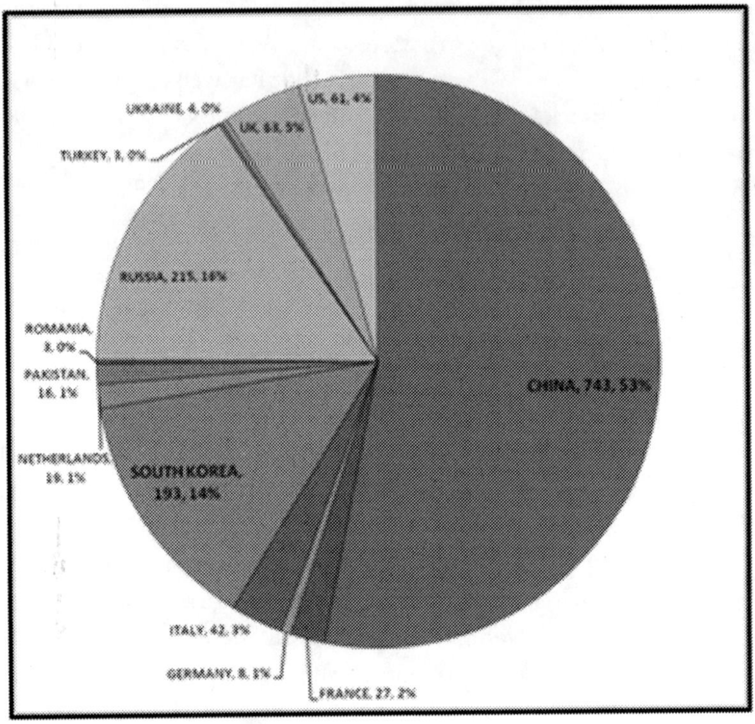

Source: SIPRI TIV Database, Author's Compilation.

Of the six contracts worth more than US$ 50 Million, four were for Chinese equipment, and one each for South Korean Offshore Patrol Vessels (OPV), and Russian MiG 29 aircraft. 19 out of 50 (38 per cent) contracts were signed with the Chinese firms during this period. Of these 19, five were sourced especially for the revitalisation of DW 2000H Frigate (BNS Bangabandhu) alone. Major naval acquisitions in future that are likely to be sourced from China include two refurbished Type 053H2 Jianghu III class FFGM as replacements for obsolete Type 41 Leopard Class Frigates; two Ming diesel electric submarines in 2019 timeframe and four new type 056 missile corvettes. The upgrade package for the refurbished Hamilton Class Cutter of American origin is also reported to include significant amounts of guided weapons from China.[24] Bangladesh though has started following a diversified pattern in its naval capabilities accretion process of late, so as to reduce single source dependencies.

Sri Lanka

The origins of a close Sino-Sri Lankan strategic partnership can be traced to the politico-military support provided by China during the fight against the Tamil separatist movement. As brought out earlier, China's focus in Sri Lanka is on infrastructure, especially port, transportation (rail/road), and power sectors. China has also provided major assistance for soft power constituencies such as:

- Confucian Centre, Kelaniya University
- Red Cross Complex at Galle
- US$ 4 Million for Internally Displaced Persons (IDP) rehabilitation effort
- Housing project in Colombo and its suburbs
- Rural electrification project (equivalent to Sri Lankan Rs. 2304 Million)

Average Sri Lankan military expenditure *vis-a-vis* national budget during the period 2000-2012, has been 16.2 per cent with a high of 21.9 per cent in 2000. The rising trend during 2006-2008 is attributed to the intense phase of military operations against the LTTE. The military expenditure in GDP terms was at an average of 3.3 per cent. During this period, Israel has been the largest military supplier to Sri Lanka valued at US$ 312 Million with 34 per cent share as can be seen at Figure 5.9. China was the second largest, worth US$ 255 Million (28 per cent). Major naval Chinese hardware imported during this period were three Type 062 Shanghai II Class FAC (G). However, the bulk of maritime response capabilities in qualitative terms during this period were provided by Israel, India, UK, and the US.

Figure 5.9: Military Imports by Sri Lanka: 2000-12
(Mn USD, constant 2011 terms)

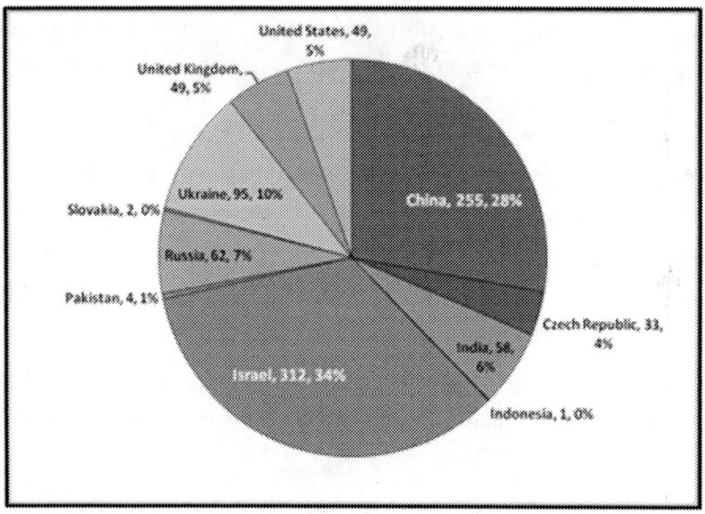

Source: SIPRI TIV Database, Author's Compilation.

Pakistan

Pakistan was one of the first countries to recognize China in 1950. As part of border settlement pact of March 3, 1963, it ceded 5160 sq km of disputed territory in Jammu and Kashmir to China. The first trade agreement was concluded in January 1963, and a joint committee for economic, trade and technology was established in October 1982. China's financial commitment and aid to Pakistan is the highest and had touched US$ nine billion in 2009 – of which 60 per cent is for developmental schemes and 30 per cent for defence sector. The principle sectors with significant Chinese involvement include telecommunications, infrastructure, energy, mining, consumer goods, automobiles and defence. The bedrock for close military-strategic bilateral ties is the 'Strategic and Defence Cooperation Agreement' of September 2005. Sino-Pak strategic relationship is the most comprehensive in the South Asian region with formal defence cooperative frameworks in critical sectors like nuclear and defence, involving joint design and co-production. Some major joint endeavours are:

- Heavy Rebuild Factory (HRF), Taxila, and Pakistan Aeronautical Complex (PAC), Kamra
- Karakoram Highway and Gwadar Port projects
- Dry Port at Sost in Pakistan occupied Kashmir (PoK).

During the period 2000-2012, Pakistan's average military expenditure *vis-a-vis* its national budget has been 22.4 per cent – one of the highest in the world. Since 2009, a downward trend is evident (attributed to adverse exchange rates) with the average military expenditure in GDP terms at 3.2 per cent. China is the leading arms supplier to Pakistan in the 21st Century at US$ 4.8 Billion (Figure 5.10). United States was the second largest arms exporter, providing 25 per cent (US$ 2.6 Billion) of its arms. 34 out of 122 (27.8 per cent) imports during 2000-2012 were of Chinese origin. Seven of these, i.e., about 20 per cent were for naval purposes. Important ones include Four (03+01) F22 frigates based on Jiangwei II FFGM, Azmat Class FAC (M), guided weapons such anti-ship and short range SAMs. However, most of advanced naval capabilities are of western origin, mainly from France, Germany, Italy and the US.

Besides military assistance through normal contractual obligations, Pakistan also receives defence equipment from China through two packages. These are:

- 'PLA Package' that provides free credit facility since 1981. Repayment is required in ten equal instalments with Pakistan receiving 100 million Yuan annually since 2004.

Figure 5.10: Military Imports by Pakistan 2000-12
(Million USD, constant 2011 terms)

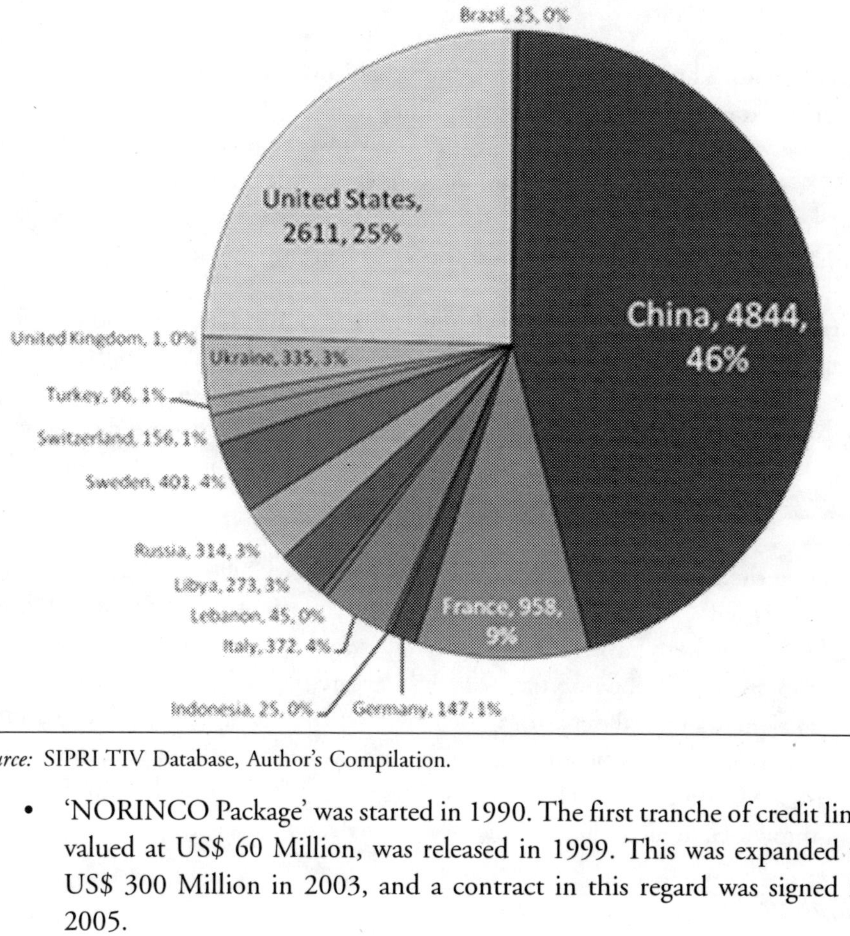

Source: SIPRI TIV Database, Author's Compilation.

- 'NORINCO Package' was started in 1990. The first tranche of credit line, valued at US$ 60 Million, was released in 1999. This was expanded to US$ 300 Million in 2003, and a contract in this regard was signed in 2005.

Interpreting Chinese Grand Strategy in South Asian Littorals

Having covered the broad shape of the country-specific Chinese engagement in the South Asian context, a critical analysis of the Chinese grand strategic posture is considered necessary. Towards this end, three important factors of behavioural pattern, strategic pillars, and vectors, besides geography and strategic context, need elaboration.

Behavioural Pattern

The changing pattern of Chinese strategic behaviour can be disaggregated in temporal dimension as follows:

Confrontation. At the height of the Cold War, during 1950s till early 1960s, the Maoist stream of communist ideology was projected as a counter to the Western capitalist philosophy.

Engagement. The deepening of Sino-Soviet schism, that started after Stalin's death, became acute and led to fierce clashes along the Ussuri River in 1969. This, and the Sino–US rapprochement during 1972-1974 were the catalyzing factors for this change in the Chinese strategic outlook. The economic reform process, initiated in 1978, under Deng Xiaoping, was a cardinal event when China started engaging with the world community beyond the 'Iron Curtain' divide.

Participation. During 1990s, with the end of confrontational bipolar politics, besides rapid expansion of geo-economic interests, and the linked political context, the Chinese behaviour was characterised by a greater participation and active engagement in the strategic sphere. Accession to WTO regime despite global scepticism and increasing participation in UN Peacekeeping Operations can be cited as apt examples in this regard.

Shaping the Environment. This trend is evident since 2000 and can be attributed to the rise of China's comprehensive power quotients. In addition, Chinese leadership seems to have realized that requisite geo-strategic heft and geo-political space exists to alter the international architecture by benign or coercive leverages. It also signals a radical departure from the essence of Deng's 24 character strategy enunciated in 1989, where the axiom of 'hide your strength, bide your time' was propagated. Some scholars have labelled the current Chinese leadership's behaviour as a throwback to 'all under the heaven' (*Tianxia*), and the ancient tributary system.[25]

Strategic Pillars

- The conventional DIME (Diplomatic, Ideological (Informational), Military and Economic) model needs adaptation while analyzing China's strategic outlook. Though ideology plays a significant role, it is more relevant for internal dynamics, so as to perpetuate the primacy of Communist Party in governance apparatus. Reduced significance of ideological preferences in foreign policy is also evident from the non-interventionist stance adopted in dealings with critical players. This has been particularly noticeable in regions where Chinese strategic influence is strong, such as in pockets of Asia and Africa. The ideological issues are put aside in situations when the national needs outweigh philosophy.[26]
- Economics and the linked politico-diplomatic milieu provide second

hierarchical imperative that drive China's outlook in contemporary environment.

- Protection of expanded economic and policy linkages is the next logical foundational pillar. Towards this end, emphasis is laid on building military security initiatives through cooperative engagements with key partners in critical geographical locations.
- The military security imperatives necessitate hard and soft (defence diplomacy) components keeping the above drivers in consideration. Strategic choices are made after careful analysis of the choices available. History, internal as well as external context, and geography are the immutable factors that shape ultimate posture. In stark opposition to the commonly held belief of Chinese strategic thought being grounded, and guided by Sun Tzsu's idioms that advocate winning with fighting (non-use), coercive options are invariably a part of strategic calculus, especially during acute crises. This unique approach by Chinese leadership to strategic affairs has been termed as 'Cultural Realism'.[27] The propensity to use 'naval nationalism' on select occasions for diverting attention away from internal causations is another factor that merits consideration while scenario building.[28]

Strategic Vectors

The critical vectors that are assessed to impinge on Chinese strategic posture are capacity, cooperation and coordination, and the role of peripheral actors. Chinese rationale – or for that matter any other dominant or emerging power – has always been endeavouring to match its military security quotient with expanding geo-strategic needs. Therefore, the Chinese efforts to build multiple-multilateral linkages for mating the 'diplomacy-economics-military' ambit highlight the aspect of cooperation and coordination.[29] Cooperation and coordination have their own internal and external locus, which undergo adaptation and calibration to obtain a win-win outcome in complex situations. Peripheral actors in China's grand strategic parlance could be equated to individual organs of the state at the operational level. In a complex, sometimes convoluted interconnected environment as it obtains today, the emphasis on socio-economic issues has indirect strategic security implications. Such tangential efforts and roundabout approaches are aimed at offsetting China's perceived, and, in some cases, valid security anxieties, given its constrained maritime periphery.[30]

Geography and Context

As has been argued by contemporary strategists, the logic of geography and contemporary context cannot be ignored.[31] The pervasive effects of physical geography in all its dimensions remain a universally accepted truism in strategic studies. In the current globalized atmosphere, the effects of politics, history, economics, society, culture, ethics, organization, information, intelligence, and technology, besides military trends, are also relevant.[32] Further, the imperatives of *context* cannot be ignored. This profound factor has been the key to international political architecture which is constantly evolving; driven by the changes in the balance across politics (policy), economics and commerce, as well as the security-stability paradigm.[33] The rapid Chinese naval developments are being perceived through strategic logics advanced by the naval strategists of yore.[34] However, it is for consideration that application of such axioms may not be the optimal interpretation of the emerging trends unless contemporary contextualization is provided to the arguments.

Primarily, maritime security imperatives for the Chinese – for that matter, every other nation – are the traditional Westphalian concepts of 'territoriality' and 'sovereignty'. It could be argued that the Chinese claims in South and East China are expansive, based on fragile legal fabric of historical *effectivités*. It could even be argued, with some justification, that the Chinese strategic discourse borders on revisionist tendencies. Nevertheless, the use of 'core interests' phraseology, when seen from Beijing's perspective, cannot be denied, howsoever convoluted may be the arguments put forth by the Chinese interlocutors. What could be contested is the proactivism, and potentially aggressive behaviour, since other claimants also have their own logic.

Strategic Underpinnings

From the discussions above, it is assessed that geo-economics and linked geo-politics are the drivers for military strategic posture, and by extension, the Chinese naval strategic signalling, force structure, deployment pattern, and cooperative partnerships. While the material focus has been on improving infrastructure, ports, telecom, transportation (rail/road), and pipelines, their use as strategic hedges in times of crisis cannot be discounted. The primary aim for these endeavours is to seek assured access to places and facilities during peace time and crisis situations at the lower end of the spectrum. In operational terms, this would translate into improved reach and sustenance. A similar end-state during acute crises and conflict, though desirable, may not be feasible by a constrained maritime periphery. As an antithesis, it could also be argued that a complementary strategic aim would be to 'restrict access' for potential adversaries in key areas by creating socio-economic and politico-military dependencies (geo-political A2AD).

While the focus has been on the 'String of Pearls' and 'Places and Bases' debate to frame the expanding Chinese maritime influence, the discourse needs enlargement after the recent postulation by the Chinese President on reviving the Land and Maritime Silk Routes during his visits to Kazakhstan and Indonesia in August-September 2013. A recent article posted on the website of the Permanent Mission of China to the United Nations gives a detailed explanation of mutually supporting 'economic belt along the historic Silk Route and establishing a new maritime silk route'.[35] The commentary identifies five links, viz, policy, road/route, trade, currency, and people, as the key constituents of this mixed continental maritime cooperative enterprise. These silk routes seek to establish a web for unhindered movement of the key constituents mentioned above, by forging a grand strategic rapprochement, that is based on a cooperative, open, as well as an inclusive framework. It can thus be seen that an *interconnected network* of pipelines, roads, rail, ports and SLOCs with a littoral focus are the key areas of geo-strategic salience for China in times to come (Figure 5.11).

Figure 5.11: From Strings to Networks

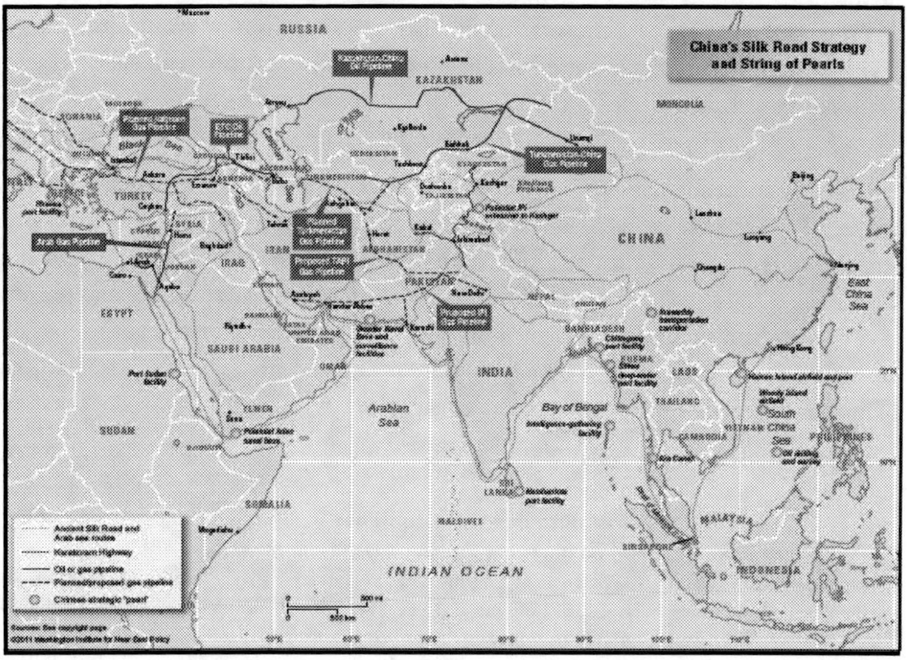

Source: Christina Lin, *The New Silk Road*, 2011.

Chinese defence diplomacy including frequent high-level visits and formalised apex level dialogues represents the benign face of managing politico-strategic perceptions. A recent endeavour has been the offer of a higher number of military training vacancies, especially for officer level courses. To cite an example, 32 Sri Lankan officers including two major generals, underwent training in China in 2011.[36] A proposal to further strengthen such linkages was also discussed during the high-level Chinese delegation visit to Sri Lanka in February 2014.[37] At this stage, it is clarified that such actions are routine for all major and rising powers, with the basic aim of fostering improved mutual perceptions, so as to ultimately shape a more favourable politico-strategic discourse. What requires a careful watch, is the trend where such endeavours are being undertaken in a much more concerted manner in countries where militaries have a significant say in the decision making mechanism, like in the majority of the South Asian countries under discussion.

Conclusion

Dissecting the Chinese 'String of Pearls' strategy through binary prisms is an archaic argument, and a more thorough comprehension of various threads of ever-expanding Chinese networks is a more appropriate course to chart. The internal dynamics of Chinese resource-security connect is another thread that has generally been disregarded in contemporary analysis.[38] As the Chinese would say, we are living in 'interesting times', and such instances require adaption and calibration of national grand strategic postures.

India and the US, with important maritime stakes in the region, need to foster an inclusive mechanism for convincing China to become a responsible global stakeholder, especially in the maritime environment where it has made impressive strides. It is imperative for the US, as the dominant maritime security provider, and a rising India, to try and transform recent the Chinese assertiveness, and prevent a spill-over into the Indian Ocean. This need not be undertaken solely through the containment and balance strategies that are military-centric, but by articulating a win-win partnership through greater engagement with Beijing as well.

NOTES

1. For detailed explanation of these sixteen indicators, see William R. Thompson (Ed), *Systemic Transitions – Past, Present, and Future* (Palgrave Macmillan, New York, 2009).
2. See Evan S. Medeiros, 'Strategic Hedging and the Future of Asia-Pacific Stability' in *The Washington Quarterly*, Issue 29:1 (Winter, 2005-06), pp. 145–167 in respect of Sino-US relations. For Japan's emerging grand strategic behaviour see Corey J. Wallace, 'Strategic Pivot South: Diversifying the Dual Hedge' in *International Relations of the Asia-Pacific*, Issue 13(3), (2013), pp. 479-517. For China's hedging behaviour in South Asian context see Rollie Lal, 'China's Relations with South Asia' in *China and the Developing World: Beijing's Strategy for the Twenty-*

First Century, Joshua Eisenman, Eric Heginbotham, and Derek Mitchell (Eds), (New York: M.E. Sharpe, 2007), pp. 133-149. Vibhanshu Shekhar, 'ASEAN's Response to the Rise of China: Deploying a Hedging Strategy', *China Report*, Vol. 48, Issue 3, August (2012), pp. 253-268.

3. Juli A. MacDonald, Amy Donahue, and Bethany Danyluk, *Energy Futures in Asia: Perspectives of India's Energy Security Strategy and Policies* (Booz Allen Hamilton, Washington, DC, November 2004).
4. Juli A. MacDonald, *Energy Futures in Asia*, Ibid, p. iii.
5. Christopher J Pehrson, *String of Pearls: Meeting the Challenge of China's Rising Power Across the Asian Littoral* (Strategic Studies Institute, U.S. Army War College, Carlisle, PA, July 2006)
6. Daniel J. Kostecka, 'Places and Bases – The Chinese Navy's Emerging Support Network in the Indian Ocean' in *US Naval War College Review*, 64, no. 1 (Winter 2011), pp. 59-78.
7. Gurpreet S. Khurana, 'China's 'String of Pearls' in the Indian Ocean and its Security Implications' in *Strategic Analysis*, 32:1 (2008), pp. 1-39.
8. 'China's foreign ports: The new masters and commanders' in *The Economist*, June 08, 2013, http://www.economist.com/news/international/21579039-chinas-growing-empire-ports-abroad-mainly-about-trade-not-aggression-new-masters (accessed February 24, 2014).
9. Alvin Toffler, *The Third Wave*, (New York: Bantam Books, 1990). The futurologist categorises various nation states into three broad categories. The lowest being the 'pre-modern' states that are largely agrarian and remain poorly industrialised. The 'modern' category is used to define the intermediate level states where industry and services sectors are fairly well developed. At the highest level of this scale are the 'post-modern' states where high-end industries, strong services sector, knowledge and advanced innovation are the core national attributes.
10. World Trade Organization, *International Trade Statistics 2013*, (Geneva: World Trade Organisation, 2014), p. 15, 52.
11. Daniel H. Rosen, 'The IMF's World Economic Outlook for China: Slower and Less Trade Surplus', October 11, 2013, http://rhg.com/notes/the-imfs-world-economic-outlook-for-china-slower-and-less-trade-surplus (accessed February 27, 2014).
12. Christina Lin, 'China's Strategic Shift toward the Region of the Four Seas: The Middle Kingdom Arrives in the Middle East,' in *Middle East Review of International Affairs*, Vol. 17, No. 1 (Spring 2013), pp 32- 55 and Geoff Wade, 'The Zheng He Voyages: A Reassessment' in *Asia Research Institute Working Paper Series*, No. 21, (October 2004), p. 18. For a recent analysis of China's expanding quest for strategic resources, see Elizabeth Economy and Michael Levi, 'By All Means Necessary – How Chinas Resource Quest is Changing the World', (New York: Oxford, 2014).
13. Kamlesh. K. Agnihotri, 'Holistic Maritime Capacity Building: New 'Route' to Chinas Rise' in *Maritime Affairs*, Journal of National Maritime Foundation of India, (Summer 2013) 9:1, pp. 30-44.
14. UNCTAD, *Review of Maritime Transport 2013*, et passim; extracted, compiled by the author, authors' interpretation emphasis.
15. This could be considered as vulnerability as well as strength in times of crisis and conflict. On one hand, it would make the Chinese merchant shipping more susceptible to interdiction, and on the other, provide greater flexibility for rerouting and diversion away from the existing International Shipping Lanes (ISLs) during difficult times because of state control.
16. Based on SIPRI Trend Indicator Value (TIV) database. The figures mentioned are in 2011 Constant Dollar terms.
17. 'China's Oil Pipeline through Myanmar brings both Energy and Resentment', February 4, 2014, http://www. indopacificreview.com/chinas-oil-pipeline-myanmar-brings-energy-resentment/ (accessed February 24, 2014).

18. For a broad insight covering the basic issues and general information in this regard, see T.C. Pharris and R.L. Kolpa, *Overview of the Design, Construction, and Operation of Interstate Liquid Petroleum Pipelines, Pub Ref- ANL/EVS/TM/08-1,* (Argonne National Laboratory, Argonne, IL, 2007).
19. Extracted from SIPRI Military Expenditure (MILEX) database. Data in local currency has been used as against normalising these to Us Dollars due to wide variation between the official and actual exchange rates.
20. Collated from *Jane's Fighting Ships* and IISS *Military Balance*, 2000-2013 editions.
21. 'Is South Asia Moving into the Chinese Orbit and Setting Off Alarm Bells in New Delhi?' July 19, 2013 in online edition of Foreign Policy Journal, http://www.foreignpolicyjournal.com/2013/07/19/is-south-asia-moving-into-the-chinese-orbit-and-setting-off-alarm-bells-in-new-delhi/ (accessed February 24, 2014).
22. 'BCIM corridor gets push after first official-level talks in China' *The Hindu online edition*, December 21, 2013, http://www.thehindu.com/news/international/world/bcim-corridor-gets-push-after-first-officiallevel-talks-in-china/article5483848.ece (accessed February 24, 2014).
23. Bernard D Cole, *The Great Wall at Sea; China's Navy in the Twenty First Century*, Second Edition, (Annapolis: Naval Institute Press, 2012), p. 54. The author stated that 'Ships are and will likely remain the most cost effective means of transporting oil; the cost of transporting one barrel of oil over a distance of 1000 km (540 nautical miles), was estimated in 2007 to be $0.163 by tanker, $0.793 via pipeline and $7.190 by train.'
24. Collated from *Jane's Fighting Ships* and IISS *Military Balance*, 2000-13 editions.
25. Edward N. Luttwak, *The Rise of China vs. the Logic of Strategy*, (Massachusetts: Harvard University Press, 2012), pp. 24-37.
26. Shee Poon Kim, 'An Anatomy of China's 'String of Pearls' Strategy' in *The Hikone Ronso*, No. 387, (Spring 2011), pp. 22–37.
27. For a detailed examination of the various streams of strategic culture and the Chinese grand strategic approach, see Alastair Iain Johnston, *Cultural Realism: Strategic Culture and Grand Strategy in Chinese History,* (Princeton University Press, Princeton, 1998)
28. For two contrasting views on this subject see Robert S. Ross 'China's Naval Nationalism' in *International Security* (2009)34(2), pp. 46-81 and, Michael A. Glosny, Phillip C. Saunders, & Robert. S Ross, 'Debating China's Naval Nationalism' in *International Security*, 35(2), (2010), pp.161-175.
29. For details, see Grygiel, Jakub J. *Great Powers and Geopolitical Change*, (Baltimore: John Hopkins University Press, 2006), Chapters 2 and 3.
30. Andrew J. Nathan and Andrew Scobell, *China's Search for Security,* (New York: Columbia University Press, 2012), pp. 155-163.
31. Gearóid Ó Tuathail, 'Thinking Critically About Geopolitics' in Gearóid Ó Tuathail, Simon Dalby, and Paul Routledge (Eds), *The Geopolitics Reader*, (New York: Routledge, 2003), pp. 1-12.
32. Colin S. Gray, 'Inescapable Geography' in Colin S Gray and Geoffrey Sloan (Eds) *Geopolitics, Geography and Strategy,* (Note 22), pp. 161-177. Also Colin S Gray, *Strategy and History: Essays on Theory and Practice*, (New York: Routledge, 2006), pp. 137-150.
33. Colin S Gray, *Another Bloody Century: Future Warfare,* (London: Weidenfeld & Nicolson, 2005), pp. 55-97.
34. For differing US perceptions about Chinese Navy by the same set of authors, see James R. Holmes and Toshi Yoshihara, *Chinese Naval Strategy in the 21st Century: The Turn to Mahan,* (New York: Routledge, 2008), Chapters 3 and 7 and James R. Holmes and Toshi Yoshihara, *China's Navy: A Turn to Corbett?* in Proceedings, Vol. 136/12/1, (December 2010), p. 294.

35. The Silk Road – From Past to the Future, March 4, 2014, on Chinese Permanent Mission to UN website, http://www.china-un.org/eng/gdxw/t1134206.htm (accessed March 5, 2014).
36. 'Chinese Army General Arrives Bolstering Existing Military Relations Further, December 13, 2013, Sri Lankan Ministry of Defence Website, http://www.defence.lk/new.asp?fname=20111213_02 (accessed March 4, 2014).
37. Shanika Sriyananda, 'Sri Lanka, China strengthen defense ties', *Asia-Pacific Defence Reporter online*, February 17, 2014, http://apdforum.com/en_GB/article/rmiap/articles/online/features/2014/02/17/srilanka-china-defense (accessed February 27, 2014).
38. Geoff Dyer, *The Contest of the Century: The New Era of Competition with China and How America Can Win*, (New York: Alfred Knopf, 2014), pp. 50-53.

6

Prospects of PLA Navy's Presence in the IOR and Impact on Regional Dynamics

Captain Gurpreet S Khurana

> *'The Indian Ocean will be one of the major problems (challenges) of the future.'*
>
> —KM Panikkar (1945)[1]

> *'The Greater Indian Ocean region...will be the centre of global conflicts, because most international business supply will be conducted through this route...it is in this region the interests and influence of India, China and the United States are beginning to overlap...two key players in this region are India and China – India moving east and west while China to the South.'*
>
> —Robert Kaplan (2010)[2]

This essay aims to discuss the prospects for PLA Navy's presence in the Indian Ocean, say in the medium-term time-frame of about 2025-30, and its impact on regional dynamics. What lies ahead flows essentially from what is China's intent in the Indian Ocean Region (IOR). Although China has been characteristically opaque in issues of national policy, it is nonetheless essential to understand China's maritime strategy for the IOR.

China's 'Blue Book' on Indian Ocean

China's 'Blue Book' on the Indian Ocean, released in June 2013, says that China has no Indian Ocean strategy.[3] This appears odd, since the following month (July 2013), the Chinese President advocated enhancement of Chinese maritime power;[4] and in October 2013, while on a visit to Indonesia, he announced the 'Maritime Silk Road' (MSR) initiative.[5] Does the 'Blue Book' then mean to merely say that China has no 'maritime military' strategy for the Indian Ocean? Possibly yes.

Be that as it may, China's 'Blue Book' does provide some valuable pointers to identify its strategy for the Indian Ocean. The salient pointers have been paraphrased as follows:

- China's intent in IOR is guided by commercial and economic (not military) interests and objectives.
- It has lagged behind India and the US thus far in securing these interests, and would now be more proactive.
- If India and/or the US impede the attainment of its objectives, it would not desist from resorting to confrontation.
- It would not permit any single power to dominate the IOR. It is prepared for jostling with such powers to establish 'a fragile'[6] balance of power equilibrium.

China's Interests and Objectives in IOR (Ends)

China's strategy for the Indian Ocean may be constructed through the 'ends-ways-means' format by examining its interests and objectives in the Indian Ocean (Ends), and a SWOT analysis. The strategy so deduced (Means and Ways) could spell out the prospects of PLA Navy's presence in the Indian Ocean, wherefrom flow the likely implications on regional dynamics.

Areas of Maritime Interest

The Western Pacific is undeniably, China's primary area of maritime interest. The IOR may be considered as its secondary area of interest. The division between China's primary and secondary areas of maritime interest may be denoted as the geographic median of the four Southeast Asian choke points (Malacca, Sunda, Lombok-Macassar and Ombai-Wetar straits), indicated in Figure 6.1 as a red line. It is interesting to note that this median nearly coincides with the line joining India's southern most territorial extremity (Indira Point of Great Nicobar Island) and the new US Marines 'place' at Darwin (Australia).

The IOR may be considered to be of level-two importance for China, but as in the case of Western Pacific, events in the IOR bear strongly on China's national security interests. In other words, the entire Indo-Pacific region (encompassing the Western Pacific and IOR)[7] may be referred to as encompassing China's geo-strategic frontiers. Hence, China is rapidly building maritime-military capacity to be able to influence events in the IOR as well. Furthermore, China's strategy for the Western Pacific is closely linked to that in the Indian Ocean.

Figure 6.1: China's Areas of Maritime Interest

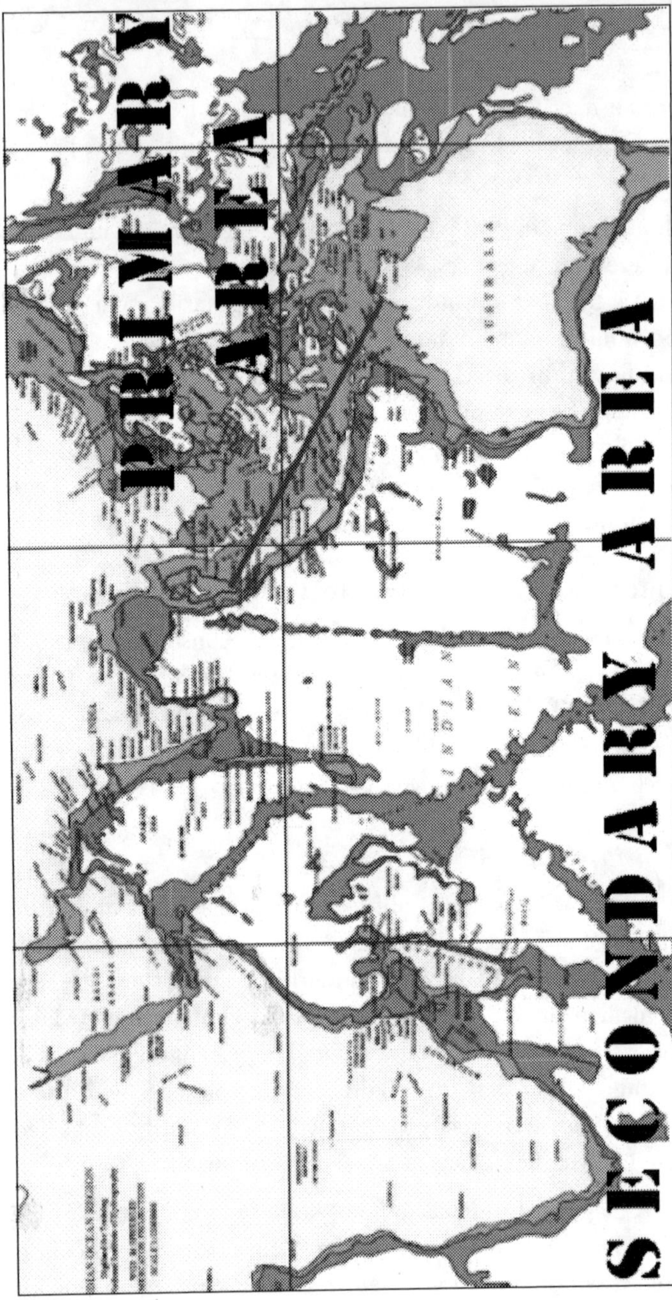

Source: Author/ National Institute of Hydrography, Goa.

Specific Stakes/Objectives

China's specific stakes in the Indian Ocean, and attendant objectives to secure these interests/objectives are examined below.

Geo-political

- Regional Polarity: Beijing has no choice but to accept a 'bipolar' world order. However, it vies for a 'uni-polar' Asia. China believes that it must be the predominant power in this region, which includes the IOR.
- Influence: China seeks symbolic influence in IOR as a major global power. Such influence is necessary for it to have a 'favourable voice' at global fora to further its quest for a redefined global order and altered global systems, and to press for its territorial sovereignty claims.

Economic

- Access to Natural Resources: China seeks an assured supply of natural resources and other raw materials to fuel its growing economy. They includes hydrocarbons and minerals,[8] including seabed minerals.[9]
- Maritime Transportation: Unrestricted use of International Shipping Lanes (ISL) for China's seaborne trade, particularly for its energy supplies, is considered to be vital. China's stakes also lie in the potential IOR feeder nodes to overland oil/gas pipelines; both under construction such as Kyaukpyu-Kunming pipeline (Myanmar),[10] and those proposed, such as Gwadar-Kashi pipeline (Pakistan).[11]
- Maritime Outlet for Continental China: Commercial maritime outlet for the western and southern parts of China through IOR littorals like Pakistan, Bangladesh and Myanmar.
- Other Commercial Interests: These include IOR markets for Chinese exports (mainly manufactured goods[12]), IOR as a source of food (agricultural produce in Africa,[13] fishing rights off Sri Lanka[14]), Chinese citizens/workforce in IOR,[15] and commercial port operations, like at Gwadar (Pakistan), Hambantota (Sri Lanka), Chahbahar (Iran)[16] and Lamu (Kenya).[17]

Military-Strategic

China's military-strategic objectives flow from the aforesaid geo-political and economic interests/objectives, with particular emphasis to catering for high-risk scenarios during war. China's key strategic objective in the IOR then is to possess the ability for unhindered maritime communications, military mobility, and maritime power projection.

SWOT Analysis

After examining China's interests and objectives in the Indian Ocean, an analysis of China's strengths, weaknesses, opportunities and threats (SWOT analysis) is undertaken below to identify its likely strategy for the Indian Ocean.

Strengths

- China's rising economic power is increasing its global clout and enabling unprecedented double-digit increases in its defence budget for its military modernization.[18]
- The PLA Navy has been a major beneficiary of China's increasing defence budget. As per the US Office of Naval Intelligence (ONI), 85 per cent of its fleet will be modern by 2020.[19] China is also rapidly developing capabilities for distant maritime power projection.
- China's influence in IOR has increased substantially over the decades. This was enabled through its multi-pronged approach, ranging from soft loans and investment in infrastructure projects, to defence equipment sales at concessional prices. China's rising influence is facilitated by its membership of UNSC and other exclusive global institutions, such as the G-8.
- China has demonstrated its ability to absorb advanced military technology, including space-based technology. It has thus developed a sound defence industrial base.

Weaknesses/Vulnerabilities

- China is a predominantly an export-led economy. Foreign trade accounts for more than half of its GDP. This leads to its overwhelming reliance on sea-borne trade.
- China is overly dependent on the IOR for natural resources. This leads to vulnerabilities, including those associated with the International Shipping Lanes (ISL), transiting the Indian Ocean.
- China is severely constrained geographically for naval access to sea areas beyond its immediate maritime periphery, and particularly so, for access to the Indian Ocean.
- The Chinese naval power is beset by capability voids in key facets of naval operations, at least *vis-à-vis* major potential adversaries in the Indo-Pacific region. This may be attributed to the lack of certain key technologies. The western arms embargo on China has also impeded PLA Navy's efforts to fill these voids. It is also pertinent to note that most of its capabilities are not battle-tested.

Opportunities

- The strategic focus of the US 'Rebalance to Asia' lies in the Western Pacific, not the Indian Ocean. Attendant to this are severe fiscal challenges for the US, for simultaneous naval focus on IOR.
- China's economic and other stakes in Indian Ocean are increasing rapidly. This justifies and legitimizes PLA Navy's presence in the area.
- India's polity has long been beset by political and security contentions with its immediate neighbours within South Asia, which strategically boxes it within South Asia, and prevents it from playing a role in the wider IOR.
- India's stance of 'strategic autonomy' would prevent it from forging a formal security alliance with any of China's potential adversaries.

Threats

- Notwithstanding the focus of the US Rebalance strategy being in the Western Pacific, there is a notable remnant US naval presence in the Indian Ocean, including military bases/ facilities, such as Diego Garcia, and the US Marine base at Darwin.
- India's geo-strategic location astride key International Shipping Lanes (ISL) transiting the Indian Ocean, and the Indian Navy's increasing capabilities pose a reckonable potential threat to China's maritime 'lifelines'.[20]
- China also perceives a major threat of its containment by the US, in conjunction with allies and partners. The increasing India-US strategic convergence in the Indian Ocean is being watched in Beijing with immense anxiety.[21]

China's Indian Ocean Strategy (Ways and Means)

The SWOT matrix could be used to outline China's likely maritime military strategy in the IOR. Its salient elements are stated in the succeeding paragraphs. While China may have no articulated strategy for the IOR, and it may profess predominantly economic interests only in the region, it is necessary to reiterate Mahan's dictum: '*Naval power, economic development and international relations are inextricably linked...*'[22]

Two-Ocean Navy

Adhering to Mahanian principles, China seeks to operate a two-ocean Navy, which it considers necessary to buttress its claim to global power status. China's growing naval presence in the Indian Ocean, its quest for membership of the Indian Ocean Naval Symposium (IONS),[23] and its 'Maritime Silk Road' (MSR) concept extending westwards from Southeast Asia to the Indian Ocean, are among the indicators of this strategy.

Diversion to Counter US Rebalance

China may have adopted a diversionary strategy for the Indo-pacific region, by seeking to increase naval presence in the IOR to relieve the pressure imposed upon it in Western Pacific by the US and its allies. Such a strategy may be becoming increasingly necessary for China, following its growing military assertiveness in the China seas, which Beijing anticipates could lead to countermeasures from the US (and allied) military forces.

Permanent Naval Presence

China is likely to maintain a permanent naval presence in the Indian Ocean through counter-piracy and humanitarian missions. It is necessary to understand that the PLA Navy's deployments in the Indian Ocean are likely to have been contemplated long before its Gulf of Aden counter-piracy mission began in December 2008. In his book authored in 2005, the eminent Indian strategist (late) Dr K Subrahmanyam recalls that as far back as in 1994, 'China had plans to deploy its navy in the Indian Ocean in the early years of the 21st Century'.[24]

In the coming years, PLA Navy's deployed force levels and missions in the Indian Ocean may witness graduated increase, with the aim of progressively attenuating US and Indian naval power in the region. Increasing numbers of China's destroyers and frigates, the new Type 056 Corvettes, and Coast Guard vessels may enable the PLA Navy to assign the other destroyers and frigates for Indian Ocean deployment. China's new Yalong Bay naval base at Hainan is likely to be the home base for such deployments.

Naval Diplomacy

Naval diplomacy/flag showing in IOR ports is a key element of China's aggressive soft power diplomacy, aimed at shaping the strategic environment, and displacing US influence in IOR. It is meant to supplement other forms of influence-building tools, like financial assistance, infrastructure development, defence equipment sales, and space & nuclear cooperation. The emphasis of China's naval diplomacy is lately directed towards certain key countries, as follows:

- **Indonesia.** Indonesia, with its maritime choke points, is critically important for China's cross-ocean naval deployments. Lately, the PLA Navy is increasingly transiting through Indonesian straits like Sunda and Lombok, as opposed to its traditional reliance on Malacca straits for its commercial shipping. This provides strategic rationale for Beijing to woo Jakarta. The Chinese President's October 2013 initiation of the 'Maritime Silk Route' initiative at Jakarta[25] may be seen in this context.

- **Pakistan.** Maritime frontage of Pakistan overlooking the Hormuz outlet of the Persian Gulf is geo-strategically valuable. A cooperative relation with Pakistan could enable China to obtain strategic and operational intelligence of this vital area. It is important to recall that the PLA Navy's first foray into the Indian Ocean in November 1985 began with a port call at Karachi. PLA Navy's interaction with the Pakistan Navy has since intensified substantially at the *Aman* exercises off Pakistan, where from both navies are increasingly operating common Chinese-made platforms/equipment.
- **IOR Island States.** The IOR island states of Maldives, Mauritius, Seychelles and Sri Lanka are all geo-strategically located astride China's 'maritime lifelines' transiting the Indian Ocean. The level of influence and presence that the PLA Navy can achieve in these states would directly affect China's ability to safeguard its strategic imports. Conversely, the influence and presence of an inimical naval power in these States would directly threaten China's 'maritime lifelines'.
- **India.** China's desire for naval engagements with India is driven by two factors. The first is its quest to undermine New Delhi's maritime-strategic partnership with China's potential adversaries like the US, Japan, and Australia. The two Malabar multinational naval exercises, conducted in 2007, had caused much anxiety in Beijing. China's February 2014 proposals for India to participate in its Maritime Silk Road concept,[26] and an institutionalised navy-level dialogue with India[27] may be seen in this context. The second driver for naval engagement with India is to seek a greater role in the dynamics of IOR, including through membership of IONS.

Naval Sustenance

The PLA Navy warships may continue to obtain peacetime naval access to IOR ports as hitherto. However, the challenge of naval sustenance pertains more to wartime facilities. The so-called Chinese 'String of Pearls'[28] may not be converted into naval bases, at least in medium term timeframe (2025-30). This is, however, unlikely to hinder the PLA Navy's operations in the Indian Ocean for the reasons mentioned below:

- **Fuel and Victuals.** International law (Law of the Armed Conflict/Law of

Neutrality) permits a 24-hour latitude to warships before departing neutral ports – a sufficient duration for the PLA Navy units to embark fuel and victuals for the next few days. Thereafter, the PLA Navy units at sea may be replenished at sea by civilian tankers that have topped-up fuel and victuals at IOR ports.

- **Machinery/Equipment Stores and Ordnance.** Increased naval hardware (including weapon) exports to IOR littorals would reduce the need for PLA Navy to source equipment/machinery stores, and even ammunition from home bases.

Naval Deployments/Power Projection

- **Surface Forces.** Notwithstanding that sustenance of naval forces may not be a serious problem, the PLA Navy is unlikely to achieve 'sea control' capabilities in the Indian Ocean in the medium-term. Its surface forces are likely to be used increasingly for peacetime missions like anti-piracy. Its aircraft carriers, major amphibious platforms, and hospital ships are likely to be used not only for humanitarian missions, like disaster relief and non-combatant evacuation, but also for low-opposition interventions.
- **Land-based Aircraft.** Conduct of maritime air operations by Chinese land-based aircraft would pose major challenges due to distance/endurance factor, the need to use airspace of IOR littorals, and the inability of PLA Navy's carrier-based aviation to establish air superiority in the Indian Ocean during war.
- **Submarines.** The PLA Navy is likely to deploy its new-generation nuclear attack submarines (SSN) armed with land-attack cruise missiles (LACM) in the Indian Ocean. Its conventional submarine construction programme is likely to plateau in favour of SSNs. Construction of SSNs is then likely to increase significantly, particularly for long-range missions, to support strategic shipments plying the Indian Ocean.
- **ASBM-based Area Denial.** The possibility of re-orientation of Chinese Anti Ship Ballistic Missile (ASBM)-based area-denial capability southwards, to target US and Indian aircraft carriers in the Indian Ocean, cannot be discounted.[29]

Impact on Regional Dynamics

That China's present emphasis in its Indian Ocean strategy is commercial may be a statement of fact. However, economic power is fungible with military power.

According to the author's broad assessment, as China accumulates economic power, it is likely to:

- Translate it into maritime military power, which is the emphasis of its military modernization program.
- Employ distant naval capabilities for missions in the Indian Ocean, where it needs increasingly greater security guarantees to cover its economic/commercial interests.

Specific aspects defining regional dynamics are discussed below.

Regional Balance of Power

Notwithstanding the modern-day dynamics of Asia, driven by geo-economics and economic interdependence, the balance of power struggles of the erstwhile era are likely to remain relevant for this region. There seems to be a likelihood of the balance of power in the IOR progressively shifting in favour of China.

The foremost of the key factors contributing to this power shift is, ironically, the US rebalance to Asia. This is premised on the reality that the focus of such a Rebalance lies in the Western Pacific, not the IOR. In any case, for the US, the western extent of Asia extends, at best, to India, and not the entire IOR.[30] The fiscal challenges for the US, for its concurrent naval attention to IOR, also need to be factored. It is pertinent to note that counter-terrorism has lately been the only major driver for the US strategic attention to the IOR.

The second factor is likely to be Russia's increasing assertiveness in Central Asia. Recent developments in this sub-region, deep in the hinterland of the Asian maritime periphery, are already demanding US's strategic attention. The third contributing factor is the stagnant maritime/defence cooperation among relevant naval powers in IOR. An apt example is the US-India Maritime Security Cooperation. The agreement has not progressed as envisaged, since it was inked in 2006.

Regional Stability and Security

Given China's growing economic/commercial stakes in IOR States, the PLA Navy could conceivably contribute positively to regional stability through stability operations, including those under the aegis of UN mandate. The PLA Navy – with its increasing force levels of policing vessels, sealift platforms, and hospital ships – could also complement the grossly feeble capacities of many IOR navies for undertaking constabulary and humanitarian missions. Noted US analysts James Holmes and Toshi Yoshihara aver that '*China's 'soft-power' strategy seems to be based on the premise that a nation can store up international goodwill by supplying 'international public goods' like maritime security, which benefit all nations with a stake in the international order.'*[31]

However, there lies a real possibility of China resorting to unilateralism dictated by self-interest to serve its geo-political, military, or commercial interests. This may adversely affect regional stability and security, particularly since there is no overarching security forum at present for the IOR that could have addressed these issues in a more broad-based manner. Some conceivable actions by China in the IOR are indicated below:

- **Politico-Military Interventions.** China could undertake politico-military intervention in an IOR State at the slightest hint of an impending political or ethnic problem, leading to regional tensions.
- **Military Coercion.** China could resort to a show of naval force to coerce an IOR State.
- **Chinese Military Activity close to IOR States.** Naval exercises or intelligence-gathering in close proximity of IOR States (or in their maritime zones) could lead to security concerns in the affected State, even though conducted in international waters. In February 2014, China carried out a naval exercise off Australia's Christmas Islands.[32] What was the intended message? Could it be an assertion against the stationing of US Marines at Darwin?
- **Chinese Stakes in Disputed Waters.** Chinese oil and gas companies could acquire offshore stakes in waters disputed between two IOR States, thereby aggravating tensions between them.
- **Chinese Arms Exports causing Instability.** Chinese defence equipment exports to IOR States may be undertaken at friendship prices to facilitate PLA Navy's sustenance in the IOR, thereby causing instability, or an arms race. In the past, the Chinese have rarely been mindful of ethical considerations while supplying arms. For example, during the Iran-Iraq war in the mid-1980s, 92 per cent of all Chinese defence exports bound for West Asia went to the two warring nations.[33] It later sold one billion US Dollars worth of weapons to both Ethiopia and Eritrea during their border conflict from 1998 to 2000.[34] In April 2008, China pushed for arms supplies to Zimbabwe against the majority global opinion that these supplies would be used by the Zimbabwean government to crush political opposition, and thereby aggravating the political crisis in the country.[35]
- **Weapons of Mass Destruction (WMD)/Missile Proliferation.** PLA Navy

forces in the Indian Ocean may shield WMD/missile proliferation to/from errant States. Pakistan's ballistic missile technology is well known to have been sourced from North Korea, which was implicitly supported by China.[36] In June 1999, Indian authorities seized the North Korean ship *Ku Wol San* at the Kandla port carrying missile components and related blueprints to West Asia and Pakistan.[37] In August 2009, North Korean vessel MV *Musen* was intercepted by Indian Coast Guard off Little Andaman Island under suspicious circumstances. A probe revealed that *Musen* had made several voyages between North Korea and China without maintaining proper records.[38] In June 2009, the US Navy tracked a North Korean ship MV *Kang Nam* along the coast of China. The ship suspected of carrying illegal weapons to Myanmar suddenly reversed its course homewards.[39]. Although China's complicity in these cases is still speculation, there are indicators in this direction.

Freedom of Navigation

PLA Navy's presence in the IOR may be conducive for freedom of navigation, given its active participation in counter-piracy efforts. This may contribute to a sense of security in the region against low-intensity threats and maritime crime; thus spur commerce and economic integration of the regional countries. However, a maritime conflict may severely impinge upon freedom of navigation, though its probability is presently low, at least relative to the Western Pacific. China has no maritime territorial claims in the Indian Ocean, but its propensity to disregard international norms with respect to freedom of navigation in the China Seas is well known. It is an indicator that China is unlikely to observe such norms with regard to the international shipping plying the Indian Ocean, while planning naval operations during conflict.

Indian Context

From the Indian perspective, PLA Navy's permanent presence in the Indian Ocean may lead to increased avenues of maritime security cooperation, but the possibility of grim scenarios cannot be discounted. The balance of power shift in the IOR in favour of China may lead to major strategic adversity for India, particularly in light of adversarial potential of India-China relations. The PLA Navy units could undertake military surveys/intelligence collection in the Indian maritime zones, thereby directly undermining India's security, and leading to the possibility of maritime skirmishes. Although China has traditionally resisted such foreign military activities off its own coast, recent instances indicate a reversal of its earlier stance. PLA Navy's conduct of such activities in the US EEZ off Guam[40] may be seen in this context. In any case, a strong Chinese naval presence in the Indian Ocean would not only hinder India's ability for maritime power projection in the IOR, but also weaken its overall conventional deterrence against China.

In case of a war with China, India would need to defend against a seaward threat to its territory and maritime interests. There are also real possibilities of Pakistan using this as an opportunity to undertake an offensive in the western maritime theatre; and of PLA Navy's use of Gwadar in a two-front scenario. In sum, from the Indian perspective, betting on China to provide regional stability and freedom of navigation is accompanied with major risks. It may be safer if the US maintains preponderance, with India onboard, for maintaining regional peace and stability.

The Way Ahead

Before suggesting a very broad way ahead, a few key questions need to be posed:

- Is the PLA Navy's emerging assertiveness in the IOR a Chinese reaction to the US rebalance? If so, could the US address such assertiveness by China?
- Can the putative balance of power shift in the IOR in favour of China be prevented, mitigated or delayed? Or at least, can the relevant naval powers act to mitigate its adverse effect on regional stability?

The common answer to these questions is probably 'yes'. On the US Rebalance to Asia strategy, Ashley Tellis says,

> "*The objective (of the US Rebalance strategy) of managing China's rise is going to be an extremely challenging one…because it requires the US to socialize China, to integrate China, to deter China, and to reassure China…all simultaneously.*"[41]

Firstly, any strategy must be continually re-appraised. Whether the US wants to tone down, maintain or ratchet up its strategic posture of Rebalance, is for the US to decide. However, it is necessary for it to consider all factors, including, particularly the following:

- The ability of the US (in conjunction with allies/partners) to sustain military-strategic escalation
- Likely effect of such escalation on regional dynamics, including regional stability, security, and economic integration
- Regional perceptions

Secondly, the US, India, and other relevant naval powers need to get their act together. Their governments and foreign policy establishments would need to adopt a more comprehensive approach, including politico-diplomatic engagement with China, to prevent the worst case scenarios to manifest. On the other hand, their maritime forces would need to prepare for such scenarios, besides assisting their governments to shape the environment favourably.

NOTES

1. K.M. Panikkar, *India and the Indian Ocean: An Essay on the Influence of Sea Power on Indian History* (London: George Allen and Unwin Ltd, 1945).
2. Robert Kaplan, *Monsoon: The Indian Ocean & Future of American Power* (Random House: Oct 10).
3. 'Development Report in the Indian Ocean', *Chinese Academy of Social Sciences* (CASS), June 6, 2013.
4. 'Xi advocates efforts to boost China's maritime power', July 31, 2013, http://news.xinhuanet.com/english/china/2013-07/31/c_132591246.htm (accessed January 21, 2014.)
5. 'The Silk Road – From Past to the Future', *Website of PRC's Permanent Mission to the UN*, April 3, 2014, http://www.china-un.org/eng/gdxw/t1134206.htm (accessed July 8, 2014).
6. The word 'fragile' possibly means that the Balance of Power equilibrium would be dynamic, and no power (or a combination of powers) would enjoy an overwhelming superiority.
7. The term 'Indo-Pacific' was first used by the author, at least within the Indian academic discourse. See Gurpreet Khurana 'Security of Sea Lines: Prospects for India-Japan Cooperation', *Strategic Analysis*, Vol. 31, No. 1, (2007), pp.139-153. Also see C. Uday Bhaskar, 'India and the Indo-Pacific: Semantic and Strategic Import', *NMF commentary*, October 8, 2013, http://www.maritimeindia.org/india-and-indo-pacific-semantic-and-strategic-import (accessed April 17, 2014).
8. Chinese companies are involved in mining operations in 13 African states and prospecting for more, Sarah Raine, *China's African Challenges*, (London: IISS/Routledge, 2009), p. 35.
9. In July 2011, China secured the permit of the *International Seabed Authority* (ISA) to undertake deep seabed mining in central Indian Ocean. Status of contracts for exploration for poly-metallic nodules, poly-metallic sulphides and cobalt-rich ferromanganese crust, *International Seabed Authority* (ISA) website, http://www.isa.org.jm/en/scientific/exploration/contractors (accessed 7 July 2014).
10. The pipeline is likely to be operational by June 2014. Du Juan, 'Myanmar-China gas pipeline completed', *China Daily*, October 20, 2013, http://www.chinadaily.com.cn/china/2013-10/20/content_17046712.htm
11. Zafar Bhutta, 'Gwadar Port: Pakistan, China all set to develop master plan', *The Express Tribune*, February 15, 2014, http://tribune.com.pk/story/671852/gwadar-port-pakistan-china-all-set-to-develop-master-plan/ (accessed February 22, 2014).
12. The proportion of machinery and electronic products accounts for more than half of China's exports to Africa. 'China-Africa Economic and Trade Cooperation', *Information Office of the State Council of PRC*, December 23, 2010, www.waltainfo.com/resource/China%20Africa%20Economic%20and%20Trade%20Cooperation.pdf (accessed February 23, 2014).
13. China had at least 63 agricultural investment projects in southern Africa ranging from small-scale farms to large cattle-raising grounds. Loro Horta, 'Food Security in Africa: China's New Rice Bowl', *China Brief, The Jamestown Foundation*, Vol. 9(11), May 27, 2009, p.10.

14. In mid 2013, Sri Lankan government accorded permission to a Chinese fishing company to use the Dikkowita harbour located north of Colombo to fish off Sri Lankan waters. See Ceylon Today, 'Indian fish workers concerned over Chinese fishing off SL', June 23, 2013, http://www.ceylontoday.lk/16-35971-news-detail-indian-fishworkers-concerned-over-chinese-fishing-off-sl.html
15. Besides numerous Chinese entrepreneurs flocking to IOR states (particularly Africa), most projects taken up by Chinese companies employ Chinese labour. At present, there are over 1 million Chinese nationals living in Africa. Yun Sun and Jane Olin-Ammentorp, 'The US and China in Africa: Competition or Cooperation?', Africa in Focus, *Brookings*, April 28, 2014, http://www.brookings.edu/blogs/africa-in-focus/posts/2014/04/28-us-china-africa-policy-sun (accessed July 8, 2014).
16. Zachary Keck, 'China Makes Play for Iran's Chabahar Port', *The Diplomat*, July 1, 2013, http:/ / thediplomat.com/2013/07/china-makes-play-for-irans-chabahar-port/
17. China offered to finance construction of Kenya's Lamu Port in Oct 11. 'Kenya says Chinese firm wins first tender for Lamu port project', *Reuters*, 11 April 2013, athttp://www.reuters.com/article/2013/04/11/kenya-port-lamu-idUSL5N0CX38D20130411
18. On March 5, 14, China announced the biggest increase in defence budget (for 2014-15) in three years at 12.2% amounting to USD 130 billion. Saibal Dasgupta, 'China increases defence budget by 12% to $130bn', *Times of India*, Mumbai, March 6, (2014), p.18.
19. 'PLA has ambitious plans to upgrade naval fleet: US report', *Want China Times*, February 8,2014, http://www.wantchinatimes.com/news-subclass-cnt.aspx?id=20140208000035&cid=1101
20. Chen Angang, 'Malacca: America's Coveted Strategic Outpost,' [*Malike Haixia: Meiguo Jiyu de Zhanlue Qianshao*], *Modern Ships* [Xiandai Jianchuan], December 2004, p. 11-14, cited in Gabriel Collins, 'An Oil Armada? The Commercial & Strategic Significance of China's Growing Tanker Fleet', in Toshi Yoshihara & James Holmes (eds.), *Asia Looks Seaward*, (Praeger Security International, Westport, Connecticut & London: 2008), p. 113.
21. In June 2012, US Defence Secretary described India as lynchpin of its Indian Ocean strategy. Address by Secretary of Defense Leon Panetta, Shangri-La Dialogue, Singapore, June 2, 2012, http://www.defense.gov /utility/printitem.aspx?print=http://www.defense.gov/speeches/speech.aspx?speechid=1681 (accessed February 17, 2014).
22. Kamphausen, Roy D. and Liang, Justin, 'PLA Power Projection' in Swaine, Michael D., Yang, Andrew N.D. and Medeiros, Evan S. (eds.) *Assessing the Threat: The Chinese Military and Taiwan's Security*. (Washington DC: Carnegie Endowment, 2007), p. 116.
23. P.K. Ghosh, 'IONS and the Indian Ocean: Reviving a listless initiative – Analysis', *Eurasia Review*, May 9, 2014, http://www.eurasiareview.com/09052014-ions-indian-ocean-reviving-listless-initiative-analysis/
24. K. Subramanyam, *Shedding Shibboleths: India's Evolving Strategic Outlook* (New Delhi: Arthur Monterio, Wordsmiths, 2005), p. 312.
25. Vibhanshu Shekhar, 'Maritime silk route: China's foothold in the Indian Ocean?' *The Jakarta Post*, February 25, 2014, http://www.thejakartapost.com/news/2014/02/25/maritime-silk-route-china-s-foothold-indian-ocean. html (accessed March 2, 2014).
26. Ankit Panda, 'China invites India to the Maritime Silk Road', *The Diplomat*, February 15, 2014, http:// thediplomat.com/2014/02/china-invites-india-to-the-maritime-silk-road/ (accessed March 2, 2014).
27. Sandeep Unnithan, 'China moots first-ever maritime dialogue with India', *India Today*, February 15, 2014, http://indiatoday.intoday.in/story/india-china-maritime-dialogue-panchsheel-diamond-jubilee-indian-navy-pla-navy-yang-jeichi/1/343577.html (accessed March 2, 2014).
28. The phrase 'String of Pearls' was first used in a 2005 report by Booz-Allen-Hamilton, 'Energy

Futures in Asia' prepared for US Defense Secretary. '*String of Pearls*' Military Plan to protect China's oil: US Report', *Space War,* January 18, 2005, http://www.spacewar.com/2005/050727.edxbxn8.html (accessed February 22, 2014).

29. Kamlesh K. Agnihotri, China's 'Anti-ship Ballistic Missile' based Anti-access Concept: Implications of a Southward Re-orientation', *Journal of Defence Studies* (Institute of Defence Studies and Analyses, New Delhi) Vol. 7, Issue 1, (2013), pp. 9-30.
30. It is pertinent to recall in this context that what Indians refer to as 'West Asia', is called 'Middle East' in the United States.
31. James R. Holmes and Toshi Yoshihara, 'Is China a 'Soft' Naval Power?', *China Brief,* Vol. 9(17), (August 20, 2009), p.5.
32. David Wroe, 'China's military might is Australia's new defence reality', *The Brisbane Times,* February 15, 2014, http://www.brisbanetimes.com.au/world/chinas-military-might-is-australias-new-defence-reality-20140214-32rb1.html (accessed March 2, 2014).
33. Yitzhak Shichor, 'Middle Eastern Perceptions of China Threat', in Herbert Yee & Ian Storey (ed.), *The China Threat: Perceptions, Myths & Reality,* (Oxon, New York: Routledge, 2002), pp. 313-316.
34. 'China Steals the March over India in Arms Sales', *Defence Digest,* September-October 2006, p. 32.
35. Celia W. Dugger and David Barboza, 'China May Give Up Attempt to Send Arms to Zimbabwe', *New York Times,* April 23, 2008, http://www.nytimes.com/2008/04/23/world/africa/23zimbabwe.html
36. Sharon A. Squassoni , 'Weapons of Mass Destruction: Trade Between North Korea and Pakistan', CRS Report for Congress, November 28, 2006, http://fas.org/sgp/crs/nuke/RL31900.pdf (accessed Jan 21, 2014).
37. 'Indian agencies to investigate North Korean ship's entry', *The Economic Times,* August 9, 2009, http://articles.economictimes.indiatimes.com/2009-08-09/news/28434630_1_security-agencies-indian-waters-k-r-nautiyal (accessed January 21, 2014).
38. Rajaram Panda, 'Is China behind Musen's intrusion to Indian Waters?', *Global Politician,* August 2009, www.globalpolitician.com/print.asp?id=5825 (accessed January 21, 2014).
39. Pauline Jelinek, 'North Korean Ship Kang Nam Turns Around', *Pacific News Centre,* June 4, 2013, http://www.huffingtonpost.com/2009/06/30/north-korean-ship-kang-na_n_223262.html (accessed March 3, 2014).
40. Kevin Kerrigan, 'FT: China begins patrolling U.S. EEZ, Possibly off Guam', *Pacific News Center,* June 4, 2013, http://www.pacificnewscenter.com/indexphp?option=com_content&view=article&id=34835:ft-china-patorls&catid=45:guam-news&itemid=156 (accessed July 7, 2014).
41. Ashley Tellis, Public Lecture on 'Pivot or Pirouette: The US Rebalance to Asia', *National Institute for Advanced Studies* (NIAS), IISc Campus, Bangalore, January 3, 2014.

7

Maritime Infrastructure-Building: Complementary Endeavours Towards Maritime Powerhood

Captain Peter Swartz (Retd.)

As the scene-setter for this theme of complementary Chinese endeavours towards maritime power-hood, this paper takes a high-level approach. It presents a series of propositions about the three related topics of port development, erection of a maritime research base, and the progress of Chinese Unmanned Underwater Vehicles (UUVs), in order to initiate discussion, debate, and additional research and analysis.

Ports[1]

The Chinese government and party see their continued power as resting on domestic social stability, achieved through economic growth, and increased living standards for the Chinese population. The Chinese economic growth hence, demands and will continue to demand, an enormous and modern port infrastructure. China has become the world's largest manufacturer and exporter, and second largest importer in the world.[2] Most of this trade – in raw materials and finished products – moves by sea. Consequently, Chinese ports have become among the largest in the world, and appear destined to remain so for quite some time. For the past three years, China has had the largest port throughput of any country in the world.[3] Shanghai is the world's busiest container port by throughput. Two other Chinese cities are in the top five and nine in the top 20, with further expansion in the pipeline.[4] The major ports are located around China's three key manufacturing hubs: The Pearl River Delta around Guangdong, the Yangtze River Delta around Shanghai, and the Bohai Rim around Beijing/Tianjin.

Chinese ports, of course, depend on a prosperous world economy to flourish. With the global economy facing challenging headwinds, China's ports have also seen a substantial slowdown in growth, with throughput in national ports up 7.2 per cent in 2012, representing a 6.1 percentage point decline from the growth rates seen a year ago. Total national container throughput fell in year-on-year growth terms by 4.3 per cent. Chinese ports are however, not solely dependent on commercial demand for their growth and development.

The Ministry of Transport regulates, manages and develops China's maritime transport industry, including its seaports. The Ministry's Tianjin Institute for Water Transport Engineering (TIWTE) is tasked with conducting research that directly supports the central government plans to develop, manage, and maintain China's domestic and foreign ports, as well as coastal and inland waterways. (Further discussion on TIWTE will follow in subsequent section). Government and private domestic investment continues to flow at a prodigious rate. In wake of the global financial crisis, Chinese foreign trade was seriously affected by weak overseas demand, but Chinese port investments have shown no sign of slowing down. Substantial investments in all kinds of economic infrastructure – including ports – have been central to the Chinese economic growth policy, and seem likely to continue to be so. Ports and shipping feature prominently in the Chinese government's 12th Five Year Plan, approved in March 2011.[5] The Plan gives particular priority to constructing coal loading ports in northern China, coal transit and storage bases in southern China, large crude oil handling terminals in Dalian, and other ports, large iron ore handling terminals in Ningbo, Zhoushan and other ports, and container terminals in Shanghai, Tianjin, and other ports. The Plan also included construction of 440 deep-water berths equipped for vessels of 10,000 tons or above. In the half year up to June 30, 2012, despite the lower throughput numbers, the Chinese fixed asset investment in the waterways sector grew by 19.9 per cent, indicating government confidence in the long-term value of port infrastructure. In September 2012, the National Development and Reform Commission (NDRC) approved the launch of seven new projects for port construction and channel reconstruction, five in the east, and two in central China.[6]

To complement the above growth pattern, foreign investment interest in Chinese port infrastructure is also increasing. Chinese infrastructure investments, including ports, are increasingly being opened to private capital. In June 2012, for example, Maersk Group and Ningbo Port signed a 4.3 billion dollar agreement to mutually invest in, and manage, new berths in the port. The Chinese ports though, are not without problem areas. These include poor stevedoring (loading/unloading of ships) practices, and managing excessive competition among ports. Dependence on the Chinese coastal ports is being decreased somewhat, through a variety of diverse efforts. The Chinese are creating and increasing road, rail, and pipeline links to Southeast and Southwest Asian ports, most famously through the construction of the Gwadar Port in Pakistani Baluchistan, and plans to link it to western China.[7]

Commercial ports can also support military forces, and the dual use of ports, for commercial and military uses, is common worldwide. China's huge civilian port infrastructure could be used for military purposes when necessary, as could any overseas ports linked to China by road and rail. It is not necessary to bring in a whole lot of military people and associated equipment for using a commercial port for military purposes. A tender could instead visit a port, and a submarine, or a destroyer would then pull up alongside that tender. One does not need large amount of ground forces, other than the domestic security forces to handle that. So one aspect that needs to be watched is whether the Chinese navy or the Chinese commercial sector for that matter, is thinking of constructing tenders or not. The US Navy went about building lots of tenders through World War II, and well afterwards, to support US warships at diverse locations worldwide. They were doing all kinds of repairs. The problem was, however, that they became personnel heavy, and were expensive. So the US Navy decommissioned most of them, except a couple now, in order to be able to rely on port facilities. However, in some situations where one should not, would not, or could not rely on port facilities, then these tenders would be very handy. Since the US Navy has those, it would be reasonable to expect that the Chinese may very well develop this capability.

Access by sea to Chinese ports though, can be threatened in peacetime, and interdicted in wartime. Blockade has become a major strategic strand in public writing on the Chinese-American military matters in the United States. Several American naval policy analysts have openly recommended that – in time of war – the United States institute a close blockade of China's ports, through the use of submarines, mines, and eventually unmanned undersea vehicles (UUVs) and – for some – long-range aircraft, as well as a more distant blockade using surface ships and aircraft, and other complementary naval operations.[8] They regard this strategy as useful, both as a deterrent to Chinese aggression, as well as a sound war-fighting strategy against a nuclear-armed, but commercially-vulnerable power.

US naval capabilities are, however, not currently optimized for blockade operations. These same writers usually also note, however, that while the United States leads the world in submarine warfare capabilities, the US Navy today has very little, by way of mine stockpiles and mine delivery systems, essential to a campaign of blockade from the sea, especially one targeted at a country with as extensive a coastline as China.[9] They also tend to take as a given that third-party shipping would drop precipitously or cease, in the face of the announcement of a blockade of Chinese ports.

Notwithstanding the debate in the US on the subject, the Chinese know very well about blockades. They have been blockaded before.[10] There are at least three important examples in modern Chinese history:

- The Imperial Japanese blockade of, and attack on the Imperial Chinese Fleet at Weihaiwei in the eastern Shandong Province, during the Sino-Japanese War of 1894-95. The naval blockade was part of a larger joint campaign that also included destruction of a Chinese fleet at sea, and extensive Japanese ground operations in Korea and Manchuria.
- A far more extensive Imperial Japanese 'pacific blockade' of Chinese ports during the undeclared Sino-Japanese War of 1937-41 – not affecting neutral ships. In this campaign, the Japanese Army conducted ground operations ashore to complement the Japanese Navy's blockade at sea.
- Taiwanese Nationalist Chinese regime's blockade of the mainland from 1949 through 1958. This blockade was the longest such campaign in modern times, and progressed through a series of stages. The blockading force consisted not only of Republic of China (RoC) naval forces, but also ground forces in the form of guerrilla groups ashore; operating from inshore island bases not far from the Chinese coast (China has some 5000 of such coastal islands). Later, RoC Air Force aircraft were also used for surveillance, and to attack shipping at sea. Mainland Chinese forces progressively rolled up most of these guerrilla bases, leading to the blockade's end in 1958.

Despite the enormous efforts expended, the two latter blockades were imperfect and only partially successful. Japan and the Nationalist Chinese regime lacked the forces to control the entire Chinese coast. Third party neutral shipping continued and the blockade thereby earned the enmity of third parties, and important alternative international land routes reduced reliance on coastal ports. On the other hand, the Chinese are probably planning blockades of their own. This is probably the case *vis-a-vis* Taiwan.[11]

It is also believed that the Chinese anti-blockade capabilities lag as opposed to those in other warfare areas. Current Chinese naval policies, however, do not seem to place high priority on anti-blockade capabilities. Chinese investments in the PLA Navy's anti-submarine and counter-mine warfare capabilities have not kept pace with those in other warfare areas, such as shore-based anti-surface warfare, including anti-carrier warfare.[12] These policies, however, could significantly change in the future. Indeed they may already be changing. As leading American analysts Lyle Goldstein and Shannon Knight have pointed out, '*the massive Chinese military industrial complex has now come around to [recognizing] the great importance of ASW, and China's substantial military and science-research energies have shifted accordingly.*' They further concluded that '*It is amply clear that China is committing significant research resources to try to detect submarines in nearby waters.*'[13]

Maritime Research Base[14]

The size and diversity of the maritime research community, as part of the general expansion of Chinese maritime research base, reflects the country's extensive maritime interests. Just as there are many bureaucratic actors involved in China's maritime affairs, there are more than 100 Chinese research organizations engaged in maritime research at the national, provincial, and municipal levels; with over a third of them directly affiliated with the Chinese government. Most of these are focused on research in the physical and natural sciences, and in engineering. Since the Chinese maritime interests are multi-faceted, it has developed a collection of research organizations that focus on a wide array of specific maritime issues, from economic to military. Chinese maritime research organizations have also tended to specialize in narrow bands of expertise that reflect the bureaucratic interests of their sponsors – such as port and waterway engineering, naval strategy, fisheries, and marine mineral resources. This high degree of specialization creates the potential for gaps, redundancies, and competition in China's collective maritime research capabilities.

Further, most of the bureaucratic actors involved in China's maritime policy do have specific economic interests in the maritime domain. As a result, many of these actors have research organizations that specialize in those areas of research which have related economic applications, such as fisheries sciences, aquaculture, marine mineral resources, ship-building, marine engineering, and hydropower. Most government research organizations specialize in some type of marine science or engineering.

The Chinese maritime research community has, hithertofore, been decentralised. There does not appear to be a central government organization tasked with coordinating state-sponsored maritime research. Consequently, PRC central government leaders might not always have been fully aware of the various research efforts being conducted by the Chinese research vessels, and this could possibly have slowed Beijing's response to incidents at sea involving Chinese research vessels. Although various Chinese bureaucratic actors involved in China's maritime affairs appear to be in agreement that sea is vital to the country's economic development and national security; it is possible – perhaps even probable – that they have been advocating competing policies for how to go about developing and securing China's maritime interests.

Reorganization of the State Oceanic Administration (SOA)

Creation of the State Oceanic Commission, and a renewed State Oceanic Administration (SOA), on the other hand, could lead to more centralization. The Chinese Government announced at the National People's Congress (NPC) in March 2013 that it would establish the State Oceanic Commission as a high-level coordination body, and consolidate the organizations, and responsibilities of under-mentioned entities under the SOA:[15]

- The previous SOA
- China Maritime Surveillance (CMS)
- Maritime police of the Border Control Department (BCD) of the Ministry of Public Security
- China Fisheries Law Enforcement Command (FLEC) of the Ministry of Agriculture
- General Administration of Customs (GAC)

This increased centralization of Chinese oceanic policy, administration, and operations may well become reflected in a more coordinated approach by the various research institutions, affiliated with, or supporting those entities. Nevertheless, the State Ministry of Science and Technology remains responsible for managing, regulating, and promoting the development of maritime science and technology at the national level. This Ministry has been responsible for the civilian underwater manned and unmanned vehicle programs, which are discussed in the latter half of the Paper.

Maritime Research Institutions

Some of the leading Chinese maritime research institutions include:

China Institute for Maritime Affairs (CIMA)

The State Oceanic Administration's China Institute for Maritime Affairs (CIMA) has been the only national-level state-sponsored civilian research organization that conducts strategic policy research on the full spectrum of civilian maritime issues. As such, it is likely to have a significant impact on the development of China's maritime policies and behaviours. CIMA plays a direct role in drafting national level maritime policy statements; and participates directly in the process of drafting and revising China's maritime laws and regulations.[16]

Naval Research Institute (NRI)

Naval Research Institute is uniquely positioned to influence the development and behaviour of the PLA Navy. NRI reports directly to the commander of the PLA Navy, it provides recommendations to senior naval officials, and helps draft naval policies and regulations. NRI's researchers are frequent commentators in the Chinese state-run media, potentially shaping views on the impact of global naval developments on China's maritime interests and the role of the PLA Navy in defending those interests.

Qingdao Institute of Marine Geology (QIMG)

The Qingdao Institute of Marine Geology's research feeds inputs for the Chinese central government's decisions about the development of marine mineral resources, including those located in disputed maritime areas. QIMG performs functions that are key to prioritizing China's interest in particular maritime areas. It investigates, surveys, and assesses oil, mineral, and gas resources in China's territorial waters, and it participates in efforts to map Chinese offshore areas.

Tianjin Institute for Water Transport Engineering (TIWTE)

The Ministry of Transport's Tianjin Institute for Water Transport Engineering (TIWTE) informs the Chinese central government decision-making system about the development of China's maritime infrastructure. TIWTE was founded in 1974. It is a large research institute with three operational laboratories, and numerous research organisations. A fourth laboratory is under construction. TIWTE's research supports China's plans related to the development, management, and maintenance of China's domestic and foreign ports, as well as its coastal and inland waterways. TIWTE consults directly with foreign and domestic port authorities, suggesting that it plays a role in China efforts to secure access to ports which are of strategic interest.

TITWE's activities include environmental impact assessments; environmental engineering studies; waterway engineering studies; surveying and mapping of coastal and inland waterways; simulations and analysis of tidal patterns; current flows, sedimentation, and other hydrological factors that affect the development; operability, and environmental sustainability of China's coastal and inland waterways; diagnostic and safety evaluations of hydraulic structures and facilities; development of software platforms for use in hydrological research; building of physical structures for use in hydrological research; development of energy-saving technologies and processes for use in port and waterway engineering; provision of facilities and equipment for hydrological, hydraulic, and hydrodynamic research demonstrations; and hydrologic engineering consultations with Chinese and foreign government organizations focused on coastal and inland waterways affairs.

Internationally, TIWTE has consulted with the governments of Pakistan, Myanmar, South Korea, Malaysia, Indonesia, and others. TIWTE is, therefore, likely to have been involved in the planning and development of foreign ports and waterways that are of strategic commercial interest to China.

PLA Navy Research Organisations

The PLA Navy also has its own research organizations, among which the most important ones are the Dalian Naval Vessel Academy and the Naval Engineering University (in Wuhan and Nanjing respectively). While they are primarily officer education institutions, important advanced technical research is conducted there as well. The Naval Vessel Academy has PhD programmes in Communications, Information Engineering and Control; and Earth Survey and Survey Engineering. The Naval Engineering University has established five research institutes.

Civilian Institutions in Support of Military Programmes and Forces

Some State-owned enterprises are also active in maritime-related research. These include the China Communications Construction Company (CCCC) First Harbour Consultants Limited, the CCCC Second Harbour Consultants Limited, China Shipbuilding Industry Corporation, and the China State Shipbuilding Corporation. As with the Chinese ports, Chinese research institutions, and laboratories – even if primarily focused on civilian and economically-relevant endeavours – can provide valuable 'dual use' support to the Chinese military, including to the PLA Navy. Chinese military and naval writers understand this, and often call for intensive cooperation between state civil maritime and military institutions. Examples of such dual use support include identifying shipments of weapons of mass destruction; surveying water areas and sea beds; monitoring commercial vessel communications and emissions, and underwater construction projects; and development of manned and unmanned underwater vehicles.

Undersea Vehicles

Infrastructure and manufacturing – both, for domestic use and export – are two main pillars amongst others, for China's economic success – and political stability. Sustenance of these pillars requires enormous amounts of raw materials. Hence, China's demand for more – and more kinds – of raw materials continues to grow. China has identified numerous new sources of raw materials to stoke its economic growth. These include domestic and foreign sources, on land and under the sea, in both China's Exclusive Economic Zone, and in international waters. China believes its Exclusive Economic Zone (EEZ) is not large enough commensurate with its perceived and desired status in the world. It views its EEZ as paltry compared to that of, for example, the United States, France, Australia, Russia, the UK, Canada, and Japan. This is a part of the larger Chinese narrative of past victimization and unfair constraints imposed by former colonial powers. Increasingly assertive Chinese sovereignty claims in the China Seas are manifestations of this view. The sea and the seabed, which are an important current and potential source of raw materials, will go a long way in supplementing the supply of such raw material from other terrestrial sources.

China is, therefore, launching a major effort to explore and exploit the international seabed. For instance, the China Ocean Mineral Resources Research and Development Association (COMRA) applied for, and received approval – through the United Nations International Sea Bed Authority (ISBA) – to exploit specific deep-sea mining sites in the Pacific and Indian Oceans in 2011. The Indian Ocean site is at the Southwest Indian Ocean Ridge, and is thought to be rich in copper, iron, lead, zinc, gold, and silver.[17] In addition to the ship-based equipment, manned and unmanned underwater vehicles would prove to be great enablers.

In 2002, the construction of China's first civilian manned undersea vehicle was approved. The China Shipbuilding Industry Corporation (CSIC) – the primary contractor for the PLA Navy and a major builder of port equipment – built and launched *Jiaolong* (Sea Dragon) in 2009.[18] With a depth capability of 23,000 feet, it is the world's second-deepest diving research submersible. *Jiaolong* was an ambitious program for a nation that had never built a manned submersible. As a result, construction time was longer than for comparable projects in the West. Its titanium pressure hull was built and tested in St. Petersburg, Russia. The hydraulic arm and syntactic foam – which withstands high pressures – were manufactured in the United States.[19] *Jiaolong* made a 23,169 foot dive in 2012 in the western Pacific's Mariana Trench that attracted significant worldwide press attention. Later that year, *Jiaolong* explored the South China Sea and areas in the North Pacific, conducting numerous dives.

In October 2013, the Chinese press reported that China's first civilian unmanned and un-tethered undersea vehicle, the 'robot' *Qianlong-1*, had conducted a dive to 5080 meters in the open sea, operating from the Chinese research vessel *Haiyang-6*. CSIC is also building a second manned underwater civilian deep-sea vehicle for the Ministry of Science and Technology, along with a dedicated mother ship. The titanium pressure hull for that will be built in China. A small two-person submersible is also planned for construction by the Shanghai Ocean University's Hadal Science and Technology Research Center.

China is now accelerating its efforts to tap mineral deposits on the ocean floor. China's manned civilian underwater deep-sea vehicle *Jiaolong* is scheduled to gather geological data in the northwest Pacific in May 2014, and in the southwest Indian Ocean in November 2014. *Jiaolong* will be supported by her mother ship *Xiangyanghong 09*. Since 2013, the COMRA has been building a new National Deep Sea Center base in Qingdao, as a home port to *Jiaolong*. It is expected to be finished in late 2014.

Most of the world's maritime powers are developing unmanned naval underwater vehicle systems and technologies. Unmanned naval systems are rapidly proliferating internationally because they are increasingly capable and cheaper than manned alternatives for certain missions.[20] China is in the forefront of these developments. In particular, China has developed a series of sophisticated unmanned underwater vehicles to complement its submarine force.[21] In 2010, Chinese researchers were testing at least seven confirmed UUV prototypes, with one of them in the initial testing phase with the PLA Navy.[22]

Undersea vehicles and undersea vehicle technology both have obvious military applications and implications. Civilian manned submersibles could also be used for tapping underwater communications cables, disrupting other nations' military sensors, retrieving foreign weapons and other military systems from the seabed, and other military tasks.[23] Protection of civilian manned submersibles deployed far forward is yet another potential rationale for a PLA Navy to forward its blue water presence in the world's oceans, including in the Indian Ocean.

NOTES

1. The basic source for much of this section is KPMG Global China Practice, *Infrastructure in China: Sustaining Quality Growth* (February 2013). Valuable insights were also provided by Mr. Matthew Fenton of the maritime services company, Brookes Bell, Hong Kong.
2. On China's economic growth, see especially Wayne M. Morrison, *China's Economic Rise: History, Trends, Challenges, and Implications for the United States*, CRS Report RL 33534 (Congressional Research Service, Washington DC, February 3, 2014). For more economic context that specifically relates to the topics addressed in this paper, see David D. Hale, *China's New Dream* (Australian Strategic Policy Institute, February 2014).
3. I am indebted to CDR Raghavendra Mishra Indian Navy for this point.
4. Data is from the World Shipping Council at http://www.worldshipping.org

5. On the 12th Five-Year Plan, see Morrison, *China's Economic Rise*, p. 32.
6. KPMG, *Infrastructure in China: Sustaining Quality Growth* ibid.
7. On the origins of the Chinese pipeline and port project in Myanmar, see Bernard D. Cole, *Sea Lanes and Pipelines: Energy Security in Asia* (Westport CT: Praeger Security International, 2008), p. 58.
8. These advocacy pieces and analyses include Col (Retd.) T.X. Hammes USMC, *Offshore Control: A Proposed Strategy for an Unlikely Conflict,* (Washington DC: National Defense University, June 2012); Capt (Retd.) Jeffrey Kline and Capt (Retd.) Wayne Hughes, 'Between Peace and the Air-Sea Battle: A War at Sea Strategy,' *Naval War College Review* 65 (Autumn 2012), pp. 35-40; Sean Mirski, 'Stranglehold: The Context, Conduct and Consequences of an American Naval Blockade of China,' *Journal of Strategic Studies* 36, (June 2013), pp. 385-421; Evan Braden Montgomery, 'Reconsidering a Naval Blockade of China: A Response to Mirski,' *Journal of Strategic Studies* (2013), pp. 616-623; and CDR (Retd.) Victor L. Vescove, '...From (Under) the Sea,' U.S. Naval Institute *Proceedings* (February 2014), pp. 53-58. Note that the centerpiece of Col Hammes's proposed strategy is distant blockade, far from the Chinese ports. Many of these arguments are made in opposition to the authors' understanding of the US Defense Department's 'Air-Sea Battle' concept.
9. See, for example, Scott C. Truver, 'Taking Mines Seriously: Mine Warfare in China's Near Seas,' *Naval War College Review* 65 (Spring 2012), pp. 30-66; and Sidney J. Freedberg, Jr., 'Deadly Serious Navy Wrestles with Mine Warfare Modernization,' *AOL Defense.com*, September 11, 2012, http://defense.aol.com/2012/09/11/navy-wrestles-with-mine-warfare-modernization. The US Navy's *Program Guide for 2014* mentions only one mine enhancement program among more than two hundred or so on-going ones discussed therein. See US Navy, *Program Guide 2014* (Department of the Navy, Washington DC, 2014), p. 104.
10. China's experience with blockades is discussed in Bruce A. Elleman and S.C.M. Paine (eds.), *Naval Blockades and Seapower: Strategies and Counter-Strategies, 1805-2005* (London and New York: Routledge, 2006).
11. The Chinese blockade option against Taiwan is explored in William S. Murray, 'Underwater TELs and China's Antisubmarine Warfare: Evolving Strength and a Calculated Weakness,' Chapter two in Peter Dutton, Andrew Erickson, and Ryan Martinson (eds.), *China's Near Seas Combat Capabilities*, (U.S. Naval War College, Newport RI, China Maritime Studies, Number 11, February 2014), pp. 17-29.
12. Ronald O'Rourke, *China Naval Modernization: Implications for U.S. Navy Capabilities – Background and Issues for Congress*, CRS Report RL 33153 (Washington DC: Congressional Research Service, February 28, 2014), p. 3 and *passim*. See also Murray, 'Underwater TELs and China's Antisubmarine Warfare: Evolving Strength and a Calculated Weakness.'
13. Lyle Goldstein and Shannon Knight, 'Wired for Sound in the "Near Seas",' U.S. Naval Institute *Proceedings,* April 2014, pp. 56-61.
14. Many Chinese research organisations have websites in both English and Chinese. Some are more detailed than others. Much of this section is derived from a series of interviews with specialists in the Washington DC area. For a related analysis of the Chinese policy research community that studies South China Sea issues, see Yun Sun, *Studying the South China Sea: The Chinese Perspective*, East and South China Seas Bulletin 1 (Washington DC: Center for a New American Security, January 9, 2012). See also Shannon Tiezzi, 'China's Academic Battle for the South China Sea,' *The Diplomat,* February 25, 2014. http://thediplomat.com/2014/02/chinas-academic-battle-for-the-south-china-sea/
15. A good description and analysis is in Masayuki Masuda, Yasuyuki Suguira and Shinji Yamaguchi, *NIDS China Security Report 2013* (Tokyo: National Institute for Defense Studies, 2014), pp. 12-13.

16. For more detailed analysis of CIMA's mandate, see Sun, *Studying the South China Sea*, p. 3-4.
17. Dolma Tsering, 'China's Deep Sea Exploration: Research and Capacity Building,' National Maritime Foundation (New Delhi: June 28, 2012). This source also has a particularly thorough accounting of the entire history of the Chinese civilian deep sea underwater vehicle program, through 2012. It is probably the best single source on the subject.
18. On Chinese civilian manned underwater deep sea vehicles, see Don Walsh, 'The Dragon Learns to Dive – Part II,' U.S. Naval Institute *Proceedings* (September 2013), 86. See also Eliza Strickland, 'China's Research Sub Dives Deep,' *IEEE Spectrum* (September 2011), pp. 11-12.
19. Arturo Perez-Reverte, 'China Seeks to Mine Deep Sea Riches,' *Guardian Weekly* (December 7, 2010).
20. For a brief overview, see Chris Rawley, 'Unmanned Systems and Distributed Operations: Out of One, Many,' Center for International Maritime Security (CIMSEC), March 6, 2014, http://cimsec.org/unmanned-systems-distributed-operations-one-many/
21. A thorough but now somewhat dated analysis is Lyle Goldstein and Shannon Knight, 'Coming without Shadows, Leaving without Footprints,' U.S. Naval Institute *Proceedings* 136 (April 2010), pp. 30-35.
22. Lyle Goldstein and Shannon Knight, 'Coming without Shadows', *Ibid,* p. 35.
23. This point is well made in Dolma Tsering, 'China's Deep Sea Exploration: Research and Capacity Building', ibid.

8

Chinese Shipbuilding Capabilities

Rear Admiral MK Badhwar (Retd.) and
Captain Pramod R Kulkarni

Introduction

Chinese commercial shipbuilding has grown very rapidly from 1990 onwards, and the country has become a global leader by displacing Japan and South Korea – both in terms of annual throughput as well as the order book position.[1] Naval shipbuilding too, has shown impressive growth over the last decade.[2] It is estimated that by 2020, China's military shipbuilding technical capabilities can become as good as Russia's, and will near the current US shipbuilding proficiency levels by 2030.[3] Majority of the Chinese shipyards have either upgraded their infrastructure or set up additional new 'greenfield' shipyards. Improvements in China's ship-design capabilities are now in line with the global state-of-the-art standards. Apart from shipbuilding infrastructure, a robust ecosystem supporting shipbuilding – such as manufacturers of engine and marine equipment – is in place. This evolution of shipbuilding capabilities over the last 30 years has facilitated an impressive transformation, enabling China to become technologically competent and fully capable of research, design, and construction of the entire spectrum of commercial as well as naval vessels.

This paper looks at the Chinese shipbuilding capabilities by presenting the role of the Chinese government in expansion and modernization of the shipbuilding industry, and reviews major shipbuilding facilities including the design, R&D, and ancillary support for shipbuilding. The paper also maps the evolution of Chinese warship and submarine building programmes, which show the transformation of naval shipbuilding capabilities, and discusses the factors that have been responsible for the impressive growth.

Major Economic and Industrial Restructuring of Chinese Shipbuilding Sector

Since the introduction of market-based economic reforms in 1978, China has become the world's fastest growing economy. Realizing the impact that the shipbuilding industry could have on the manufacturing sector, the Chinese political leadership decided to patronize the shipbuilding industry and undertook the following major economic and industrial restructuring decision for this sector:[4]

- In 1982, the sixth Ministry of Machine Building was corporatized into the China State Shipbuilding Corporation (CSSC), which became the starting point of China's growth story in shipbuilding.
- The growth of CSSC far exceeded the initial expectations of the Chinese Government. Therefore, in 1999, it was decided to partition CSSC into two organizations, primarily for more effective management, but also as an anti-monopoly initiative, bringing in a limited amount of free-market competition. Thus, a second corporation known as China Shipbuilding Industrial Corporation (CSIC), was created by grouping the shipyards and subsidiaries in locations north of Shanghai. CSSC continued to control the shipyards and related subsidiaries in Shanghai and south of river Yangtze.
- Around the same time, it was also decided to integrate the military and commercial sides of Chinese shipbuilding; as a result of which, Chinese shipbuilders have become far more efficient, better skilled, and more sophisticated in designing and building commercial as well as naval ships.

Statistics of the Chinese Shipbuilding Industry

Though the Chinese shipbuilding industry aggressively moved into building commercial ships from the 1990s, the story of the Chinese shipbuilding industry during the last decade has been particularly impressive. Chinese shipyards penetrated the global market by producing low complexity ships, such as dry bulk carriers and oil tankers, at a lower price than their competitors in South Korea and Japan. China then gradually entered into producing medium complexity ships, and thereafter attempted to learn the skill of outfitting technically complex vessels, such as Liquefied Natural Gas (LNG) as well as passenger vessels and cruise ships.[5]

In 2010, China became the world leader in commercial shipbuilding both in terms of annual throughput, as well as the order book position. The impressive growth can be seen from the following statistics[6]:

- The relative world share of actual shipbuilding completions (Figure 8.1) has changed over the last 10 years for different players. It can be seen that:
  - China's share has risen from less than 8 per cent in 2002 to over 40 per cent in 2012.
  - Korea's share rose from 31 per cent in 2002 to 35.4 per cent in 2008, but fell thereafter to less than 28 per cent in 2012.
  - Japan's share fell from 31 per cent in 2002 to around 17 per cent in 2012.
  - Europe's share fell from 21.6 per cent in 2002 to less than 4 per cent in 2012.

Figure 8.1: Growth of Commercial Shipbuilding – Shipbuilding Completions

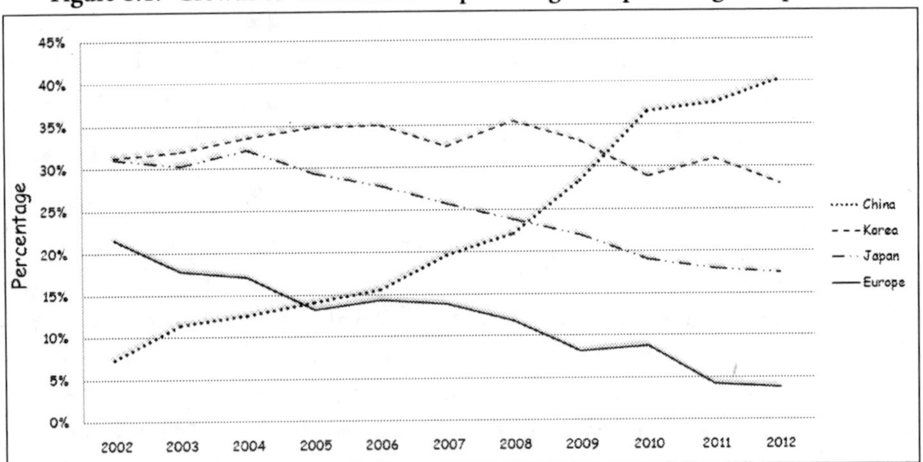

Source: Data from Report on China's Shipbuilding and Offshore Industries: Translating Crisis into Opportunities (SeaHow Consulting, Shanghai, 2013), p. 8.

- Figure 8.2 shows the share of new shipbuilding orders. It can be seen that:
  - China's share rose from 11 per cent in 2002 to 42 per cent in 2008, and then reduced, but was still over 33 per cent in 2012
  - Korea's share rose from 30 per cent in 2002 to 44 per cent in 2003, but then fell to less than 28 per cent in 2012
  - Japan's share fell from 37 per cent in 2002 to around 17 per cent in 2012
  - Europe's share moved up from nine per cent in 2002, to about 18 per cent in 2005, and then came down to less than six per cent in 2012

Figure 8.2: Growth of Commercial Shipbuilding – New Orders

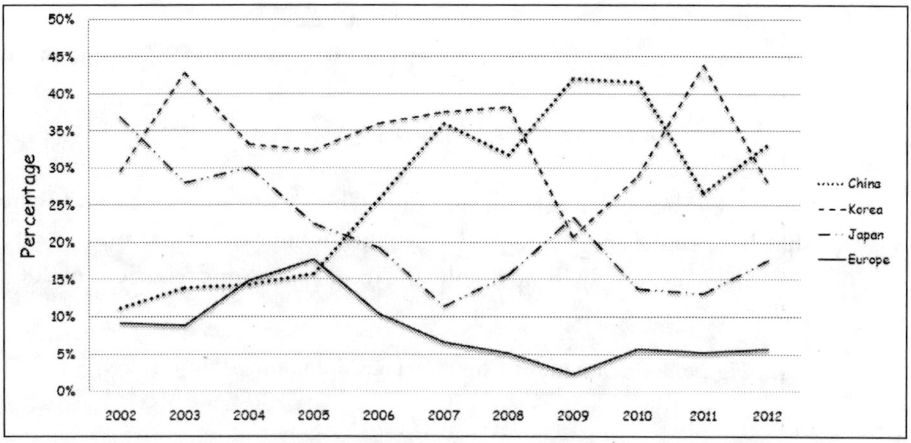

Source: Data from Report on China's Shipbuilding and Offshore Industries: Translating Crisis into Opportunities (SeaHow Consulting, Shanghai, 2013), p. 9.

- Figure 8.3 shows the resultant share of shipbuilding order books. It can be seen that:
    - ❑ China's share has risen from 12.3 per cent in 2002 to over 33 per cent in 2012

Figure 8.3: Growth of Commercial Shipbuilding Order Books

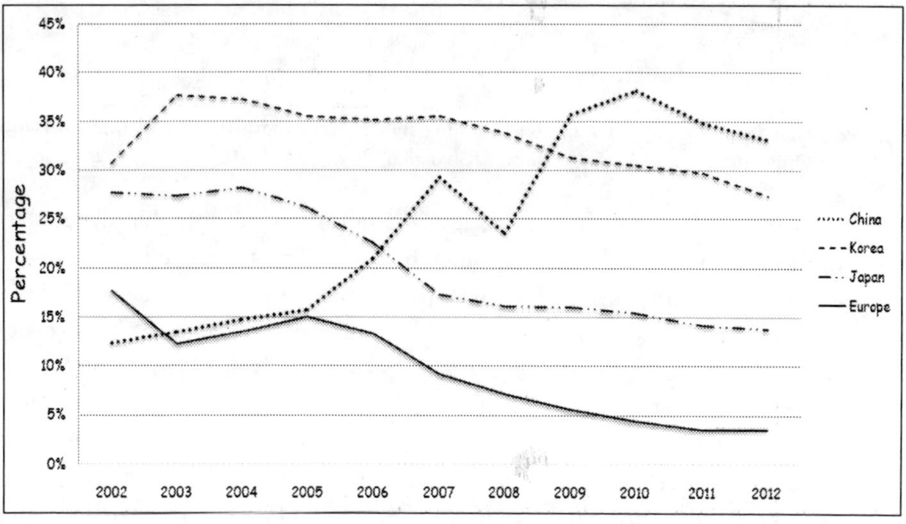

Source: Data from Report on China's Shipbuilding and Offshore Industries: Translating Crisis into Opportunities (SeaHow Consulting, Shanghai, 2013), p 10.

- Korea's share rose from 31 per cent in 2002 to 37.7 per cent in 2003, but fell to less than 28 per cent in 2012
- Japan's share fell from 37 per cent in 2002 to around 17.4 per cent in 2012
- Europe's share fell from 17.7 per cent in 2002 to less than four per cent in 2012

• Figure 8.4 shows that that it is not only China's percentage of world share that has been rising, but also the net throughput over this entire period has been handsomely rising despite the recent economic recessions of 2008 and 2012.

Figure 8.4: Growth of Commercial Shipbuilding Output

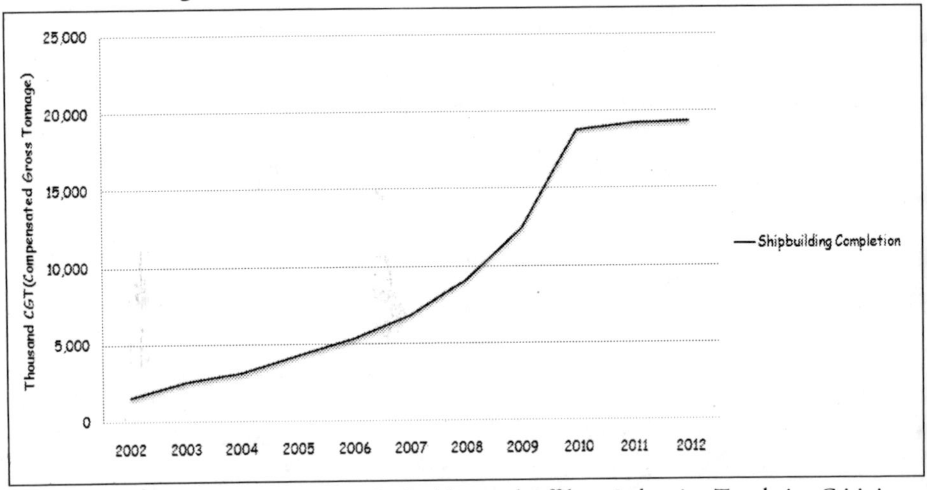

Source: Data from Report on China's Shipbuilding and Offshore Industries: Translating Crisis into Opportunities (SeaHow Consulting, Shanghai, 2013), pp. 8-10.

Notwithstanding the above statistics, it is important to note that in terms of contribution of individual yards to the global capability, the three largest Korean yards – Hyundai and Samsung (each with 5.4 per cent), and Daewoo (5.2 per cent) – are still far ahead of the largest Chinese yards – Dalian (2.2 per cent), Jiangnan (1.9 per cent), and Jiangsu (1.7 per cent). Even in terms of average Compensated Gross Tons (CGT) of ships built, Korean yards are much better placed with 28,600 CGT as compared to 16,800 CGT for the Chinese. However, the Chinese shipyards have been gradually learning the skill of outfitting more complex vessels with the help of Japanese, Korean, and German shipyards through various joint ventures and are already executing orders for such vessels.

Role of the Government in Expansion and Modernization of Chinese Shipbuilding Industry

The Chinese government has been playing a very constructive role in the transformation of the Chinese shipbuilding industry.[7] Shipbuilding was declared a strategic industry, because it was realized that promoting that industry would result in the growth of the complete manufacturing sector and in turn, the national economy. Also, the Chinese government did not step aside after formulating policy guidelines, but has been watching the performance of this industry very closely. It has been introducing midstream changes to suit the needs of the day. For example, in 1982, the government corporatized the entity that ran the shipyards, giving them a high degree of market based financial autonomy. When it realized the necessity of nurturing quality workforce, it gave the shipyards the bureaucratic freedom to hire and fire. When it found that CSSC had become too large to manage as a single corporation, it carved out another entity – CSIC – out of it. When poor quality of the Chinese built ships found mention in the international media, the government was quick to insist on minimum quality standards, and threatened to revoke licenses of yards that were found guilty of producing poor quality vessels.[8]

Some of the important initiatives taken by the Chinese government for consolidation of their shipbuilding industry have been as follows:[9]

- Direct subsidy of up to 17 per cent to Chinese ship buyers, if the vessel in ordered on domestic shipyards
- Loss reimbursement to any domestic shipyard provided it is assessed to have made high contribution to the nation
- Sovereign refund guarantees for the advances received by shipyards from foreign clients
- Refund of Value Added Tax (VAT), Zero Custom Duty, and exemption on Income Tax
- Allowing accelerated depreciation and providing working capital at nominal rates
- Restructuring and modernization assistance
- Introduction of 'Issue 55' to enhance quality of ships built, safe working conditions, and environment protection. The Ministry of Industry and Information Technology (MIIT) directive – 'Issue 55' – became a law on December 1, 2013. As part of the law, the government demanded the compliance of the following from the shipyards:[10]

    - ❑ Limit energy consumption to equivalent of 0.2 tonnes of coal for every RMB 10,000 (US$ 1650) revenue earned

- Exceed steel utilization rates of 90 per cent
- Exceed automatic and semi-automatic welding rates of 65 per cent
- Comply with all relevant (national and international) standards for safety, environmental protection, and energy efficiency
- Establish R&D departments and invest 2 per cent revenue in it

Major Chinese Shipbuilding Facilities

Though hundreds of shipyards have had to shut shop in the last few years because of financial difficulties and inefficient operations, there are still around 1800 functional shipyards reported in China. Overall, the Chinese maritime industry employs about 34 million people and contributed about 5 trillion Yuan to the China's GDP in 2012. This, according to some experts, could rise to about 20 trillion Yuan by 2020.[11] The major shipbuilding activity in China, tends to be concentrated in specific locations, namely Dalian, Shanghai, and Guangzhou; either in the coastal areas, or along the mouths of the three major rivers – Yellow River, Yangtze River and Pearl River. It can be seen from the map in Figure 8.5 that:

Figure 8.5: Location of Major Shipyards

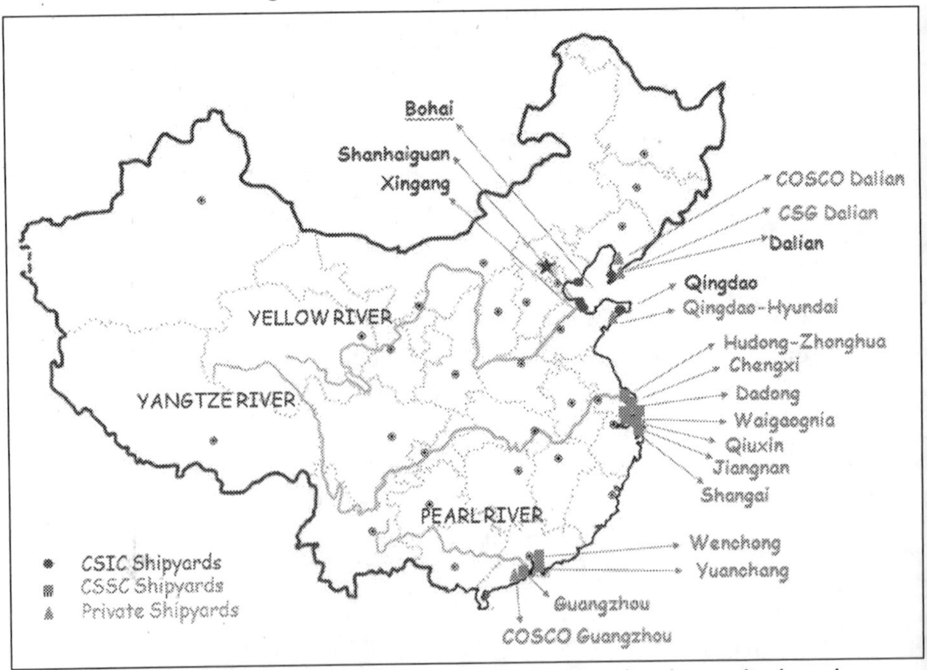

Source: The blank map has been taken from one website. Thereafter, the river has been drawn on it by the authors. Further, information about the location of shipyards has been compiled from different documents and have then been incorporated in the map by the authors.

- Area extending from Yellow River to Heilong River in the north has fostered major yards like Dalian, Bohai, Wuchang, Qingdao, Shanhaiguan, Xingang, all belonging to CSIC, and private yards like CSG Dalian, COSCO Dalian and Qingdao- Hyundai.
- The Yangtze River Delta around Shanghai has a concentration of major CSSC yards like Waigaoqiao, Hudong-Zhonghua, Chengxi, Shanghai, Jiangnan, Dadong, and Qiuxin shipyards.
- The remaining CSSC yards like Guangzhou, Wenchong and Yuanchang, and a private yard, COSCO Guangzhou, are located along the South China Sea coast, in the mouth of the Pearl River.

Contributors to the Transformation of China's Naval Shipbuilding Capability

Apart from the government policies, thrust and encouragement for the shipbuilding industry, there have also been other contributors of the transformation of China's naval shipbuilding capability.

Commercial Vessel Design Capability

According to several foreign experts who have been interacting with Chinese shipyards for years, their commercial ship design capabilities are in line with the global state-of-the-art ship design standards. Major ship design houses like the Shanghai Merchant Ship Design & Research Institute (SDARI), and Marine Design & Research Institute of China (MARIC), as well as design houses of all major Chinese shipyards, use the latest CAD/CAM software. Even in as early as in 2005, 13 of the world's largest shipyards using the Swedish software TRIBON were claimed to be Chinese; and at least 40 other shipyards in China were using this software. Widespread use of this state-of-the-art ship design software has certainly helped in improving the Chinese ship design, structural tolerance control and faster pre-outfitting.

Many large commercial vessel designs are jointly prepared by the Chinese and foreign firms. It is learnt that both CSSC and CSIC organize numerous study tours abroad for their designers, and also have ongoing partnerships with foreign design firms. According to a RAND Report,[12] even in 2005, there were more than 500 vessel designs completed by the Chinese ship designers. In recent years, Chinese shipyards have been designing and building more complex ships like the Ro-Ro ships.

Warship Design Capability

China initially took help of the Russian warship and submarine design organizations. Some cooperation between French warship design houses and Chinese designers is also indicated.[13] However, the Chinese designers have been largely consolidating their expertise through reverse engineering, and incremental learning process. They have been incorporating lessons learnt from preceding designs in their new design work, and evaluating their impact.[14] It is estimated that by 2020, China's military shipbuilding technical capabilities can become as good as Russia's and will near the current US shipbuilding proficiency levels by 2030.[15]

Research and Development

China operates a wide variety of R&D institutes devoted to shipbuilding. Many of these have strong linkages with the Chinese and foreign universities and shipyards. These institutes have provided the Chinese shipbuilding industry access to modern R&D techniques, production technologies, and best management practices.[16]

Ancillary Support

In terms of ancillary support, Sino-foreign joint ventures are required to set up 'special technology centres', aimed at providing a short-cut to close gaps between the Chinese shipbuilding and established European shipbuilding industry. Joint ventures and subsidiaries, with the help of Koreans and Japanese shipyards, and with European equipment manufacturers like Sulzur, Caterpillar, B&W (Burmeister & Wain), MAN (Maschinenfabrik Augsberg Nurmberg), ABB (Asea Brown Boveri), MTU (Motoren und Turbinen Union), and Wartsila, are some such examples. With shrinking market and high cost of labour in their countries, most of these equipment manufacturers find China an attractive place to do business. It is reported that under pressure of recession in the commercial shipbuilding orders, the Chinese shipyards are shifting attention to manufacturing marine engineering equipment; the results of which are already showing. In 2013, the Chinese maritime industry has received new equipment orders for almost US$13 Billion, which is almost 26 per cent of the world demand. In 2012, the Chinese share was only 13 per cent.[17]

Naval Shipbuilding Capability[18]

Just like commercial shipbuilding, the naval shipbuilding in China too has shown impressive growth since 2001. Interestingly most of the major Chinese shipyards build commercial as well as naval ships. Also, each type of warship is built at more than one shipyard and each shipyard is capable of building more than one type of warship. While on one hand, this enables the shipyards to mitigate their risk due to market ups and downs; on the other, it stimulates healthy competition among the yards, enabling the PLA Navy to demand best prices and 'build periods' for their ships.[19]

While in the 1970s, the main focus of the PLA Navy was rapid expansion by way of indigenous construction of warships; in the 1980s, the focus shifted from 'numbers only' to building quality warships. As the Chinese shipbuilding industry aggressively moved to building commercial ships over the next two decades, it also managed to leverage these efforts towards design and construction of better naval vessels. China's overall fleet of front-line combatants has already grown from 172 ships in 2005 to 221 in 2012, and has improved substantially in qualitative terms. The evolution of different types of naval vessels in Chinese inventory is presented in succeeding paragraphs.

Submarines

Since the mid 1990s, China has laid emphasis on the submarine force as one of the primary thrusts of its military modernization effort. Besides acquiring 12 Russian Kilo Class non-nuclear attack submarines, China has also put into service at least four new classes of indigenously designed submarines, which are regarded as more modern and capable than China's aging older-generation submarines.[20]

Nuclear Submarines

- Jin class or Type 094 – Three of these new nuclear-powered ballistic missile submarines (SSBN) are already operational and up to five more may enter service before China proceeds to its next generation SSBN (Type 096) over the next decade.
- Shang class or Type 093 –Two Shang nuclear-powered attack submarines (SSN) are already in service, and it is reported that four improved variants are under construction to replace the aging Han class SSNs (Type 091).

Non-nuclear Submarines

- Yuan class or Type 039A – A non-nuclear-powered attack submarine (SSG) design, with Air independent propulsion (AIP). China may construct up to 20 of this class.
- Song class or Type 039/039G – A fairly new non-nuclear-powered attack submarine (SSG) design.

Ballistic Missile Test-Bed Submarine

In 2011, China is reported to have commissioned a new type of non-nuclear submarine built in Wuchang shipyard called the *Qing* class (about one-third larger than the Yuan-class design), which will be used to test ballistic missiles, as well as a new vertical launch system. With about 6800 tons displacement, this is one of the largest non-nuclear submarines in the world.

Destroyer Program

During 1980's, China modified several Luda III–class Destroyers at Guangzhou and Dalian to augment their capabilities. In the 1990s, it commenced development of its second-generation Destroyers which were substantially more modern in terms of their hull designs, propulsion and weapon systems. A total of six new indigenous destroyer designs have been developed and built in the recent times:[21]

- Luhu (Type 052) – China's first of second-generation Destroyers
- Luhai (Type 051B) – Only one ship of the class built-1998
- Louzhou (Type 051C)
- Luyang I (Type 052B)
- Luyang II (Type 052C)
- Luyang III (Type 052D) – China's third-generation Destroyer

The *Luyang* II (052C class) destroyer has a phased array radar, which would be used with the vertical launch system (VLS) air-defence missiles. Both these systems are a first for Chinese combatants, and gave the PLA Navy its first fleet of air-defence vessels. Incorporating further improvements, the lead ship in the follow-on class, the Luyang III (Type 052D), named *Kunming*, entered service in 2014. The Luyang III incorporates the PLA Navy's first multipurpose vertical launch system, capable of launching ASCM, LACM, SAM, and AS rockets. There are strong indications that Type 052D – a capable guided-missile destroyer may become a standard surface combatant, which could be the central element of Beijing's new blue-water Navy.[22] China is projected to build more than a dozen of these ships to replace its aging LUDA-class destroyers.

Frigates

Since early 1990s, China has put into service four new classes of indigenously built Frigates, which are essentially variations of two designs. These are:

- Jiangwei I (Type 053H2)
- Jiangwei II (Type 053H3)
- Jiangkai I (Type 054)
- Jiangkai II (Type 054A)

Like China's new destroyers, the latest frigate (Type 054A) design has a more streamlined form, very small superstructure, low radar cross-section (RCS), and larger displacement, thereby augmenting its war-fighting capabilities and seaworthiness. Type 054A also offers greater flexibility in terms of payload. Some observers indicate that the new frigate will have a significantly enhanced set of weapon capabilities over the Jiangwei-class frigates, possibly including VLS capabilities. With 16 ships currently in the fleet and four in various stages of construction, a total of at least 20 are eventually expected.

Corvettes

China is building a new type of corvette called the Jiangdao class (Type 056). At least six of these were launched in 2012. The first nine of these ships entered service in 2013. China may build 20 to 30 ships of this class.

Fast Attack Craft (FAC)

In 2004, China embarked on the construction of a 400 tonne missile FAC, called the *Houbei* class (Type 022), that uses a stealthy wave-piercing catamaran hull made of an aluminum alloy. Each boat can carry eight C-802 ASCMs. The *Houbei's* ability to patrol coastal and littoral waters and react at short notice allows the PLA Navy's larger combatants to focus on offshore defence and out-of-home area missions, without leaving a security gap along China's coastline. The *Houbei* class was concurrently built in at least six shipyards. In just seven years, the PLA Navy has inducted 83 of these.

Amphibious Ships

- **Yuzhao (Type 071) Amphibious Ship.** China put into service a new class of amphibious ships called the *Yuzhao* class [Type 071 LPD (Landing Platform Dock)]. The lead ship entered service in 2007. The second and third ships of this class entered service in 2012. A fourth ship has also been launched.
- **Type 081 Amphibious Ship.** China has reportedly begun construction of a larger amphibious ship, called the Type 081 LHD (Landing Helicopter Dock). It has resemblance to the French Mistral. Displacing about 35,000 tonnes, it is expected to have a length of 211m, maximum speed of 23 knots, endurance of 25-30 days at sea, accommodation for 1,068 embarked marines, and will be able to embark eight helicopters with hangar space for four.

Aircraft Carrier

China had initiated studies on possible aircraft carrier options in the 1990s. They have been consolidating their expertise, while fitting out *Liaoning*, a 60,000 tonne conventionally powered carrier, which was originally bought from Ukraine. Having commissioned Liaoning in Sep 2012, China now plans to build three more carriers that will be domestically designed. Work on the first domestic carrier (Type 001A class) has reportedly started in the second half of 2013 in the Dalian shipyard (which did the refitting work for *Liaoning*).[23]

Carrier Aviation

China has developed a carrier-capable fighter Shenyang J-15 or 'Flying Shark', reverse engineered from a Russian Sukhoi Su-33, also bought from Ukraine. Although the J-15 has a land-based combat radius of 1200 km, the aircraft will be limited in range and armament, when operating from *Liaoning*, due to limits imposed by ski-jump takeoff and arrested landing. This implies that the aircraft exploitation would currently be restricted to limited air superiority operations and ship defence. China will therefore be looking at acquiring a 'catapult-assisted take-off but arrested recovery' (CATOBAR) capability in its future carriers, so that the J-15, which is a multirole fighter, can carry a heavier payload and thus launch attacks against ships and ground targets as well.

Factors Responsible for Growth of Chinese Naval Shipbuilding Capability

In addition to the factors listed in the earlier sections of this paper, some other factors that have helped accelerate China's rise as a world-class military shipbuilder are as follows:[24]

- **Use of modular mass production techniques** – Chinese yards have been quick to adopt modern shipbuilding techniques like modular construction, which significantly enhances the productive efficiency, particularly when the series are large. Jiangnan Shipyard is using modular construction to build Type 052D Destroyers. Hudong-Zhonghua shipyard also appears to be using modular construction for the Type 071 LPDs. It is reported that this yard has been able to significantly speed up the construction of successive ships of the class – with the time gap of nearly four years between the first and second vessels, reducing to 10 months between vessels 2 and 3, and only four months between vessels 3 and 4.
- **Sharing design and production information across company lines** –

Historically, CSIC built all the Chinese submarines. It is now reported that submarine construction expertise is growing outside of CSIC, which could mean that the companies and their design institutes are being asked to share the design and construction information. This suggests that standardized designs and production approaches are being adopted across shipyards.

- **Infrastructure to indigenously build aircraft carriers** – China has seven shipyards with sufficiently large berths to assemble carrier hulls. These yards are equally dispersed between CSSC and CSIC; and are located in Dalian (CSIC), Qingdao (CSIC), Huludao (CSIC), Shanghai (CSSC), and Guangzhou (CSSC). CSIC's Bohai Complex (where China builds its nuclear submarines) is a front-runner due to large covered building sheds where carrier parts could be fabricated in modular fashion, out of the view of satellite surveillance. The company has the largest indoor ship construction facility in China. This facility, together with CSSC's large new Changxing Island yard, and CSIC's Dalian yard – which fitted out the *Liaoning* carrier – are the three leading candidates to build China's indigenous carriers.
- **China's military shipbuilding cost advantage** – Chinese shipbuilders have a substantial labour cost advantage over their counterparts in South Korea, Japan, and the US. CSSC's Jiangnan shipyard can deliver a Type 052C destroyer for 24 per cent less cost than Korea's Hyundai Heavy Industries can to produce a KDX-III destroyer. Wuchang shipyard can produce a late model diesel electric submarine such as the Type 041 for roughly 47 per cent less than it would cost South Korea's Daewoo Shipbuilding & Marine Engineering (DSME) to make a Type 209 submarine.
- **Export of Naval vessels** – China's shipbuilders are becoming increasingly competitive in terms of the ratio of 'cost to combat power' that they can deliver. Chinese yards are also willing to design and build ships according to the requirements of foreign navies; and thus have been successful in getting export orders from many countries. For instance, China is supplying six AIP equipped submarines to Pakistan for as little as one-third the unit price, at which European shipyards would be able to supply comparable boats. The export version of Russia's Steregushy-class corvette, called *Tigr*, currently costs around US $150 million. As China's Type 056 production run continues to expand, it would not be a surprise to eventually see the PLA Navy's unit cost reduce to US $100-110 million per ship. Similarly, the type 022 missile FAC's cost is in the region of merely US$40 million.[25]

Conclusion

Chinese shipbuilding industry has consolidated its capabilities, particularly over the past decade, not only handsomely overshadowing its nearest rivals, Korea and Japan in commercial shipbuilding but also creating and consolidating its expertise in design and construction of all types of military vessels – a process that continues to gain steam to this very day. Chinese shipbuilding infrastructure and the know-how that has been built up is fully capable of building greater numbers of large modern warships, such as frigates, destroyers, submarines, amphibious support vessels and even aircraft carriers simultaneously, if a political decision is made to increase the PLA Navy's size and capabilities significantly.

Acknowledgement

The authors acknowledge the contribution of Mr. P.V. Kaushik, student of IIT Delhi, for assisting in researching for this Paper.

NOTES

1. S. Navaneetha Krishnan, 'Analysis of Chinese Shipbuilding Industry: Strategic Lessons for India', Maritime Affairs, Vol. 7, No. 2, (Winter 2011), pp. 66-84.
2. Ronald O'Rourke, 'China Naval Modernization: Implications for U.S. Navy Capabilities – Background and Issues for Congress', *Congressional Research Service, 7-5700*, September 30, 2013.
3. Gabe Collins and Andrew Erickson, 'The engine of China's naval rise has flown under the radar until now', November 1, 2012, http://thediplomat.com/2012/11/u-s-navy-take-notice-china-is-becoming-a-world-class-military-shipbuilder/ (accessed February 24, 2014).
4. For details, see S. Navaneetha Krishnan, *Prosperous Nation Building Through Shipbuilding* (New Delhi: Knowledge World Publishers, 2013), pp. 115-133.
5. S. Navaneetha Krishnan, *Prosperous Nation Building through Shipbuilding* ibid, pp. 115-133. Also see the presentation 'Chinese Shipbuilding and Shipbuilding Capacity' by Li Zhengyu, November 2011, http://www.google.co.in/url?sa=t&rct=j&q=&esrc=s&source=web&cd=2&cad=rja&uact=8&ved=0CCQQ FjAB&url=http%3A%2 F%2Fwww.marinemoney.com%2Fsites%2Fall%2Fthemes%2Fmarinemoney%2Fforums%2Fchina11%2 Fchina presentations%2 FLiZhengyu.pdf &ei=sJ8aVNBcz5S4BKSzgJAM&usg=AFQjCNHspVIynJMOOzz42XeKm_kaipU8DQ&bvm=bv.75097201,d.c2E (accessed February 24, 2014).
6. Shipbuilders Association of Japan, 'Shipbuilding Statistics', September, 2013, www.sajn.org.jp/e/statistics/ Shipbuilding_Statistics_Sep2013e.pdf (accessed February 24, 2014).
7. S. Navaneetha Krishnan, *Prosperous Nation Building through Shipbuilding* ibid, p. 115.
8. Naval Architect, 'Deconstructing China's shipbuilding industry', *RINA* (Royal Institution of Naval Architects), (February 2014), pp. 30-33.
9. S. Navaneetha Krishnan, *Prosperous Nation Building through Shipbuilding* ibid, pp. 115-133.
10. 'Deconstructing China's shipbuilding industry', *Naval Architect, RINA*, ibid, pp. 30-33.
11. 'Chinese Shipbuilding and Shipbuilding Capacity' ibid. Also see, 'Hudong-Zhonghua led by innovation', *In-Depth China Ship News, Naval Architect, RINA*, February 2014, pp. 26-28.
12. Evan S. Medeiros, Roger Cliff, Keith Crane, James C. Mulvenon, 'A New Direction for China's Defense Industry', *RAND Report* MG-334, 2005.

13. Ronald O'Rourke, 'China Naval Modernization' ibid; Evan S. Medeiros et. al., RAND Report MG-334 ibid.
14. Gabe Collins and Andrew Erickson, 'The engine of China's naval rise has flown under the radar until now' ibid.
15. P.R. Kulkarni, 'Review of Global Naval Shipbuilding Trends and Lessons for Indian Shipbuilding Industry', being published in *Maritime Affairs* Journal of the National Maritime Foundation, Winter 2014 edition.
16. S. Navaneetha Krishnan, *Prosperous Nation Building Through Shipbuilding* ibid, pp. 115-133.
17. S. Navaneetha Krishnan, 'Analysis of Chinese Shipbuilding Industry: Strategic Lessons for India' ibid.
18. The data and statistics cited in this section are sourced from Ronald O'Rourke, 'China Naval Modernization' ibid, unless mentioned additionally or otherwise.
19. Evan S. Medeiros et. al., RAND Report MG-334 ibid.
20. Commander Kamlesh K. Agnihotri, 'The Chinese Navy's Submarine Arm: Lynchpin of 'Active Defence', *Maritime Affairs* Journal of the National Maritime Foundation, 8:2, (2012), pp. 95-122.
21. '2013 Chinese Naval Review', December 25, 2013, Posted by Feng, http://www.information dissemination.net/2013/12/2013-chinese-naval-review.html (accessed March 5, 2014).
22. Jonathan Marcus, 'Buzz over China's new prototype warship', September 13, 2012, http:// www. bbc.com/news/ world-asia-china-19553811 (accessed February 24, 2014).
23. '2013 Chinese Naval Review', December 25, 2013, Posted by Feng, www.informationdissemina tion.net (accessed March 5, 2014).
24. 'The Shipbuilding Industry in China', OECD Report No. C/WP6 (2008)7/REV1, June 26, 2008.
25. Gabe Collins and Andrew Erickson, 'The engine of China's naval rise has flown under the radar until now', ibid.

9

Polar Security Issues: An American Perspective

Captain Mark E. Rosen, JAGC, USN (Retd.)

Introduction

The Polar Regions have re-emerged as a significant policy issue due to increased international awareness of their abundant fishery, energy and mineral resources – particularly in the Arctic North. As climate change makes these areas more accessible, the question becomes whether these are areas of global opportunity or a venue for friction and confrontation.

This paper will examine the security issues in the Polar Regions; although the primary focus will be on the Arctic, since this region is receiving the greatest amount of attention and an increased human presence. The Arctic is far more likely to be an area of political and military competition because it can be accessed by sea, and there are demonstrable resources in the littoral areas which are important to fast growing economies. Another very important fact is that global climate change patterns resulted in long term ice regression trends in the Arctic Ocean; but that is not the case in Antarctica. Earlier predictions of ice regression in Antarctica are now being reexamined.[1]

Legal Structure: Antarctica versus the Arctic

Even though international organizations like the International Maritime Organization (IMO) have shipping guidelines that deal with 'polar' operations, the fact is that the legal structure of the Arctic is completely different from Antarctica.

Firstly, Antarctica is a continental land mass which is roughly twice the size of Australia. There are no permanent human residents, but anywhere from 1,000 to 5,000 people reside throughout the year at research stations scattered across the continent. In contrast, the Arctic region is essentially a maritime region. The Arctic Ocean is the smallest and the shallowest of the five major oceans. Owing to its size, and the fact that it is completely surrounded by Eurasia and North America, some classify the Arctic as a Sea. This small size and the close proximity of land in all directions means that coastal countries have significant legal interests in the water column, due to the entitlements of States under the 1982 UN Law of the Sea Convention (UNCLOS). This relationship is shown in Figure 9.1. All areas outside of the red hatched line are unquestionably under the legal and resource jurisdiction of coastal countries. Owing to the shallow depth of the continental shelf in much of the Arctic Ocean, the actual amount of the area which is clearly beyond the jurisdiction of any coastal country is estimated at about 15 per cent.

Figure 9.1: The Arctic Ocean

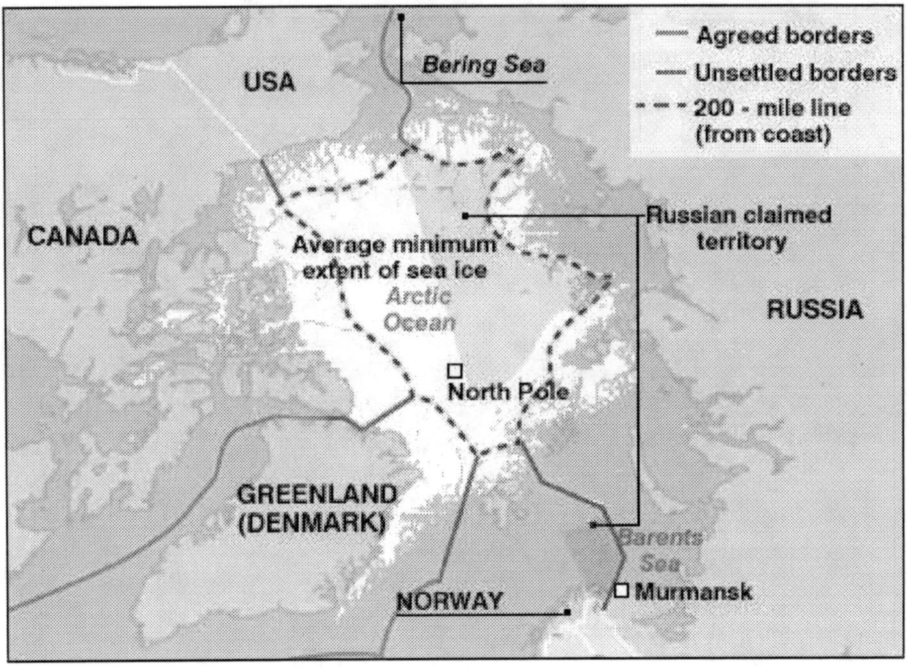

Source: 2012 US Coast Guard Briefing.

Antarctica is entirely different. Like outer space and the deep seabed, it is legally classified as 'Global Commons' because it is not under the jurisdiction of any single country. Antarctica's special status as part of the 'global commons' was established in the 1961 Antarctic Treaty that shelved the claims of seven countries which had prior claims. It declared that no new claims to sovereignty could be asserted.[2] Nearly 50 years have elapsed without any serious dispute as to the essential international character of Antarctica as an international research venue; although from time to time, countries have reserved their rights to establish claims in the future. Military bases, fortifications, maneuovres, and weapon testing are banned in perpetuity on Antarctica and there have been no serious challenges to that moral, and legal imperative since after the Treaty was concluded.

Consistent with this international character, management of the affairs of Antarctica is done via Treaty organizations which regulate fishing and mining.[3] The fisheries organization is quite active and licenses a large amount of fisheries each year. Figure 9.2 depicts the fishing areas which the Antarctic Commission has licensed to specified vessels (by fish species).[4]

Figure 9.2: Antarctic Fishing Zones

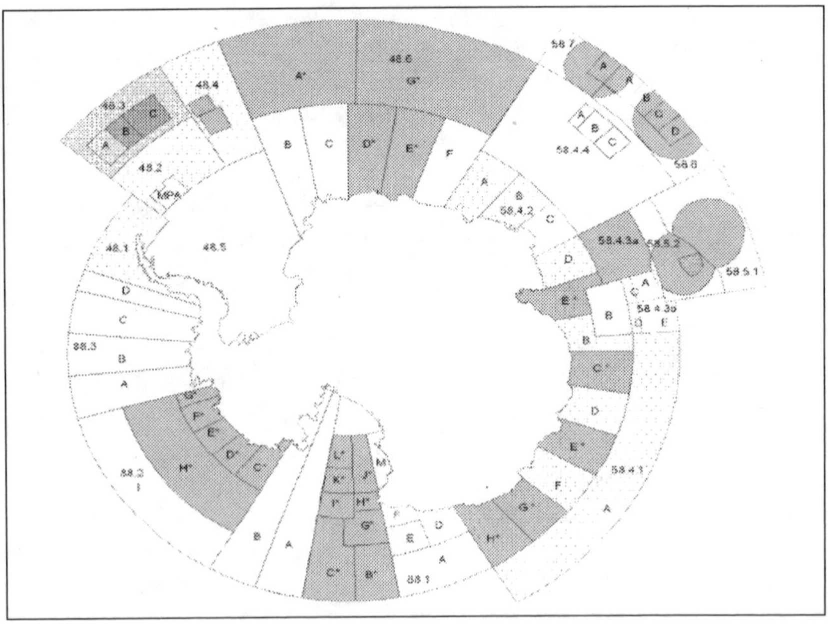

Source: CCAMLR.

Some minerals have been found in Antarctica, but a 1991 Protocol on Environmental Protection to the 1961 Treaty places a moratorium on mineral extraction until at least 2048.[5] Though not explicit, one must assume that the moratorium on mineral extraction in the Protocol would cover all offshore oil and gas activities within 200 NM of Antarctica's coastline.

Resource Scarcity and the Poles

An increasing amount is being written about how declining stores of accessible resources will inevitably lead to conflict. China is often featured in the centre stage in those discussions, as is the Arctic. In a recent book by the Council on Foreign Relations, Scholar Elizabeth Economy chronicles China's worldwide quest for resources and discusses the implications of those activities.[6] China's dependence on foreign oil imports, for instance, has increased nine times in the past ten years, and analysts estimate that in 2013, China will have imported 60 per cent of its total oil supplies.[7] This dependence is expected to increase in the future. Ms. Economy concludes that global resource wars are 'far down on the worry list', but she did not rule out the potential for localized conflicts, especially in the South and East China Sea, where ownership of fisheries, and oil and gas are at the heart of current sovereignty and other maritime disputes. However, it is unquestionable that China will need access to resources to be able to fuel its economy, and in her view – which the author supports – international law frequently does not provide many solutions. Given that, she postulates that '...rising Chinese Nationalism and military capacity…make a confrontation appear increasingly attractive to many in Beijing.' This risk could intensify if the Chinese economy or political leadership is substantially weakened. It could 'tempt the Chinese leadership to distract citizens from problems at home by provoking international confrontation.'[8]

The preceding discussion singles out China but it could have just as easily included other fast growing economies that have large energy appetites, like Korea, Japan, and India, among other countries that will be seeking access to Arctic mineral, oil and gas, and fisheries resources. As regards the Arctic, the resource projections are breathtaking; although they must be taken in the context that little actual oil and gas prospecting has taken place. Over 80 per cent of its unrecovered natural gas, and 70 per cent of Russia's unrecovered petroleum, are in the Arctic regions, primarily in the Barents and Kara Seas, and in the Timan-Pechora basin.[9] According to a 2008 US Geological Survey (USGS) report, 'extensive Arctic continental shelves may constitute the geographically largest unexplored prospective area for petroleum remaining on Earth.' The USGS estimates that 13 per cent of the world's undiscovered oil reserves (90 billion barrels) and 30 per cent of the undiscovered gas reserves (1,700 trillion cubic feet of natural gas, and 44 billion barrels of natural gas liquids) are in the Arctic. These estimates are in addition to more than 240 billion barrels of petroleum reserves that have already been discovered.[10]

Even though the annual temperature in the Arctic is rising faster than predicted, there remain significant challenges to all of the Arctic littoral countries to harvest these resources, because there is no shore infrastructure to serve as oil and gas terminals. Further, the rig operations remain a dangerous proposition for much of the year because of the dangers of sea-ice (which destabilises the rig's buoyancy), extreme cold, and severe storms. Also, responsible ship- owners complain about the scarce availability of reasonably priced insurance products for voyages into Arctic waters. Despite these challenges, several countries – along with corporations like ExxonMobil, STATOIL, and Royal Dutch Shell – are preparing to exploit the region's enormous oil and natural gas reserves; although Shell recently took a pause in its exploration activities because of a number of 'close calls' they had experienced in their offshore drilling in the American Chukchi Sea area.

However, the mineral extraction is taking place at present. The Arctic currently supplies more than 90 per cent of Russia's nickel, cobalt, and platinum, as well as 60 per cent of Russia's copper. 90 per cent of Russian diamonds and 24 per cent of its gold is mined in the Arctic region of Yakutia. One of the world's largest phosphate mines is located on the Kola Peninsula. In addition, Arctic Russia has significant deposits of silver, tungsten, manganese, tin, chromium, and titanium The US Arctic is home to one of the largest zinc and lead mines in the world which is located in northwest Alaska (Red Dog Mine). The Government of Norway attributes the following percentages of worldwide mineral production to the Arctic:

> Nickel (11 per cent), cobalt (11 per cent), tungsten (9 per cent), zinc (8 per cent), palladium (40 per cent), platinum (15 per cent), gem-grade diamonds (26 per cent), industrial-grade diamonds (24 per cent), and apatite (11 per cent)[11]

The upshot of all of this is that the Arctic is quite likely to be an area that will be very attractive to investors and prospectors who need the raw materials to fuel their economies. This necessarily means that the area will almost certainly see increased level of foreign investment, and also increased 'destination' shipping to mine, and perhaps, oil and gas sites.[12] Likewise, the area is also likely to see increased fishing as it becomes more accessible. With this increased human traffic will come the potential for vessel accidents, oil and gas spills, rig accidents, protest activity,[13] and possibly clashes between military or law enforcement vessels with unlicensed fisherman or other 'foreign' vessels, which are considered unseaworthy, or might be carrying dangerous cargoes that threaten the marine environment.

Security Implications of the Legal Differences between the Poles

The security implications of increased demand for potential untapped polar reserves are unquestioned when one looks at the relation between various conflicts in the Middle East involving the US – and other western countries – and its regional importance as an exporter of oil and gas. However, increase in natural gas supplies as a result of fracking has reduced the urgency by which states might wish to pursue polar hydrocarbon resources. It is, however, anyone's guess as to how long this situation will persist; and nations are wise to take a long-term view because the world's economies are not standing still, and fossil fuel and mineral consumption demand from China and India, amongst others, is projected to increase in the long term.

Security Issues Concerning the Antarctic

As noted above, the current Antarctic Treaty structure bans mining and drilling – both, continental and offshore – until 2048. That ban was the result of an initiative by France and the UK (versus the US). It is, therefore, difficult to envision that China or other states would be able to muster the political consensus to unmake the taboo against mining or offshore drilling there. One could possibly envision scientific expeditions by countries that are, in fact, a stalking horse for oil and gas exploration. However, sustained activities in Antarctica are readily observable by others and clandestine mining or oil and gas drilling would be met with immediate international condemnation.

Even though oil and gas is a powerful lure, the recent debacle in December of 2013 involving the stranding of a Russian research ship and the Chinese icebreaker Xuelong or Snow Dragon (in which both vessels became stuck in the thick summer ice) demonstrates that Antarctica is an especially remote area. It cannot be easily reached by ship – even when temperatures are highest – and air transport of bulk commodities would be prohibitively expensive. Unlicensed fishing is another matter. The UN fisheries oversight agency reported an upswing in unlicensed fishing in portions of Antarctica's EEZ; presumably because these fishermen have assessed their freedom from arrest, which justifies the hazards of making the voyage.

In terms of inter-state conflict over Antarctic resources, it is a fundamentally different proposition to extract resources in Antarctic versus the Arctic. There are formidable political barriers to building airheads or bases of operation that would be able to support some sort of mining or drilling operation. Also, the costs of mounting and insuring a safe operation would be staggering. Given that, it appears unlikely that Antarctica will become an area of intense commercial activity or concomitant conflict over territory or resources – apart from the occasional arrest of illegal fishing vessels.

Security Issues Concerning the Arctic

The Arctic is a different story. It is a more fertile area for competition and conflict zone for a number of reasons; mostly geography. Firstly, the Arctic is accessible by sea, and the long-term trend is towards increased maritime access due to the effects of climate change. Secondly, since the Arctic is a maritime region, coastal states have no authority under UNCLOS to prevent foreign ships from either entering most Arctic waters, or passing through.[14] Coastal States also have no authority to specify whether ships meet the 'polar class' equipment standards – for training, equipment, crew composition – unless the particular foreign ship is entering a port in the area and that country specifies that the ship meet certain standards.[15] Thirdly, there are already established patterns of resource development. Significant mining activity is occurring in all of the Arctic littoral States, and countries outside of the Arctic are now investing in major new mining sites in Canada, Iceland, and Greenland. Despite the current surplus of natural gas in world markets, the shallow continental shelf in much of the Western Arctic makes it an exceedingly attractive target for foreign offshore oil and gas exploration. Shell's exploratory well in the United States' Chukchi Sea was about 75 miles offshore but the water depth was only about 150 feet. This is in sharp contrast to other drilling operations like *Deepwater Horizon*, that must operate in waters over 5,000 feet in depth.

Fourthly, the regression of Arctic ice is making fisheries much more accessible; including some Far North fisheries, which are beyond the management control of any single nation. Obviously, if these far North fisheries are not managed, it could affect worldwide fishing stocks. However, lack of a management structure will not deter fisherman from entering these waters. Finally, the Arctic has become much more accessible because Russia is making the development of its Northern Sea Route (NSR) a national priority.[16] This is not all bad since Russia appears to be doing a responsible job administering the NSR. However, future political and economic pressures may result in a relaxation of important safety and monitoring standards, and create a permissive environment for undesirable shipping to enter the Arctic. Undesirable shipping could put the marine environment at risk or sow the seeds of conflict if that shipping becomes involved in illegal activities, such as unlicensed fishing, smuggling and piracy.

Arctic Security in Context

The Arctic used to be a very 'hot' national security domain. The US and Canada operated a network of surveillance systems based in the far North, including the 'Dew Line', which was a network of radar stations to detect and give early warning of attacking Soviet bombers. The actual 'Dew Line' comprised the uppermost constellation of radar stations that were situated north of the Arctic Circle, primarily on Canadian territory. The Arctic seas were also a venue for interaction and competition between the US and the Soviet submarine forces. Both routinely operated in this region, because of the proximity to strategic bases and choke points of the other country. The 1963 thriller (and movie) *Ice Station Zebra* portrays a fictional conflict between the US and Soviet forces, in which a US nuclear submarine is involved in rescuing of the members of a remote drifting Arctic ice station which was handling important satellite intelligence data.

Military competition in the Arctic has cooled down since the days of *Ice Station Zebra,* but President Putin has been gradually increasing the size of the Russian military contingent in the Arctic. Shortly after sending the scientific mission to the Arctic ridge, Putin ordered the resumption of regular air patrols over the Arctic, by strategic bombers and anti-submarine patrol aircraft.[17] There have been similar announcements that the Russian Navy is increasing its naval deployments in its claimed continental shelf areas.[18]

O'Rourke's excellent paper on changes in the Arctic[19] discussed how the US, Canada, and Denmark have continued their annual Arctic exercises and NATO, to some extent, has followed suit. However, there is a schism in NATO. Even though the text of the 1949 NATO Mutual Defence Treaty can be easily read to include the land territory and the sea boundaries (EEZ and continental shelf areas of the US, Canada, Greenland, Norway, and Iceland), there is no consensus within NATO that the Arctic should be an area of military concern. Some states would like to have a more robust military presence in the Arctic; and others, like former NATO Secretary General Jaap de Hoop Scheffeer, have urged that NATO member countries should go to great pains in not allowing the Arctic to become an area of military competition.[20] As of this writing, NATO continues to be a forum for discussions of Arctic affairs, but Russia's NATO ambassador and President Medvedev has made it clear that Russia would not cooperate with NATO on Arctic matters.

On November 22, 2013, US Department of Defense (DoD) unveiled its new strategy for the Arctic; the roll-out occurring in a speech given by Secretary of Defence Chuck Hagel, in Halifax, Nova Scotia, that same day. The DoD strategy complements the May 2013 policy issued by President Obama, and does not dwell on security threats or issues. In a press conference held in conjunction with the rollout, DoD senior defence officials asserted that there is 'no assumption of an emerging military threat…[and the strategy seeks to]…keep the region as peaceful as it already is.'[21] However, Secretary Hagel said that the rush by nations to exploit the substantial oil and gas reserves cannot rule out the possibility that a greater military presence will be necessary to ensure peace as mankind discovers this 'next frontier'. As Hagel put it, 'throughout human history, mankind has raced to discover the next frontier. And time after time, discovery was swiftly followed by conflict. We cannot erase this history, we can assure that history does not repeat itself in the Arctic.'[22]

The new DoD Policy[23] states that DoD will continue to build on its strategic partnerships to increase its regional expertise and obtain 'small footprint' cold weather operational experience. This is in addition to the sizeable US Coast Guard, US Air Force, and Army Corps of Engineers footprint in Alaska.[24] The February 2014 US Navy 'Arctic Roadmap' accentuates an increase in the US Navy's role in the Arctic relating to forecasting, maritime domain awareness, information sharing and hydrographic surveys/charting. In general, however, DoD will play a supporting role and contribute its expertise and resources in such areas as international Science and Technology (S&T) cooperation, disaster & emergency response, regional maritime domain awareness (MDA), ice & weather forecasting, and hydrographic charting & mapping. Engagement of Russia in these cooperative activities and the role of NATO in Arctic affairs are not directly addressed in the DoD policy. Not much is said about whether, and how, DoD will fund these enhanced missions. The policy makes it very clear that DoD's activities in the Arctic will have to compete with other budget priorities; mainly because the US defence planners feel that the Arctic should remain free of military competition for the foreseeable future.

Will the Arctic Go Like the South China Sea?

Before assessing external security threats to the Arctic, it is important to first assess whether there are serious underlying differences between the main Arctic players – the US, Russia, Canada, Norway, and Greenland (Denmark) – that could create internal friction and would stimulate military competition, or make it politically impossible for the main players to reach an agreement on regional matters in the Arctic Council, and elsewhere.

The US has two disputes with Canada that involve delineation of their adjacent boundary in the Beaufort Sea, and a longstanding disagreement over the status of Canada's Northwest Passage. There is a small dispute between Canada and Denmark over the status of Hans Island, which lies roughly equidistant from Canada and Greenland in the upper reaches of the Baffin Bay. Russia and Norway still have to delineate their EEZs in the Barents Sea, west of the Svalbard Islands. Even though there was a stunt in which Russia planted a flag on the seabed of the North Pole in 2007, in the vicinity of the Lomonosov Ridge[25] – stimulating various press agencies to speculate that Russia was engaged in an Arctic 'land grab' – the reality is that Russia has been fully complying with the process to lay claim to an extended continental shelf in the Arctic.[26] The UN Commission of the Limits of the Continental Shelf (CLCS) will probably take years to help the parties demarcate the outer limits of their extended continental shelf, since Russia's submission is far more advanced than that of Canada and Denmark.

Most of these disputes are highly technical and will be resolved in due time, and in an appropriate manner. None of these disputes dominate the headlines, and none have led to a breakdown in diplomatic communications between the contestants. In case of the limits of extended continental shelf claims, there is an impartial intermediary – the CLCS –to steer the parties to agreement. Besides, most of these disputes involve areas that are extremely remote, and it is highly questionable that these areas will ever be exploitable because they are ice-bound for most of the year. As a result, most of the countries are quite content to put these minor disputes on the back-burner, because there are plenty of other undeveloped areas which are far more accessible for development. In this region at least, there appears to be sizeable consensus among the five major states over how the Arctic is to be governed, and territorial and other types of legal disputes are unlikely to fracture that consensus.

UNCLOS Revisionism from Asia?

Another dimension of Arctic Security centres on the keen interest of outside states, particularly China and India, to petition for observer status in the Arctic Council. One can debate whether the interest of these states is to passively secure access to resources, or is there something more? Writing for Naval War College, David Curtis Wright[27] and Shiloh Rainwater[28] assert that China has aspirations to reorder the legal regime of the Arctic so that the resources in that region become part of the global commons, because these areas are the 'common heritage of mankind'. How exactly those policies would be implemented is unclear, since under UNCLOS, five littoral states in the Arctic control roughly 85 per cent of the water space and the resources in the water column, and the seabed. If Rainwater is correct, this type of thinking which articulates that the Arctic resources are part of the common heritage is certain to galvanize opposition from the US, Russia, Canada, and almost every other country that relies upon principles of UNCLOS to legally support their offshore resource activities. This type of thinking was expressly rejected in the UNCLOS negotiations. The compromise, of course, is that the international community has resource rights in those areas that lie beyond a coastal state's continental shelf and EEZ. The only possible way for this type of thinking to advance peacefully would be through an action at the United Nations to negotiate some sort of protocol to UNCLOS which deals with the Arctic. The US and Russia are certain to oppose such an effort, but countries such as China might be successful in mustering the votes in the UN General Assembly for an international arrangement by arguing that the Arctic – which today is largely unregulated[29] – needs to placed under some sort of governance controls to restrict fishing, and oil & gas exploration, since imprudent development of those resources affects worldwide fisheries, and water quality. They would certainly cite the Antarctic Treaty as precedent. Even though the Antarctic Treaty deals with a polar region, the ownership scheme and geography are different, as analyzed above.

The argument that international management is needed to protect the world's fisheries is a stretch, but is not beyond the realm of possibility if China, and perhaps others, will use 'lawfare' as a method of dislodging the superior legal rights of the US, Russia, Canada, and others. Were China and other countries to seriously embark on such an effort, they would invite serious trade retaliation, given the huge economic stakes involved, and might have the unintended consequence of making the US and Russia into stalwart allies.

Buying an Arctic Coastline

If you can't beat them, join them. This is one way to explain the sudden interest of Korea, Japan, Singapore, India, and China[30] to join in the activities of the heretofore moribund Arctic Council, as observers. Their inclusion in May 2013 stimulated a healthy dose of paranoia in Washington, Oslo, Ottawa, and Moscow, given that the Arctic Council has no real legal powers, and has been little more than a talk shop since its formation in 1996.[31] More likely than not, the new entrants to the Arctic Council – including China – have no serious intention of turning the entitlements in UNCLOS on their head. Rather, the weight of authority supporting the notion that China seeks to take advantage of the Arctic economic opportunities as strategic competition for control of the region, will increase. Chinese diplomats and military strategists have stated that China's interests in the Arctic remain chiefly economic, and that it intends to contribute to the region's peaceful development.[32] This same sentiment has been expressed to the author in multiple meetings that he has had with senior officials of the PLA and the Chinese government.

Assuming then that the new observers do not wish to provoke a conflict with the US and others over their resource rights in the Arctic, the question now becomes but as to how exactly will China, India, and the others assert their rights to make Arctic resource investments. Whether and how China and others will make investments in the Arctic is increasingly becoming a moot point. According to *The Guardian*, Greenland's self-governing parliament is considering approving a $2.3billion mining project north east of the capital Nuuk, which would be led by the UK-based London Mining plc., and which will supply China with 15 million tons of iron ore annually. The project, which may kick off in summer 2014, would require a team of 3,000 Chinese workers, adding more than 4 per cent to the country's population of 57,000.[33] In 2010, China provided Iceland with a $500 million-plus currency swap to support the struggling Iceland bank system. Also in 2010, Denmark signed deals with China worth $740 million in the areas of power, green economy, agriculture, and food security.[34] Finally, in March 2013, the Russian Government licensed the China National Petroleum Corporation to conduct a joint venture with the Russian oil company Rosneft to explore three offshore Arctic oil and gas sites.[35]

In the face of increased Chinese investment in Canadian oil sands, Ottawa passed new laws limiting foreign direct investment in certain Canadian natural resource projects. This came on the heels of recent reports of Chinese investments of over $400 million in various Canadian mineral and petroleum projects.[36] According to Yale University's *Environment 360* publication, Iceland '...twice rejected a Chinese plan to buy a 115 square mile farm along its northern coast for a proposed golf course resort'. The island nation, which is located at the confluence of the North Atlantic and Arctic oceans, feared that the proposal was part of a thinly veiled plan to build an Arctic port.[37] Even though this particular land deal was blocked by the Iceland Government, China has signed high level political agreements with Iceland concerning trade and investment; and China has purchased large stakes in Icelandic fishing companies. It also expanded the size of its Reykjavik Embassy to accommodate up to 500 persons.[38]

What are the implications of this strategic direct investment? Rob Huebert, an associate professor at the University of Calgary, who follows China's economic and strategic Arctic investment says, 'They have demonstrated that they will play hardball politics in terms of their interests.'[39] Also, the preceding patterns of direct investment, which include large number of foreign workers and tracts of land, suggests that China is not engaged in strictly passive foreign direct investment activities.

Future Collision Course?

Since territorial and boundary disputes are unlikely to be a driver for conflict, it is useful then, to reflect on seminal security interests of the US and the other Arctic littoral states, which could lead to serious political instability or conflict. These interests are as follows:

- Perfection and international recognition of legitimate claims over resources in the EEZ and continental shelf. including fisheries and hydrocarbons
- Preservation of political independence of the five primary littoral Arctic Countries (Denmark, Norway, Canada, Russia, and the US)
- Protection of the Arctic marine environment from ship or oil & gas pollution

Protection of Claims

The entitlements to assert claims to the maritime regions in the Arctic are determined almost exclusively by UNCLOS, since the Arctic is a maritime region. Four of the five Arctic Countries are parties to the 1982 UN Law of the Sea Convention, and the US has declared that it will abide by and respect UNCLOS in all of its dealings, including its assertion of maritime claims. Areas of disagreement between the five main Arctic states are small, and none will do anything to contest the resource entitlements of the others. If for no other reason, the fact that the Arctic is a closed sea, there is a strong geographic reason for the countries to be cooperative on matters such as maritime boundaries, fisheries management, and protection of the marine environment.

Political Independence

No serious scholar has suggested that China or any other resource dependent country will invade the Arctic to seize its riches. Doing so would invite massive retaliation from the US and Russia; and would likely implicate NATO, given that Canada, Norway, and Greenland (Denmark) are involved. While Rainwater's report on the Chinese aspirations contains quotes which suggest that some in China would like to alter the legal landscape by instigating action at the United Nations, the weight of evidence is that China will take a long term view to increase its influence in the region, in order to preserve access to its recourses. The same can also be said about the other new observers to the Arctic Council (Singapore, Japan, Korea, and India), but their modalities for increasing their influence would probably be more subtle.

The biggest challenges facing the Arctic have to do with ensuring that the region is developed in an economically sane manner, with proper controls in place to protect the marine environment. Since the Arctic is a closed sea, Arctic countries nations are more interdependent than in other regions, because a pollution event in one part of the Arctic Ocean is likely to affect the fisheries and marine environment of others. Consequently, the long-term security of the Arctic is very much dependent on a high degree of regional cooperation in which the countries act according to a set of shared economic development and environmental protection parameters.

Projecting shared values in the economic and environmental area means that each of the five Arctic Countries is able to exercise political free will, which is devoid of undue political or economic pressures. This is the Arctic's greatest vulnerability, because China has shown willingness to use its foreign direct investments to leverage political influence. The instances of foreign direct investment in Iceland, Canada, and Newfoundland have not led to a loss of political independence, but the parallels between what is happening in the Arctic, and what has happened in Africa and South America is instructive.

In *By All Means Necessary,* Elizabeth Economy chronicles how China has been involved in the acquisition of agricultural and mining sites worldwide. Economy notes that China secures political concessions to import its own workers.[40] On occasions when they do hire, they pay local workers considerably less than rates paid by multinationals and ignore workers rights – including safe working conditions.[41] In one case involving a Chinese acquisition of the Marcona mines in Peru, Economy reported that the mine became highly profitable after importing several hundred Chinese workers; and in the overall process, amassed complaints about its safety and environmental practices.[42] Among mine workers in Zambia, the workers will gravitate to mines owned by Canadian and Australian companies, but avoid mines owned by Indian or Chinese firms, because of safety and low wage conditions.[43] Finally, Economy cites case examples involving oil and gas and extractive industries in Zambia, Ghana and Mozambique where 'environmental protection has taken a back seat to rapid economic development', because Chinese investors have used bribery and offers of investment or employment to ignore proper standards.

It is unlikely that Economy's tale of what has happened in parts of South America and Africa would play out exactly the same way in the Arctic, because the latter is more prosperous. Yet it would be foolhardy to think that Chinese oil & gas, and mining investors will not actively seek (and obtain) environmental and safety concessions from landowners and licensing officials in Russia or Greenland.

If this happens to some degree, it could create political friction among the Arctic powers. It is for just this precise reason that analysts argue that the Arctic Council needs to assume a more prominent role in promoting harmonized environmental standards (especially as regards operation of oil rigs[44]); or perhaps, standards for foreign direct investment in natural resource projects.

Outside Shipping

While access will increase as the ice regresses, the maritime region remains a challenging place to either live, work, or transit. The past year (2013) witnessed the least amount of ice coverage in recorded history, but the stormiest one on record. Only a small percentage of the Arctic has been surveyed to enable safe navigation. Navigation and communications system commonplace in other regions of the world are absent or spotty in the High North. The physical infrastructure to support resource extraction, commerce, environmental response, and inevitable search and rescue operations is scarce. The US Coast Guard and Navy, stretched thin by other global obligations and significant budget constraints, must now add the 'high north' to their areas of operations. So too must the US National Oceanographic and Atmospheric Administration (NOAA). It is chronically underfunded, but has announced that it has over 50 years of work ahead of it to survey the newly accessible US EEZ, both North and South of the Bering Strait.

Legal schemes for maritime transit routes and standards for polar shipping are evolving, but the fundamental basis for addressing resource claims and disagreements will be the 1982 UNCLOS, a treaty to which the US regrettably is not party. Since UNCLOS predetermines most rights for maritime actors, there has been no compelling need for additional regional rule-making. However, UNCLOS was negotiated well before the physical changes in the Arctic began to manifest; and serious questions have been raised whether the 'usual UNCLOS rules', which rely on flag state regulation of shipping are sufficient.[45] UNCLOS provides Coastal States a right under Article 234 to enact non-discriminatory pollution control measures in areas which are ice-bound most of the year. As of yet, there is no universal agreement on what Article 234 means and how far States can go to regulate ships that are transiting through their maritime regions. In this regard, it is important to keep in mind that Coastal States generally have no authority to interfere with transiting vessels, and also no authority to specify how ships will be constructed, crewed, or trained.

The most substantive effort to establish legislation affecting the Arctic has been ongoing at the International Maritime Organization (IMO). Various international treaties establish standards for ships in terms of safety, pollution prevention, and security. Most of these general standards are established in the 1960 SOLAS Convention, the 1973 MARPOL Convention, and the Standards for Training, Certification and Watch-keeping for Seafarers (SCTW), which was adopted in 1978. SOLAS and SCTW in particular, have various provisions which deal with shipboard operations in polar waters; but as of now, there is no overarching instrument which is legally binding in the Arctic.

IMO is currently attempting to create a mandatory code of safety rules for ships navigating in both polar regions. The 'Polar Code' is using existing conventions that encompass safety (SOLAS) and environmental protections (MARPOL) to address a variety of Arctic specific issues in the realm of ship design, safety equipment, training, operational procedures, and communications. This important move to develop a mandatory code follows the adoption, by the IMO Assembly in 2009, of the non-mandatory 'Guidelines for Ships Operating in Polar Waters' (Resolution A. 1024 (26)). The Polar Code remains a work in progress because of disagreements among some key participants, and the slow pace of regulatory development at the IMO. Also, the Polar Code does not address issues related to pollution control equipment, mandatory insurance, and liability limits for ships operating in the Arctic; given the anticipated high costs associated with any type of rescue or cleanup action.

Over time, the Arctic Council – even though not having any legal authority to enact regulations, enter into contracts, or take any actions – has assumed greater prominence in Arctic affairs. The Council has been responsible for brokering two international instruments: a 2011 Agreement on Cooperation in Aeronautical and Maritime Search and Rescue in the Arctic (SAR Agreement), and a 2013 Agreement on Marine Oil Pollution Preparedness and Response in the Arctic. These agreements help identify regional goals and points of contact for cooperation, but they do not commit any of the states to regulatory activities or any funding. Whether the Arctic Council needs to be invigorated to deal with the trans-boundary implications of oil & gas exploration and international shipping, is something that is currently being debated.

Policy analysts will likely be dismissive of the preceding discussion of technical standards for shipping and pollution risks as anything close to a security concern. However, those opinions are ill considered, because if in present times there were an incident of the proportion of *Exxon Valdez* or *Deepwater Horizon,* it would have global implications, and almost certainly invite broad-based international controls for international management of the Arctic. Depending on who was at fault, and whether there was a financially responsible actor involved, it could fracture the political consensus which largely exists among the five major Arctic players, and lead to possible arrests, seizures, and perhaps, violence.

Final Thoughts

In Washington and other capitals, the Arctic continues to generate a lot of heat in policy discussions, but there have been no formal diplomatic or other actions initiated yet, to deal with the range of risk, liability, financing, and infrastructure issues being discussed. This is probably understandable given that the cost of developing proper legal and physical infrastructure to support increased human activity is staggering. However, even though policy developments may be slow in coming, economic activity in the oil & gas and mining sectors continues to increase in the US, Canada, Greenland, and especially, Russia.

Reasonable minds can differ as to the timing for future development in the Arctic, but it would be extremely deleterious if individual states 'broke out' and implemented unilateral standards for development, as opposed to complementary ones – since all of the states have shared interest in protecting the marine environment in the Arctic. As the US assumes leadership of the Arctic Council, it is sure to help formalize and preserve this consensus. Building this political consensus will take time and one can only hope that it does not fall victim to the desires of some coastal community or outside investors, to lower the bar, in order to make a quick buck.

NOTES

1. Peiser B., 'Antarctic Sea Ice Sets New Records', *Canadian Free Press*, February 3, 2014, http:// canadafreepress.com/ index.php/article/60904
2. 12 UST 794, TIAS 4780, December 1, 1959, entered into force in 1961. Prior to the conclusion of the 1961 Treaty, seven nations – Argentina, Australia, Chile, France, New Zealand, Norway, and the United Kingdom – claimed sovereignty over areas of Antarctica on the basis of discovery, exploration, or geographic propinquity. The 1961 Accord did not expressly renounce those claims. However, the agreement did declare (Article IV) that 'No acts or activities taking place while the present treaty is in force shall constitute a basis for asserting, supporting or denying a claim to territorial sovereignty in Antarctica or create any rights of sovereignty in Antarctica. No new claim or enlargement of an existing claim to territorial sovereignty in Antarctica shall be asserted while the present treaty is in force.'
3. Fishing is regulated by a Treaty based Commission for the Conservation of Antarctic Marine Living Resources (CCMLR) which is based in Tasmania.
4. Unlicensed fishing of tooth-fish and other species continues to be a problem in Antarctic waters. Since there is no sovereign government in charge of these waters, enforcement actions have been lacking.
5. The Environmental Protocol can be found at http://www.ats.aq/e/ep.htm. The Protocol entered into force in 1998. A 1988 Convention on the Regulation of Antarctic Mineral Resources (CRAMRA) envisioned a scheme under which mining could be conducted under the auspices

of the International Seabed Authority. That 1988 Convention failed to secure sufficient ratifications and was effectively overtaken by the 1991 Environmental Protocol which states in Article 7 that 'any activity with respect to mineral resources, other than scientific research, shall be prohibited….'

6. Elizabeth Economy and Michael Levi, *By All Means Necessary: How China's Resource Question is Changing the World Economy* (Oxford University Press, 2014).
7. Caijing Magazine, 'China's Foreign Oil Dependence to Rise to 60 Percent This Year: Former Energy Chief', September 22, 2013, http://english.caijing.com.cn/2013-09-22/113326662.html; Huang Ye, 'Dependence on foreign oil increases 9 times over 10 years', *International Finance News* (Guoji Jinrong Bao), February 5, 2013, http://paper.people.com.cn/gjjrb/html/2013-02/05/content_1196107.htm?div=-1; 'China's foreign oil dependence to rise, but 2015 limit set at 61% of needs', *Platts.com*, January 24, 2013, http://www.platts.com/latest-news/oil/singapore/chinas-foreign-oil-dependence-to-rise-but-2015-8086747.
8. Elizabeth Economy and Michael Levi, *By All Means Necessary* ibid, p. 163.
9. D. Gautier et al., 'Assessment of Undiscovered Oil and Gas in the Arctic', *Science No. 5931*, (2009), pp.1175-79.
10. US Coast Guard, *Arctic Policy* (2013), pp. 11-12.
11. US Coast Guard, *Arctic Policy* ibid, p.13.
12. There is a large debate whether the Arctic will become a transit route from Asia to Europe in the foreseeable future. The jury is out on that question although Russia is betting that this type of 'transit' shipping will take place and is making investments in its Northern Sea Route (NSR). If this type of transit shipping is to occur, it will magnify the issues discussed in this paper since coastal state control is lowest over ships that are simply in transit.
13. This of course refers to the September 2013 attempts by Greenpeace to board Gazprom's Prirazlomnaya platform in the Russian Arctic waters. Russian authorities arrested the Greenpeace vessel and this led to an action by Greenpeace and the Dutch government in the International Tribunal for the Law of the Sea (ITLOS) to secure the vessel's prompt release. ITLOS decided the case in Greenpeace's favor and ordered the vessel's release. Russia has declared that it will ignore the court order.
14. Under UNCLOS, coastal states have no right to regulate the passage of ships either on the high seas (to include Exclusive Economic Zones) or through territorial seas provided the vessels comply with the regime of innocent passage i.e., continuous and expeditious passage.
15. There is an evolving Polar Code, which is being developed at the IMO. However, that Code is not likely to be finalized for a number of years. Also, even when the Code is adopted by the IMO, Flag States will have to adopt it and begin enforcing it with their vessels. The Arctic littoral countries could short-circuit this process by requiring that ships calling on any of their ports comply with the Code. However, such a specialized 'port state control' agreement does not currently exist. Whether that will occur is questionable given the differences between Canada and Russia during the Polar Code negotiations over permissible discharge levels and the 'grandfathering' of less technically capable Russian coastal vessels.
16. The Russian government considers improvements to infrastructure and it regulatory authority over the NSR as a lynchpin in its plan to develop the natural resource deposits in its part of the Arctic and establish Russia (and the NSR) as the commercial gateway to the Arctic.
17. Blank S., *Russia in the Arctic* Strategic Studies Monograph (July 2011).
18. In October 2012, Russia conducted a major command post exercise that included a significant Arctic component. As part of this exercise, coastal defense forces engaged in a sea-borne landing on Kotelny Island in the Novosibirsk Archipelago in order to conduct reconnaissance and to field test military equipment in Arctic conditions. This was Russian military exercise focused on civilian facilities in the Arctic. The Russian Navy is also participating in exploration work

along the Arctic continental shelf. The deep water submarine *Losharik*, was involved in the Arktika-2012 exploration mission that collected samples for use in Russian efforts to prove that the Lomonosov and Mendeleyev Ridges are part of the Russian continental shelf. Source: Gorenburg, D.P. *Arctic International Actors*, CNA Corporation (2014 Unpublished – Copy on File with Author).

19. O'Rourke et. al., 'Changes in the Arctic: Background and Issues for Congress', Congressional Research Service (2013).
20. O'Rourke et. al., 'Changes in the Arctic' ibid, p. 55.
21. Inside Defense, '*DOD* Arctic Strategy Assures Region's Place as Military Focus Area', posted on *InsideDefense.com*, November 22, 2013.
22. Barnes and Entous, 'Hagel Outlines Pentagon's Arctic Strategy in an Era of Climate Change', *Wall Street Journal* Online, November 22, 2013, http://online.wsj.com/news/articles/SB10001424052702304607104579214332434305064
23. See www.defense.gov/pubs/2013_Arctic_Strategy.pdf
24. The US Coast Guard has a significant budgetary footprint in the Arctic to implement its traditional fisheries enforcement, search and rescue, safety of navigation (and maintenance of navigation aids) and oil spill response. The Coast Guard's 17th District consists of roughly 2500 personnel who are posted both at bases, air stations and as well as boat stations and hangers where boats and aviation units are housed. The 17th District also includes medium and high endurance cutters, buoy tenders, 12 helicopters and four C-130 aircraft. The DOD has a number of major bases in Alaska and funds a variety of research activities. Most of the Arctic research funding has historically been done by various Navy components and the Army Corps of Engineers (headquartered on Fort Wainwright). The Corps has the responsibility for various military construction projects as well as sizable number of civil public works projects to build and maintain harbors along Alaska's coast, restore former DOD lands, provide floor and erosion control, and construct facilities on tribal lands.
25. The area of the Lomonosov Ridge is a contestable feature in the continental shelf of three countries, namely, Russia, Canada and Denmark (Greenland).
26. Russia made its submission to the UN Commission for the Limits of the Continental Shelf in 2001.
27. Wright, David Curtis, 'The Dragon Eyes the Top of the World', *Naval War College, China Maritime Studies Institute*, No. 8, (August 2011).
28. Rainwater, Shiloh, 'Race to the North: China's Arctic Strategy and Its Implications', *Naval War College Review,* No. 62 (Spring 2013), p. 66.
29. Rosen M, and Asufu Heim P, 'Gaps in Arctic Governance', Stanford University (Hoover Institute) November 2013, http://www.hoover.org/publications/monographs/168846.
30. Rosen M, Arctic Council Adds Six Members Including China, http://www.nytimes.com/2013/05/16/world/ europe/arctic-council-adds-six-members-including-china.html?_r=0.
31. In 2008, the five states bordering the Arctic Ocean, affirmed in the Ilulissat Declaration that sovereign rights in the Arctic are predetermined by UNCLOS and that the affected states remain 'committed to th[at] legal framework....' In other words, since UNCLOS predetermined most rights, there was no compelling need for additional regional rule-making. The Declaration also stated that the five Arctic littoral states would work together 'through the IMO to strengthen additional measures and develop new measures to improve safety of maritime navigation and prevent or reduce the risk of ship based pollution...' Over time, the Arctic Council assumed greater prominence in Arctic Affairs as well as expanded its membership to eight states plus six observer nations, including China, Japan and India. Formed in 1996, the Council calls itself an 'intergovernmental forum' for high-level dialogue. It does not have any legal authority to enact regulations, enter into contracts, or take any actions on behalf of the eight members.

32. Degategno P., 'Arctic International Actors', *CNA Corporation* (2014 Unpublished – Copy on File with Author).
33. 'China Arctic Mineral Investment', http://www.theguardian.com/world/2013/mar/18/china-arctic-mineral-investment.
34. Guschin Arthur, 'Understanding China's Arctic Policies', *The Diplomat*, November 14, 2013, p. 2, http://thediplomat.com/ 2013/11/understanding-chinas-arctic-policies/1/
35. Katakey R. and Kennedy W., 'Russia Lets China into Arctic Rush as Energy Giants Embrace', *Bloomberg Sustainability Newsletter*, March 25, 2013, http://www.bloomberg.com/news/2013-03-25/russia-cuts-china-into-arctic-oil-rush-as-energy-giants-embrace.html.
36. China – North Canada's Resources and China's Arctic Long-Game, I Politics (Canada), December 31, 2012, http://www.ipolitics.ca/2012/12/31/china-north-canadas-resources-and-chinas-arctic-long-game/.
37. 'Chinas New Arctic Presence Signals Future Development', http://e360.yale.edu/feature/chinas_new_arctic_ presence_ signals _future_development/2658/
38. Einarsson Sveinn, 'China Foreign Direct Investment in the West: Is there a Security Threat?', *Kennitala* 2013, http://skemman.is/stream/get/1946/14799/35223/1/China$00b4s_FDI_in_the_West.pdf
39. I Politics, supra, http://skemman.is/stream/get/1946/14799/35223/1/China$00b4s_FDI_in_the_West.pdf
40. Economy quotes one Chinese MFA official who explains that the motivating factor for China importing Chinese labor into Africa is that such labor will 'work seven days per week on longer shifts at lower pay. The official also justified this trend because African workers 'have unions' 'they want to go to church' 'they refuse to work on weekends' and 'they like to sing and dance.' Economy, *supra* note 6 at 93.
41. Elizabeth Economy and Michael Levi, *By All Means Necessary* ibid, p. 89.
42. Elizabeth Economy and Michael Levi, *By All Means Necessary* ibid, p. 91.
43. Elizabeth Economy and Michael Levi, *By All Means Necessary* ibid, p. 92.
44. Rosen M., 'Arctic Council Adds Six Members Including China' ibid.
45. Rosen M., 'Arctic Council Adds Six Members Including China' ibid.

10

Dynamics of Diplomatic and Security Developments in South China Sea

Chintamani Mahapatra

If at all there is going to be a major conflict in the future involving major powers in Asia, it will be in the South China Sea. Recent security developments in this region indicate a trend that may culminate in armed conflict over maritime disputes that would directly involve China, and indirectly rope in the US and Japan into it. India may stay off, but cannot remain unaffected. Recent developments in the South China Sea signify that relative peace in the Asia Pacific has given way to complex dynamics of conflict; and the lowest common factor in it happens to be the Chinese muscle flexing, its mounting assertiveness, and unreasonable claims of sovereignty over vast swathes of the South China Sea.

Intricate Scenario

The security dynamics of this region are rather intricate in view of a number of problematic facts. First of all, half a dozen littoral countries in the South China Sea, namely China, Vietnam, the Philippines, Malaysia, Taiwan, and Brunei have incompatible claims of sovereignty over islands, reefs, rocks, and other geographical features. Secondly, there is immense asymmetry in the size, wealth, governing structures, and naval/military capabilities among these claimants. Thirdly, four out of these six countries, namely the Philippines, Vietnam, Brunei, and Malaysia are part of the vibrant Association of Southeast Asian Nations, where as the other two are entangled in another tortuous conflict, with China considering Taiwan to be part of its mainland, and Taiwan, in principle, considering the Chinese mainland to be part of it. Fifthly, one country, the Philippines, is a strategic ally, and Vietnam has been a fast emerging strategic partner of the US. Last, but not the least, the South China Sea has witnessed, in recent years, use of force, occupation of island groups, clashes between security forces and fishermen from rival countries, and harassment of oil and gas companies of one country by security forces of the other.

Further, the conflicts of this kind have not abated, despite China's growing trade and investment cooperation with other disputants; rather have dragged the US and China into periodic wars of words. Seriousness of the security environment in the South China Sea, in addition, is marked by the importance of Sea Lanes of Communication that are used by myriad countries, including India and Japan, whose trade passes through this sea. There are other countries whose energy companies have developed stakes in exploration of the sea-bed resources. Significantly, about five trillion dollars worth of trade passes through this sea every year.[1] According to the US Energy Information Administration (EIA), the South China Sea bears about 11 trillion cubic meters of gas, and several billion barrels of oil reserves.

The sheer number of stakeholders involved in the peace and development of the South China Sea makes it imperative on their parts to ensure conflict prevention at best, and conflict management in the very least. However, the same fact also signals the dangerous level that any armed conflict can escalate to, unless timely action is taken to de-escalate any tension in this region.

Root Cause of the Problem

Once the Cold War tensions disappeared in early 1990s, the Asia-Pacific region turned into a quintessential model of regional stability and economic growth. The post Cold War peace dividend was witnessed more in this region than even in Europe. China's persistently positive economic growth, expansion of ASEAN to include countries of Indo-China peninsula and subsequently Myanmar, China's projection of a theory of 'peaceful growth' and Vietnam's economic liberalization, the creation of ASEAN Regional Forum, the successful regional multilateralism and formation of an East Asia Summit, were all welcomed by the rest of the world. Strategic analysts began to claim that the centre of gravity of the global economic activities and dynamism had shifted to the East from the West.

The traditional animosity and historical grievances in the region involving China, Japan, and South Korea, had not surfaced as yet to create regional tension. North Korea's nuclear ambition united almost every regional country to address the issue. Also during all these years, regional conflicts in Europe and the Middle

East kept the US engaged. Bosnia-Herzegovina, Kosovo, 9/11 terrorist attacks on the US, and subsequently, the war on terror, the political upheaval in the Arab world, the economic crisis in the European Union (EU), and Iran's nuclear ambition, were the headlines news of those days.

The peaceful environment in the Asia-Pacific region was however, jolted when China, after achieving unprecedented economic growth, and undergoing robust military modernization, slowly began to assert its newly acquired power and influence in the region. One of the theatres that had faced a critical challenge to its stability since then, has been the South China Sea. As mentioned earlier, China, as the emerging superpower began to claim about 90 per cent of the South China Sea waters as its own.[2] Other claimants to sovereignty over islands, reefs, and shoals in this sea are relatively smaller countries with weaker navies. In the face of China's flexing of its naval capabilities, and making new rules and occupying islands or conducting aggressive patrolling, the Philippines and Vietnam have been trying to resist, and other countries have either verbally protested, or remained quiet.

As China drew nine-dash lines in a cow-tongue shaped area, in a communication to the United Nations in 2009, and claimed complete sovereignty over this water body, it sent shock waves around, and even the US did not remain immune to it.[3] It would certainly affect the uninterrupted trade and commerce of its allies, but could also challenge the movement of the American naval ships and military aircraft in the South China Sea. Operation of the US naval and air forces in this self-declared Chinese Exclusive Economic Zone (EEZ) could lead to tense encounters, any one of which could become a confrontation. In fact, such encounters have already taken place.[4] Bonnie S Glazer, a US analyst, has warned that 'China routinely intercepts US reconnaissance flights conducted in its EEZ, and periodically does so in aggressive ways that increases the risk of an accident, similar to the April 2001 collision of a US EP-3 reconnaissance plane and a Chinese F-8 fighter jet near Hainan Island.' China has also been accused of occasionally harassing US naval surveillance ships. The incident related to USNS *Impeccable* and USNS *Victorious* in June 2009 provides a good example.

Beijing does not make all the strategic moves in one go, instead it makes one claim after the other; and expects one issue to cool down before it makes the next move. Just to give a few examples instead of a detailed chronology: China's nine-dash line claim and declaration of the South China Sea as its core interest were made in 2010. In 2012, Chinese naval vessels occupied the Scarborough shoal claimed by the Philippines. When the Filipino fishermen went near the shoal to fish, the Chinese ships used water cannons to drive them away. China soon began to deploy Coast Guard and surveillance ships around some islands, and began to threaten those who entered adjacent waters. In 2012 itself, Beijing once again established a government headquarter and military garrison on Woody Island in the Paracel group, which China seized from Vietnam in 1974.

More recently, in January 2014, the Chinese government issued a decree requiring fishermen in the South China Sea, even beyond China's exclusive economic zone, to obtain fishing permits from China.[5] Those who did not oblige were to be accordingly punished. The Philippines lodged a formal protest with Beijing, after a Chinese law enforcement vessel reportedly sprayed the two Filipino fishing boats with water cannons, in a disputed area of the sea. However, the protest apparently fell on deaf ears. Yet another aggressive move by China, on January 20, 2014, was marked by a naval exercise of capturing a shoal, followed by the conduct of an oath taking ceremony with a vow to protect Chinese maritime rights and sovereignty. Three Chinese ships – *Changbaishan* Amphibious Landing Craft and *Wuhan* and *Haikou* destroyers – first conducted drills off the Paracel Islands, including amphibious landings 'on every reef guarded by China's Navy', and then sailed south to the Spratly Islands after a few days.[6] When the ships reached James Shoal, 80 kilometres off Malaysia's Sarawak province, the sailors vowed to protect Chinese interests.

No other claimants of sovereignty in the South China Sea have been as aggressive as China. Those who appear to be, by way of statements of protest and harsh words, do so out of desperation. So asymmetrical is the power differential among the littorals of the South China Sea that even the combined strength of other countries would be of no match to China's military right. Also, not many of them appear to be completely reliant on external allies to come to their rescue during confrontations, especially which are categorized below serious armed conflicts.

Nervous Neighbourhood

Consequently, developments in the South China Sea have created a nervous neighbourhood. Out of extreme anxiety over the Chinese use of force to enforce its proclaimed rights, President Benigno S. Aquino III of the Philippines once compared China's claim in the South China Sea with Nazi Germany's demands for Czech territory in 1938.[7] China, no doubt, expressed its displeasure at such a comparison. A Chinese spokesman remarked, 'It is inconceivable and unreasonable to place China-Philippines South China Sea disputes in the same category with the WWII history.'[8]

The Philippines has often tried to confront China's aggression, as exemplified by the Sino-Philippines stand-off in the Mischief Reef. In January 2014, Manila increased its public boldness, and Emmanuel Bautista, the Philippines Armed Forces' Chief of Staff, stated in a television interview, that Filipino fishermen should not obey the new fishing regulations issued by Hainan province under threat or intimidation. Subsequently, Filipino Secretary of Defence, Voltaire Gazmin, stated that the Philippines would provide escorts to Filipino fishermen in the West Philippines Sea 'if necessary'. It was indeed a brave proclamation, but when the Chinese patrols used water cannon against Filipino fishermen, there was little Manila could do.[9]

On February 4, 2014, President Benigno Aquino of the Philippines, in an interview with *The New York Times*, appealed to the international community to lend its support to resist China's claims in the South China Sea. The Philippines also moved the international tribunal to legally fight for its claims in South China Sea under the UN Law of the Sea Convention. However, China refused to be part of the arbitration, and reiterated its policy of bilateralism.

The international community cannot come to the rescue of the Philippines, if ASEAN members continue to be divided over the merits of the South China Sea disputes. When the ASEAN Foreign Ministers met in Bagan, Myanmar, to discuss this matter along with other issues, Philippines Secretary of Foreign Affairs, Albert del Rosario, called on ASEAN to 'maintain regional solidarity' in response to China's highhandedness. However, ASEAN did what was expected of it. The ASEAN Ministers 'expressed their concerns on the recent developments in the South China Sea. They further reaffirmed ASEAN's Six-Point Principles on the South China Sea, and the importance of maintaining peace and stability, maritime security, freedom of navigation in- and over-flight above the South China Sea.'[10] The ministers also reiterated ASEAN's customary position that all disputes should be resolved by peaceful means in accordance with international law and that all parties should show 'self-restraint in the conduct of activities'.

The ASEAN has often tried to calm tempers in the South China Sea. At one time, it sought to develop a 'code of conduct' that none adhered to. A call for a multilateral solution to the disputes has not materialized, as China is vehemently opposed to any solution, other than through bilateral negotiations. When Indonesia proposed an unofficial draft 'code of conduct', suggesting avoidance of routine military exercises in disputed waters, and settling disputes according to the UN Law of the Sea, or little-used ASEAN procedures, China promptly disagreed. Beijing would just not accept any push that would prevent it from conducting naval exercises in its area of 'core interest'!

Vietnam is another strong opposer to China's outlandish claims of sovereignty over the South China Sea Islands. China's major strategic move in this direction, in fact, began with the capture of Paracel Islands from Vietnam in the 1970s. There was none to question China at that time, since Washington had signed the Paris Agreements to end its war in the Indo-China region. Before that, the Nixon Administration had successfully established détente with China. The Soviet Union was in no position to fill the vacuum left by the departing Americans in Indo-China. At this critical juncture, Beijing moved in to capture the strategic islands that were under the control of the Vietnamese.

While Sino-Vietnam relations have improved considerably in the post-Cold War era, and China's trade and investment relationships with its immediate neighbours have become robust, Vietnam finds it harder to deal with a China that is an economic partner, yet a perceived island grabber. There have been several 'minor' confrontations between China and Vietnam, particularly with Chinese vessels cutting off cables of Vietnamese oil exploration ships, occupying islands, setting up government offices, and more recently, ramming Vietnamese ships.

While the Philippines and Vietnam have been unable to resist the Chinese advances, interestingly, these two parties to the dispute do not support each other, either. Vietnam, for instance, does not support Manila's recourse to legal means to resolve the issue. Malaysia seems to be ignoring the Chinese advances for reasons best known to its government. When the Chinese naval ships visited James Shoal, and vowed to protect Chinese interests, Malaysia pleaded ignorance, and did not even recognize that such an event took place.

Cold Confrontation

While the South China Sea neighbours of China appear nervous, and have trying hard to protect their interests in the face of Chinese assertiveness, all eyes have been fixed at Washington. China expects the US to keep out of the maritime disputes in its sphere of influence, whereas the American allies and partners look up to the US leadership to stand up to China's belligerent behaviour. The US has had a very delicate balance to make. Not standing by the allies and potential partners at this hour of challenge from America's principle competitor will be hazardous for the long term US presence in the region. Confronting China directly with military show of force, or open backing to the allies would mean the US seriously putting its economic interests in China into high risk.

Consequently, the South China Sea has become a potential battle-ground of what may be termed as an emerging 'Cold Conflict' between the US and China –

the reigning superpower and an aspiring one. China's ability to defy the US and assert its position in the wake of its economic rise and military modernization has, to a certain extent, circumscribed the US influence in the region. China's policy of asserting its power and influence through systematic steps to protect its 'rights and sovereignty' in the South China Sea has put the US in a dilemma – to turn a blind eye to China's claims, or back the allies. It has, however, sought to navigate whether in these tough political waters. While not taking sides with the 'sovereignty issue' in the South China Sea, the US has opposed China's unilateral moves and use of force against other disputants.

In very many ways, the US has sought to express its displeasure, or quietly warn China, or even indirectly extend support to its allies in this region. In February 2014, as the Sino-Filipino spat over ownership of reefs appeared serious, Admiral Jonathan Greenert, Chief of Naval Operations of the US Navy, remarked that the US would fulfill its obligations under the Mutual Defence Treaty to help the Philippines, if it is under attack.[11] It is a rare show of US support to the Philippines by the Pentagon, although the State Department and the White House maintained silence over this issue. The message nonetheless, went across and Hua Chunying of the Chinese foreign ministry responded by saying that 'the US, who is not a party concerned in the South China Sea dispute, should honour its commitment of not taking sides on the territorial sovereignty issue, be discreet in word and deed, and do more for peace and stability of the Asia-Pacific, rather than the opposite.'[12]

Of course, when the Philippines resorted to legal recourse and went to the international tribunal to resolve the maritime disputes with China, the US Secretary of State John Kerry lent support to the Philippines by saying; 'With respect to the South China Sea, its important to resolve these differences in a peaceful, non-confrontational way, that honours the law of the sea and honours the rule of law itself.'[13] Again, China responded promptly by rejecting the idea of resolving the issue in the international tribunal, despite being a signatory to the UN Convention on Laws of the Sea, and reiterated its bilateral approach to dispute resolution.

After distancing itself from the South China Sea disputes for some years, China decided recently to break its silence, in the face of what Assistant US Secretary for East Asian Affairs, Danny Russel, calls China's 'incremental pattern of assertiveness'.[14] Russel pointed out that 'no one can justifiably, in compliance with international law, simply assert the right to exercise control over great swaths of a sea.'[15] China's response was swift yet again and the Foreign Ministry in Beijing argued that the US, being a non-party to the disputes, 'should keep its commitment of not taking sides on issues of territorial sovereignty, and be cautious in words and actions.'[16]

The Sino-US differences became especially marked when China announced its control over nine-dash line, apparently threatening the hitherto unhindered movement of the US Navy in the Asia-Pacific. A quest for anti-access and area-denial capability by the Chinese Navy doubled the American apprehensions about Beijing's motivations. The US then openly opposed the Chinese claim of sovereignty over the area enclosed by the so-called 'nine-dashed lines'.

Chinese academics contend that shipping of other nations would not be affected by China's 'nine-dash line' declaration, and quote their government's position that 'there is freedom of navigation within the nine-dash line."[17] However, such polite explanations raise doubts all around when China springs surprises by its actions or declarations. One such surprise announcement was Beijing's declaration of an 'Air Defence Identification Zone (ADIZ)' in East China Sea. This zone had little to do with the South China Sea. However, soon speculations were rife that the next zone could very well be over the South China Sea.

The Obama administration took swift action; it flew two B-52 bombers over the zone, and encouraged Japan and others to do so as well. It was a symbolic protest since flying of military aircraft was not against international law. The Chinese and the others, however, knew the signal Washington sought to send across. Subsequently, Assistant Secretary Russel told the American legislators that 'we neither recognize nor accept China's declared ADIZ', and added that the US had "made clear to China that it should not attempt to implement that ADIZ, and should refrain from taking similar actions elsewhere in the region.'[18] China understood the US signal, appreciated the eventual advice by the US government to American commercial airlines to respect the Chinese ADIZ, but reiterated its position that 'as a sovereign state, China has the right to act in order to defend its air security.'

Concluding Observations

The South China Sea disputes, and an upward trend in tensions in the region need to be seen in a larger perspective of systemic transformations taking place in the Indo-Pacific region. Rise of the Chinese power, emergence of India as a major player, the US strategy of rebalancing towards the region, Japan's efforts towards becoming a 'normal' country, and several other related developments have had a cause and effect impact upon China's assertive behaviour and aggressive posture in the South China Sea. It is not just coincidence that China has demonstrated its belligerence on disputes with mainly those countries that are either strategic allies of the USA, or its new strategic partners. China's pushy policies in the South China Sea have also been directly influenced by the Obama administration's 'pivot to Asia' or 'rebalancing strategy'. Beijing sees this as a renewed American effort to stem the further rise of China, or as a veiled containment strategy.

In response, China has sought to convey the costs of any such policy by the US to contain its rise. Unlike the old '*Cold Warriors*' – the US and the USSR – China and the US as potential '*Cold Warriors*' are economically interdependent. Therefore, Cold War-type action-reaction is unlikely due to its lose-lose consequences for both the parties. Moreover, the Sino-US cooperation in handling difficult concerns of WMD proliferation, climate change, and many other issues, is an imperative that will prevent a Cold War between these two countries. Yet another complicating factor lies in China's close economic ties with countries that have maritime disputes in the South China Sea. Some of them do more trade with China than with the US. However, such economic considerations have thus far, not prevented tension in the region. In fact, all these economic considerations have served to limit tensions and the result is a 'Sino-US cold confrontation'.

While a cold confrontation is much below the threshold of armed conflict, the danger of escalation remains, either due to misperception or accidents. The US Cowpens incident involving the American and the Chinese navies is a case in point that highlights the danger of 'cold confrontation'. It is difficult to predict the future, but the American determination to implement the Asia 'rebalancing' strategy and China's efforts to maintain and enhance its new hegemony in Asia-Pacific, is likely to make cold confrontation inevitable.

Many countries in the region, including India, will find it difficult to navigate with ease in the troubled political atmosphere of the Sino-US 'cold confrontation'. China's spat with Japan in the East China Sea, Chinese naval inroads into the Indian Ocean, and the new US strategic initiative in the Indo-Pacific region will be influenced by developments in the South China Sea and *vice versa*. These developments raise serious questions for India *vis-a-vis* India-China relations. Some that readily come to mind include:

- Will China allow uninterrupted Indian energy activities in the South China Sea in exchange for Indian support to its proposal for a maritime silk road?
- China opposes any oil and gas exploration in the disputed sites of South China Sea. Will this stand lead to tensions in Sino-Indian relations?
- China has invested a lot of its capital in port developments in the Indian Ocean region, close to India. Will China raise objections to future Indian port development activities in Indo-China?

- What kind of role will India play in the cold confrontation between China and the US?
- How will India respond to the US plan to make India a 'lynchpin' of the Indo-Pacific strategy? Will it negatively impact Sino-Indian relations?
- Should India allow China to exercise a veto to its policy towards the US?
- If India refuses to play the role of a 'lynchpin' in the American strategy, will it, in any way, lead to improved ties with China?
- How will China perceive the rising strategic cooperation between Japan and India?
- Japan is concerned about China's behaviour in the East China Sea and India is apprehensive over Chinese ambitions in the Indian Ocean. Also, both Japan and India use trade routes passing through the South China Sea. Will it lead to enhanced Indo-Japan naval cooperation?
- What will be its impact on the Indo-Pacific dynamics?

All these questions should keep the policy makers, strategists, and the scholarly community engaged in years to come.

NOTES

1. http://www.reuters.com/article/2014/02/24/us-asean-china-code-idUSBREA1N1RR20140224
2. Reuters.com ibid.
3. US Congressional Research Service, Maritime Territorial and Exclusive Economic Zone (EEZ) Disputes Involving China: Issues for Congress, August 5, 2014, http://fas.org/sgp/crs/row/R42784.pdf. p. 15.
4. Congressional Research Service, Maritime Territorial and Exclusive Economic Zone (EEZ) Disputes Involving China ibid, p. 4.
5. James R. Holmes, 'The Return of China's Small-Stick Diplomacy in South China Sea,' *The Diplomat*, January 9, 2014, http://seasissues.org/category/analysis/
6. For detailed account of Chinese assertive and aggressive moves in South China Sea, see Carl Thayer, 'Tensions set to Rise in South China Sea', February 19, 2014, http://thediplomat.com/2014/02/tensions-set-to-rise-in-the-south-china-sea/
7. 'Chinese State Media Slam Disgraced Aquino over Nazi Germany Comparison,' *South China Morning Post online*, http://www.scmp.com/news/china/article/1421480/chinese-state-media-slam-disgraced-aquino-over-nazi-germany-comparison?page=all
8. 'The truth must be told: China is the Nazi Germany of the contemporary world order,' *China Daily Mail*, February 9, 2014, http://chinadailymail.com/2014/02/09/the-truth-must-be-told-china-is-the-nazi-germany-of-the-contemporary-world-order/
9. For detailed account of Chinese assertive and aggressive moves in South China Sea, see Carl Thayer, 'Tensions set to Rise in South China Sea', February 19, 2014, http://thediplomat.com/2014/02/tensions-set-to-rise-in-the-south-china-sea/
10. Walter Lohman, 'A China Focused Policy for Southeast Asia', March 13, 2014, http://www.heritage.org/research/testimony/2014/03/a-china-focused-policy-for-southeast-asia
11. http://johnib.wordpress.com/2014/02/15/secretary-of-state-john-kerry-welcome-back-to-asia-the-south-china-sea/

12. Keith Bradsher, 'South China Sea Tensions a Backdrop to Kerry's China Visit', *New York Times*, February 14, 2014, http://sinosphere.blogs.nytimes.com/2014/02/14/south-china-sea-tensions-a-backdrop-to-kerrys-china-visit/
13. http://www.state.gov/secretary/remarks/2014/02/221658.htm
14. This statement was made on February 4, 2014. See http://www.taiwandc.org/twcom/tc145-int.pdf
15. http://www.voanews.com/content/us-pushes-for-greater-transparency-in-south-china-sea-claims/1852273.html
16. www.wantchinatimes.com/news-subclass-cnt.aspx?id...cid=1101
17. Wantchinatimes.com ibid
18. 'US Presses Beijing on South China Sea Claims', February 5, 2014, http://www.spacedaily.com/reports/ US_presses_Beijing_on_South_China_Sea_claims_999.html

11

China's Coast Guard: Implications for Maritime Disputes

Gerald Meyerle

Introduction

In July 2013, China merged five different maritime enforcement agencies – each reporting to a different ministry – under a single organization known as the Chinese Oceanographic Administration (COA). Analysts have dubbed the new entity the Chinese Coast Guard (CCG). These reforms have met with mixed responses in Asia, and among analysts in the US.

Many initially welcomed the move as a reasonable attempt to increase the coordination among agencies with overlapping responsibilities and areas of operation, while reducing friction and the risk of mishaps. The move appeared to be a natural outgrowth of China's overall economic and political development. For some analysts, it represented a welcome reprieve from reports of the growing Chinese military capabilities.

There has been growing concern, however, that China intends to leverage the new CCG to more aggressively – and effectively – pursue its claims to parts of the East and South China Seas, leading to growing tensions with countries in the region. Stepped-up patrols in and near disputed waters and growing tensions between China and its neighbours have lent credence to these concerns. This paper outlines the formation of the new CCG and provides a brief description of its constituent parts. It examines the new force's potential benefits to regional stability, as well as concerns that it may play a destabilizing role. The paper then discusses potential implications.

Formation of the Chinese Coast Guard

Analysts in China have been talking since at least the early 2000s about merging various 'white hull' maritime enforcement organizations and streamlining their operations. The main impetus originally was the recurring coordination problems between the different agencies, especially in the South and East China Seas. In July 2013, five key maritime enforcement entities were merged into a new and more robust coast guard. These five agencies include:

- China Maritime Surveillance (CMS), under the State Oceanographic Administration, part of the Ministry of Land and Resources. The CMS's main responsibility is maritime research and enforcement of China's EEZs. It has a relatively expansive fleet of long-range vessels – some of them armed – and some aircraft.
- The Fisheries Law Enforcement Command (FLEC), under the Ministry of Agriculture. The FLEC enforces Chinese regulations on fishing and the preservation of fish stocks, an important concern for China. The FLEC also escorts Chinese fishing boats. Its vessels are largely unarmed.
- The Maritime Safety Administration (MSA), under the Ministry of Transport. The MSA is the largest of the maritime enforcement organizations in terms of personnel, with more than 20,000 in its ranks. It registers and inspects foreign and Chinese vessels, regulates marine traffic, maintains navigation aids, conducts search and rescue and other similar missions.
- Maritime anti-smuggling force, under the General Administration of Customs. Its main responsibility is counter-drug operations. It operates a fleet of relatively small vessels, some of them armed.
- The Coast Guard, under the Ministry of Public Security. It operates a number of long-range armed vessels – some of them decommissioned navy warships. It is mainly a maritime border protection force, and reportedly the best armed of the five agencies.

These five organizations were brought under the control of the State Oceanographic Administration (SOA) which is part of the Ministry of Land and Resources. SOA operates a large headquarters staff to administer the five organizations, and streamline their reporting and operations. The new and expanded CCG will include an estimated 16,300 personnel, and will be split among three operational areas off the north, central, and southern areas of China's coast.[1] The organization is roughly at par with other coast guards in the region, though much smaller than Japan's.

The SOA is, by and large, not a security or paramilitary organization. Prior to 2013, the organization's primary responsibility was enforcement of maritime economic and environment regulations. The COA will now assume the missions of four additional agencies, but will nonetheless remain outside the direct purview of China's defence and security ministries. The Ministry for Public Security will reportedly exert some 'operational direction' over the newly formed CCG, the details of which are not yet clear.[2] The new CCG is still a work in progress. It will take years for differences to be ironed out among these five different agencies that had hitherto operated under different ministries. Though the five agencies have been brought under the SOA, they remain separate entities with different missions, cultures, capabilities, and means of communication, which have yet to be fully integrated and reorganized. It is likely that there will be additional reforms to the CCG structure as time goes on.

China is building a large number of maritime surveillance vessels, many of which will be armed. It is speeding up the construction of 20 new inspection ships and transferring additional decommissioned naval warships to the new CCG. Many of the vessels being built are long-range surveillance craft capable of operating far from the shore, and carrying heavy weapons.[3] The CMS, which is the largest of the five agencies in the new CCG, is expected to more than double its fleet of over 200 vessels by 2020, and expand its modest fleet of aircraft and helicopters.

China's development of its coast guard forces has occurred along with substantial expansion of its naval and air capabilities – including the acquisition of new platforms such as destroyers and frigates capable of patrolling farther ashore, and backing up coast guard vessels under attack. The PLA Navy ships are capable of operating further ashore in the 'far seas' while coast guard vessels take more of the burden in the littorals. The PLA Air Force (PLAAF) has acquired a number of shorter and longer range aircraft, particularly those capable of operating over the sea in support of naval and coast guard vessels.[4]

Potential Benefits of a More Unified Coast Guard

The initial impetus for the unification of the five agencies under a more robust CCG was to increase coordination, and improve capacity to enforce laws and regulations in the maritime realm, particularly those viewed as important for economic development. Chinese official statements and plans suggest that the original intention behind these reforms was simply to improve maritime governance and reduce coordination problems. In China's five-year plan covering the years 2011-2016, there is particular emphasis on maritime economic activities and increasing Chinese capacity to develop and enforce regulations in the littorals.

Beijing apparently chose not to place the five agencies under the old coast guard, which fell under the Ministry for Public Security. This would have been the most obvious choice – especially if China intended to use the new force to project power and press its claims in the East and South China Seas; or simply follow the example of the US Coast Guard, which is considered a military service. Instead, the organizations were brought under the SOA, which – though it operates a relatively extensive fleet of long-range patrol vessels and aircraft – is not a military or paramilitary organization. The message appears to be that China intends to use the new force mainly to police its shores and further its economic development.

Compared to Japan and South Korea, China has relatively little capacity in the area of maritime enforcement. China has invested heavily in its navy, which has become increasingly formidable. The country also has a robust land border force, and an impressive fleet of commercial vessels. Its capacity to protect its maritime boundaries, however, remains relatively undeveloped.[5] As China has built up its navy, increasing the capacity of its coast guard and unifying various agencies appears to be a natural step. It is possible that more effective and professional maritime enforcement may further integrate China with the world economy, and bring its policies more in line with international norms. As China develops its coast guard, it may look to other coast guards, especially that of the US, as a model and seek to regularize its patrols. China conducts occasional exercises with the US Coast Guard, and sends a small number of officers for short courses in US Coast Guard training centers.[6]

Consolidation of the five agencies is likely to reduce the risk of accidents and unwanted escalation. There will be less incentive for different agencies with separate chains of command to compete for resources and attention, and therefore work at cross purposes. Other coast guards and navies will have a single point of contact for dealing with Chinese maritime enforcement vessels. The latter is likely to facilitate communication and timely negotiation of disputes – assuming both sides seek resolution.

International Concerns and Regional Security Implications

There is considerable concern among countries in the region that as the CCG's capacity grows, China is likely to become increasingly assertive with regard to maritime disputes. This may lead to greater tensions between China and its neighbours.[7] Indeed, this has largely been the trend since the CCG was stood up. In less than a year, there has been a notable increase in patrols, and heightened tensions in the East and South China Seas. These developments have led to considerable concern in the region – and increasingly, in the US as well – that China intends to use these forces to press its claims in disputed waters.

As recently as February 2014, the chief of the Philippines Armed Forces claimed that Chinese coast guard vessels used water cannons against Filipino fishermen in the disputed Scarborough Shoal in the South China Sea. The coast guard boats reportedly employed water cannons to force those fishermen out of the area. China responded to the accusation by insisting that it has undisputed sovereignty over those waters, and is using its coast guard vessels to police its claims through regular patrols.[8] In January 2014, three CCG vessels reportedly spent about two hours in Japan's territorial waters near one of the Senkaku/Diaoyu islands. This happened while the Japanese Prime Minister Shinzo Abe was in New Delhi for talks about strengthening defence cooperation with India, including increasing the number of maritime exercises. Abe compared Japan-China relations at present with those between Britain and Germany during the run-up to World War I.[9]

Within weeks of the CCG's formation, four ships were deployed to the East China Sea near the Senkaku/Diaoyu islands.[10] China also deployed an early warning aircraft in the vicinity of the vessels, prompting Japan to scramble jets to shadow the Chinese plane. The incident was viewed as potentially escalatory, especially with the involvement of military aircraft.[11] In September 2013, manned Chinese bombers reportedly flew near Okinawa, but did not cross into the Japanese airspace, prompting considerable concern in the Japanese air command.[12]

These incidents suggest that China intends to use CCG vessels to press Japan over the islands, and perhaps plans to back these vessels with military aircraft.[13] In a separate incident near the islands, Japan scrambled its jets to shadow a Chinese surveillance drone that strayed over Japan's territorial waters. China has invested heavily in UAV capabilities, which are becoming increasingly integrated, and capable of flying at longer ranges and higher altitudes. Like the coast guard vessels, these surveillance drones may be another less escalatory means to probe Japan's defences and red-lines; and press China's claims to the Senkaku/Diaoyu islands.[14]

China's use of maritime patrol vessels to push territorial claims predates the formation of the CCG. Chinese patrol vessels began conducting patrols near the Senkaku/Diaoyu islands in the East China Sea as far back as 2008. In 2010, a Chinese fishing vessel rammed two Japanese coast guard ships near these islands, prompting high-level exchanges between China and Japan.[15] In 2011, there were a number of surveys conducted by Chinese research vessels.[16] In 2008, PLA Navy vessels patrolled the entirety of the Spratly Islands in the South China Sea, and conducted regular patrols there into 2009. Chinese ships also left markers in the southernmost part of the islands.[17] In 2012, there were serious confrontations between unarmed Chinese patrol vessels and Philippines' ships in the disputed Scarborough Shoal.[18]

Lyle Goldstein, author of the most comprehensive study to-date on China's maritime enforcement capabilities, noted in his report that coast guards are often used as buffers between maritime forces.[19] China appears to be using its coast guard forces as a less escalatory means to press maritime claims, and test other countries' maritime defences and red lines. 'White hull' ships are a means to establish control and enforce claims with less risk of confrontations; and also provide additional options at the lower levels of escalation.[20] They allow China to pursue its claims, even engage in persistent coercion, while keeping the conflict localised. As Zia-ul Haq, Pakistan's military dictator in the 1980s, once said about supporting insurgents against the Soviet army in Afghanistan, 'the pot must boil at the right temperature'.[21]

James Holmes at the US Naval War College, has argued that China may use its growing 'white hull' capability to selectively deny access to commercial and military vessels of other countries. Just as China has continually tested Japan's red lines, and tested Southeast Asian countries over disputes in the South China Sea, China may continually test the boundaries of what the US and the international community will accept, when it comes to the 'freedom of navigation'. Holmes has termed such 'salami-slicing' tactics as 'selective access-denial'.[22]

Though China may rely increasingly on the CCG to secure its maritime claims, the PLA Navy could intervene at any time – to back up patrol vessels under fire or to intentionally escalate. This would send a strong message to smaller powers engaged in confrontation with the Chinese patrol vessels. There is little need for the PLA Navy to become involved directly – or for its involvement to be explicitly threatened or even mentioned – for its presence to have impact. If needed, China may climb the escalation ladder – a game it is likely to win against the smaller powers of Southeast Asia.[23] Some analysts have argued that the reorganization and growth of the CCG will free up the PLA Navy to pursue its blue water ambitions further afield. They see an evolving strategy, whereby China relies on its coast guard forces to pursue its claims close to shore, and to keep these conflicts limited and localized, while the PLA Navy projects power further outward. The implication is that the development of the CCG may lead to a more capable – and possibly more assertive – PLA Navy.[24]

It is both possible and likely that more CCG vessels will be armed in the future, perhaps with heavier weaponry, and that interoperability with the PLA Navy will improve. The CCG already operates a number of decommissioned PLA Navy vessels, many of which are equipped with deck-mounted guns.[25] CMS, one of the five agencies consolidated into the new CCG, has at least two destroyers decommissioned from the PLA Navy, and is likely to receive more in future. The destroyers are reportedly armed with 130mm deck-mounted guns with 29km range, as well as possible anti-ship missiles.[26]

Other countries in the region are likely to respond to China's growing 'white hull' capability by growing their own coast guards, including inducting ships with longer ranges and more weaponry. It may become increasingly difficult for the countries to deploy 'grey hull' naval vessels against the much smaller Chinese coast guard boats without appearing overly aggressive and creating needless escalation. This also may lead to increased demand for more 'white hull' vessels by countries in the region.

Implications for the US

It may become increasingly difficult for US naval vessels to confront the Chinese Coast Guard ships without appearing unnecessarily escalatory. 'White hull' patrols are best met in kind. Furthermore, as China builds more coast guard vessels, it may be increasingly difficult for a limited (and relatively static) number of US Navy ships to cover down on China's growing fleet of smaller boats patrolling further ashore, and across a larger area. It will be increasingly necessary for the US to invest in capacity building among Asia's coast guards and smaller naval vessels.

China appears to be using its newly formed CCG to continually test the responses of the US, its Asian allies, and other countries in the region. Beijing has relied on maritime surveillance vessels to repeatedly test red lines, probe weaknesses in maritime defences, send messages, and keep disputes at a low boil. For the US, these tactics raise some difficult questions about an escalation. For instance:

- Is the US willing to force a confrontation and risk escalation over relatively small, discrete actions by China on issues in which it has relatively little at stake?
- Would US threats be credible under these circumstances?
- Is the US Navy prepared to respond aggressively to efforts by Chinese 'white hull' ships to limit access to commercial or fishing vessels, deep water surveys, or even limited military exercises on discrete occasions in particular locales?
- Is the US prepared to respond aggressively, perhaps disproportionately, in every instance?

It will be increasingly necessary for the US to develop a wider array of discrete options, particularly at the lower levels of escalation, aimed at deterring further encroachments by Chinese maritime vessels. The American way of war, which tends to favour overwhelming firepower to secure rapid and complete defeat, will need to become more calibrated. More options will be needed between the extremes of inaction and an all-out war. It will be necessary to better integrate military postures and operations with diplomacy in ways that, at the very least, match the level of sophistication demonstrated by China in pursuit of its maritime claims. There is a strong incentive for Japan and other affected US allies and partners in the region to respond forcefully to China's 'gradualist' tactics. It is possible that Japan, in particular, may respond more sternly in the future, and perhaps even provoke a crisis in order to send a message to Beijing, and deter further attempts at escalation at the lower levels. Such dynamics threaten to draw the US further into the region's maritime disputes.

Conclusion

Disagreements over the implications of China's new Coast Guard mirror a larger debate over China's rise – between those who argue that China's intentions are largely benign and defensive in nature, and those who insist that China intends to build military capacity in order to project power and aggressively coerce its neighbors. In many ways, it is the same debate that political scientists and historians have been having for generations – over whether rising powers will become more passive as they become more integrated with the world economy, or whether they will use their newly acquired resources to build more powerful militaries with which to pursue their interests and threaten their neighbours. Given its dual role in economic development and domestic law enforcement on the one hand, and as a source of military power and force projection on the other, the future evolution and activities of the Chinese Coast Guard may prove a valuable indicator of China's future direction.

NOTES

1. 'Maritime Authority to Boost Capabilities', *China Daily*, July 10, 2013, http://www.china.org.cn/china/2013-07/10/content_29377089.htm (accessed March 10, 2014).
2. 'Maritime Authority to Boost Capabilities' ibid. also See Bonnie Glaser and Brittany Billingsley, 'The Promise and Peril of China's New Coast Guard', *The Diplomat*, August 7, 2013.
3. 'China Ramping Up Navy with More Ships amid Maritime Disputes', *Press Trust of India*, January 17, 2014, http://articles.economictimes.indiatimes.com/2014-01-17/news/4630230 (accessed March 10, 2014).
4. Ronald O'Rourke, 'Chinese Naval Modernization: Implications for U.S. Navy Capabilities – Background and Issues for Congress', *Congressional Research Service*, April 8, 2011.

5. Lyle J. Goldstein, 'Five Dragons Stirring up the Sea: Challenge and Opportunity in China's Improving Maritime Enforcement Capabilities', *Naval War College*, April 2010.
6. Goldstein, 'Five Dragons Stirring up the Sea' ibid.
7. James Holmes, 'No, China's Coast Guard Won't Reduce Tensions', *The Diplomat*, July 29, 2013.
8. Zachary Keck, 'China Fires Water Cannons at Philippine Fishermen', *The Diplomat*, February 25, 2014.
9. 'China Tests the Waters with Coastguard Ships Near Japan-Controlled Islands', *Agence France-Presse*, January 27, 2014, http://www.globalpost.com/dispatch/news/regions/asia-pacific/china/140127/china-tests-the-waters-coastguard-ships-near-japan-c (accessed March 10, 2013).
10. Bonnie Glaser and Brittany Billingsley, 'The Promise and Peril of China's New Coast Guard', *The Diplomat*, August 7, 2013
11. Michael Cole, 'Japan Alarmed by China's Air and Naval Surveillance', *The Diplomat*, July 26, 2013.
12. Mira Rapp-Hooper, 'The Battle for the Senkakus Moves to the Skies', *The Diplomat*, November 12, 2013.
13. Rapp-Hooper, 'The Battle for the Senkakus Moves to the Skies' ibid.
14. Rapp-Hooper, 'The Battle for the Senkakus Moves to the Skies' ibid.
15. Yuki Tatsumi, 'Senkaku Islands/East China Sea Disputes – A Japanese Perspective', *CNA Maritime Asia Project*, August 2013.
16. State Oceanic Administration, *China's Ocean Development Report 2010* (Beijing: Ocean Press, 2010), p. 45.
17. China's Ocean Development Report 2010, ibid, p. 100.
18. James Holmes and Toshi Yoshihara, 'Small-stick Diplomacy in the South China Sea', *The National Interest*, April 23, 2012.
19. Goldstein, 'Five Dragons Stirring up the Sea' ibid.
20. For more on this, see Goldstein, 'Five Dragons Stirring up the Sea' ibid.
21. Steve Coll, Ghost Wars: The Secret History of the CIA, Afghanistan, and bin Laden from the Soviet Invasion to September 10, 2001 (New York: Penguin Books, 2004), p. 63.
22. James Holmes, 'China's Selective Access-Denial Strategy', *The National Interest*, December 3, 2013.
23. Holmes and Yoshihara, 'Small-stick Diplomacy in the South China Sea' ibid.
24. Patrick Roberts, 'China's New Coastguard: Not Handing out Many Carrots (But Definitely Starting to Wield a Big Stick'. RUSI Analysis, January 23, 2014. See also Holmes Yoshihara, 'Small-stick Diplomacy in the South China Sea' ibid.
25. Glaser and Billingsley, 'The Promise and Peril of China's New Coast Guard' ibid.
26. Michael Cole, 'China's Maritime Surveillance Fleet Adds Muscle', *The Diplomat*, January 3, 2013.

12

Geopolitics of Deep-Sea Mining and China

Sunil Kumar Agarwal

The rising demand for strategic minerals and rare earths has triggered countries to search for 'non-traditional' sources, viz. polymetallic nodules, seafloor massive sulphides, and cobalt rich ferromanganese crusts, occurring within and beyond the national jurisdictions. This has resulted in the emergence of deep seabed mining as a major new strategic issue. This new maritime frontier threatens to stir new conflicts among States for securing rights to access and exploit mineral resources beyond national jurisdiction, which are considered to be 'Common Heritage of Mankind' under the 1982 UNCLOS. There is growing concern that China's quest for deep-seabed minerals is part of its maritime strategy and it is likely to use that as a political lever to enhance its geopolitical influence. This, in turn, would change maritime power equations in the world. In this scenario, growing competition over resources poses potential threat to maritime peace and security, especially in the IOR.

Introduction

Deep-seabed mining is a significant new and emerging activity for usage of the global oceans.[1] The principal drivers of this new interest are largely the result of a combination of technological advances in marine deep-seabed mining and processing; a dramatic increase in demand for metals, primarily fuelled by emerging economies, leading to a rise in metal prices; a decline in the grade of land-based nickel, copper, and cobalt sulphide deposits; and increased demand and reduced

Figure 12.1: Jiaolong Submersible Plants China's Flag on the Seafloor

Source: China Daily, August 27, 2010.

supply of rare earth minerals.[2] The surge in searches for alternative sources of supply of strategic minerals and rare earths has also been ongoing since China – the predominant supplier of rare earth minerals – announced its decision to reduce its export quota in September 2009. China, which produces about 97 per cent of rare earth minerals in the world, allegedly restricted exports in order to conserve supplies for its own high-tech and green industries.[3]

As a result, there has been a shift of mineral exploration and development activities to 'non-traditional' sources, viz. polymetallic nodules, seafloor massive sulphides, and cobalt-rich ferromanganese crusts, occurring within and beyond the national jurisdictions. Such deposits also have the potential to contain rare earth elements, something that is likely to enhance their attractiveness as targets for seabed resource development.[4] Interest in deep-seabed mining began in the mid-1960s with the publication of a book by J N Mero entitled *The Mineral Resources of the Sea*,[5] which provided the estimates of manganese nodules present on the floor of the Pacific Ocean. Those estimates led many to envision manganese nodules as the vast reserves of strategic minerals. Over the next 20 years, countries such as the US, France, and Germany conducted research projects on nodule mining, but these were eventually abandoned after realizing their commercial non-viability.

However, over the past decade, the demand for strategic resources in various countries – especially China, Japan, Korea, India, and Brazil – has led to a resurgence of interest in sea-bed minerals. The private sector and the financial institutions that support such interest believe that deep-seabed mining can be commercially viable.[6]

It is pertinent to note that mineral resources beyond national jurisdiction are the 'Common Heritage of Humankind' (CHM) under the 1982 UNCLOS. The mineral resources of the common heritage are administered by the International Seabed Authority (ISA) under Part XI of the UNCLOS. Accordingly, offshore deep-seabed mining beyond national jurisdiction can only be undertaken through application for a license from the ISA. This article outlines the legal aspects of deep-seabed mining and analyzes China's efforts to secure the rights to explore and exploit marine resources and its geopolitical implications in IOR.

Mineral Resources of Deep-seabed

Commercial interest is currently focused on three types of deep-seabed mineral resources: polymetallic nodules, polymetallic sulphides or seafloor massive sulphides and cobalt-rich ferromanganese crusts deposit. Table 12.1 shows the location, oceanic area and metal constituents of these marine resources.

Table 12.1: Important Deep-seabed Mineral Resources

Resource	*Location/ Depth*	*Oceanic Area*	*Key products*
Pollymetallic nodules	deep-seafloor, deep-water abyssal plains (4,000-6,000m)	Clarion-Clipperton zone, Peru Basin, Southern Ocean, North Indian Ocean	Manganese, nickel, copper, cobalt, iron, rare earths
Polymetallic Sulphides	hydrothermal vents, submarine volcanic ridges (500-4,000m)	Southwest Indian Ridge, East, southeast and northeast Pacific Rise; Red Sea	Copper, zinc, lead, gold and silver
Cobalt-rich manganese crusts	seamounts (800-2,500m)	South Pacific island states	Cobalt, manganese, nickel, rare earths, tungsten, tellurium

Source: Greenpeace, Deep-seabed Mining (2013).

Polymetallic Manganese Nodules

Also known as manganese nodules, these are rock concretions formed of concentric layers of iron and manganese hydroxides around a core. They occur on the seabed at depths of 4000-6000 m. While the nodules tend to vary in size, the average size ranges from 2 to 10 cm in diameter, about the size of potatoes. They take a million years to grow by one millimeter. Their formation requires a nucleus, low sedimentation rate, oxidizing conditions, and low velocity bottom currents. They occur throughout the ocean and are found lying on the seafloor in the abyssal plains, often partially buried in fine grain sediments. These nodules contain a wide variety of metals including manganese, iron, copper, nickel, cobalt, lead, and zinc, with important but minor concentrations of molybdenum, lithium, titanium, and niobium, among others. While they occur in all oceans, deposits in the Clarion Clipperton Zone (CCZ) in the eastern Pacific are considered to be among the richest, containing high grade and high abundance nodules.[7] It is estimated that the CCZ contains a potential resource of 62 billion tonnes of nodules, comprising 17,500 million tonnes of manganese, 761 million tonnes of nickel, 669 million tonnes of copper and 134 million tonnes of cobalt 6.[8] Other areas of potential interest are the Central Indian Ocean basin and the exclusive economic zones (EEZs) of the Cook Islands, Kiribati, and French Polynesia.

Polymetallic Sulphides

Polymetallic sulphides are also known as Seafloor Massive Sulphides (SMS). They are rich in copper, iron, zinc, silver, and gold. Polymetallic sulphide deposits are concentrated over thousands of years by seafloor hot springs at sites along an active global submerged volcanic mountain range that extends through all the ocean basins of the world. These deposits also occur at sites associated with volcanic island chains, such as those along the western boundary of the Pacific Ocean, tectonic plate boundaries along the mid-ocean ridges, back-arc ridges, and active volcanic arcs, typically at water depths of around 2,000 m for mid-ocean ridges. These deposits are formed over thousands of years through hydrothermal activity, which is when metals precipitate from water discharged from the Earth's crust through hot springs, at temperatures of up to 400°C. These hydrothermal vents are often referred to as 'black smokers' because of the black plumes formed by the activity. The International Seabed Authority database contains locations of about 350 known sites of hydrothermal activity; but it is estimated that vents are likely to occur at approximately 100 km intervals along the 60,000 km mid-oceanic ridge system that encircles the globe, including in some EEZs.

Cobalt-Rich Manganese Crusts

These are generally found on hard-rock sub-stratas throughout the ocean basins. They form at the seafloor on the flanks and summits of seamounts, ridges, plateau, and abyssal hills where the rocks have been swept clean of sediments intermittently for millions of years. Ferromanganese crusts contain sub-equal amounts of iron and manganese, and are specially enriched in cobalt, manganese, lead, tellurium, bismuth, and platinum, relative to their lithospheric and seawater concentrations. These crusts are precipitated over millions of years on the submerged flanks of inactive underwater volcanoes from metals dissolved in seawater, and also derived from input of metals by both rivers and seafloor hot springs. These are found at water depths of about 400–4,000 m, with the thickest and most cobalt-rich crusts occurring at about 800–2,500 m. The most prospective area for cobalt crusts is the Magellan seamounts in the Pacific Ocean, east of Japan and the Mariana islands.

Legal Regime of Deep-seabed Mining

The 1982 UNCLOS[9] sets out the legal framework for uses of the ocean space as well as ocean activities. Establishment of maritime zones, and the rights and duties of states within them, is at the core of the UNCLOS. Maritime zones, as outlined by UNCLOS, are: the territorial sea, the contiguous zone, the exclusive economic zone, the continental shelf, the high seas and the Area (seabed outside national jurisdictions). Article 1(1) of the UNCLOS defines Area as 'the seabed and ocean floor and subsoil thereof, beyond the limits of national jurisdiction'.[10] Activities in the Area are governed by the provisions of Part XI of UNCLOS. Section 2 of Part XI provides the fundamental principles governing the Area. One of the fundamental principles governing this regime is that the Area and its resources are the 'Common Heritage of Mankind'.[11] Section 133 of UNCLOS defines 'resources' as 'all solid, liquid or gaseous mineral[12] resources *in situ* in the Area at or beneath the seabed, including polymetallic nodules.'

Legal regime for the administration and development of the mineral resources of the Area is provided in the Part XI[13] of the UNCLOS, and in Annex III to the Convention, which contains the 'basic conditions of prospecting, exploration and exploitation' with respect to the resources of the Area. Annex IV contains the statute of the Enterprise, the operating arm of the International Seabed Authority, and the 1994 Agreement,[14] which modified Part XI and the Annexes in significant ways.[15] Regarding dispute settlement, Annex VI of the UNCLOS provides for the establishment of a 'Seabed Disputes Chamber' of the International Tribunal for the Law of the Sea (ITLOS).[16] The Seabed Disputes Chamber has jurisdiction in disputes with respect to activities in the Area.[17]

The regime for seabed mining under Part XI has undergone significant changes by virtue of the 1994 Agreement. The 1994 Agreement has made important adjustments to the substantive provisions in the Convention which were initially contentious and delayed the entry of the UNCLOS into force. It provides that the obligations applicable to 'private contractors' shall also apply to the 'Enterprise'. This removes any competitive advantage for the 'Enterprise' over 'private contractors'.[18] The provision relating to the mandatory transfer of technology by the contractor to the 'Enterprise', or to a developing country's operators, has been substituted by a "general duty of cooperation by sponsoring States to facilitate the acquisition of deep-seabed mining technology, if the Enterprise or the developing country is unable to obtain such technology in open market, or through joint-venture arrangements".[19] The financial terms of the contract are modified to a single market-oriented system with a preference for the 'simple royalty' system. The decision-making process in the ISA has been modified by the Agreement which requires that all organs of the ISA, including the Assembly, should make efforts to arrive at decisions by way of consensus, as a first step.[20]

Through its terms, the 1994 Agreement forms an integral part of the UNCLOS. It states that Part XI of the UNCLOS shall be interpreted and applied together as a single instrument. In the event of any inconsistency between this Agreement and Part XI, the provisions of the Agreement shall prevail. Where a provision of Part XI, Annex III, or Annex IV is affected by a provision of the Agreement, the effect of the relevant provisions of the Agreement is addressed in the UNCLOS in each individual article. Exploration and exploitation of mineral resources in the Area has to be carried out in accordance with regime Part XI, adapted by the 1994 Implementation Agreement. The mining regime for the Area is given practical effect by providing for an institutional framework in the form of ISA through which States Parties[21] are required to organize and control activities in the Area, particularly with a view to administering the resources of the Area by adoption of regulations.[22]

Activities in the Area shall be carried out by the Enterprise,[23] or in association with the Authority by States Parties, or state enterprises, or natural or juridical persons which possess the nationality of States Parties, or are effectively controlled by them or their nationals, when sponsored by such States.[24] Article 137(3) of the UNCLOS provides that 'no State or natural or juridical person shall claim, acquire or exercise rights with respect to the minerals recovered from the Area except in accordance with this part. Otherwise, no such claim, acquisition or exercise of such rights shall be recognized.'

General Principles Governing Deep-seabed Regime

Some of the important principles governing the deep-seabed regime are as follows:[25]

- Area and its (mineral) resources are the common heritage of mankind; i.e. rights over resources are vested in mankind

- ISA shall act on behalf of 'mankind'; all Parties in the UNCLOS are responsible for organizing and controlling mining activities in the Area
- Mining activities shall be carried out for the benefit of mankind; implies equitable sharing of economic benefits
- No State shall claim or exercise sovereignty or sovereign rights over any part of the Area or its mineral resources

Common Heritage of Mankind[26]

Common Heritage of Mankind (CHM) is a relatively novel concept in international law and politics in ensuring a new place for the regime of the Area. UNCLOS provides that the Area and its resources are neither subject to claims of sovereignty by any state, nor subject to appropriation by any state or natural or juridical persons; and are to be used for peaceful purposes only.[27] All rights in the resources are vested in mankind as a whole, with the ISA acting as a type of trustee on behalf of 'mankind'.[28] Activities in the Area are to be carried out for the benefit of mankind as a whole.[29] These concepts are further defined under Article 136 of UNCLOS as related to 'the seabed and ocean floor and subsoil thereof, beyond the limits of national jurisdiction.' By extension, it can be argued that there are four core components of CHM that govern exploitation, resource recovery, and utilization, of the deep-seabed resources:

- There can be no private or public appropriation; no one legally owns common heritage spaces
- Representatives from all nations must manage resources contained in such a territorial or conceptual area on behalf of all, since a commons area is considered to belong to everyone. This is the reason for establishing ISA to coordinate shared management
- All nations must actively share the benefits acquired from exploitation of resources from the common heritage region, with each other. This requires restraint on profit-making activities of private corporate entities, in accordance with the concept of a global public good
- The commons should be preserved for the benefit of future generations

Although the CHM sets forth the overarching framework for deep-seabed mineral exploitation, the actual implementation is broadly governed by the 1994 Agreement on the Implementation of Part XI (sections 6 and 8 of the Annex). Section 6, on production policy, emphasizes that the development of resources of the Area shall take place in accordance with 'sound commercial principles'; that 'there shall be no subsidization of activities in the Area'; and that 'there shall be no discrimination between minerals derived from the Area and from other sources.'

Section 8, paragraph 1, on financial terms of contracts provides that:

- The system of payments to the Authority shall be fair to both, the contractor and the Authority; and shall provide adequate means of determining compliance by the contractor within such system
- The rates of payment under the system shall be within the range prevailing in respect of land-based mining of the same or similar minerals, in order to avoid giving deep-seabed miners an artificial competitive advantage or imposing on them a competitive disadvantage
- The system should not be complicated and should not impose major administrative costs on the Authority, or on a contractor. Consideration should be given to the adoption of a royalty system, or a combination of a royalty and profit-sharing system.
- The system of payments may be revised periodically in light of changing circumstances.

Institutional and Regulatory Framework

The ISA is one of the most important institutions established by the 1982 UNCLOS. It came into being on November 16, 1994, upon the entry of the UNCLOS into force. The membership of the ISA consists of all parties to the 1982 Convention who are *ipso facto* members of the Authority. The need for an international machinery to administer the Area arose from the fact that investors in seabed mining activities could not exercise exclusive rights over parts of the seabed where they could explore and exploit the mineral resources. Those areas would otherwise be subject to the 'freedom of the high seas' and would be accessible to nationals of other States in the exercise of their own 'high seas freedom'. The ISA, therefore, provides an essential safeguard for investors who intend to undertake long term development of the resources of deep-seabed areas by giving them exclusive rights to the resources of those areas for the duration of their contracts or licenses with the Authority.

Powers and Functions of ISA

The mandate of the ISA is to administer the mineral resources of the deep-seabed which is beyond national jurisdiction, and is referred to as the Area and to organize, carry out, and control activities in the Area on behalf of mankind with a view to administering the resources therein.[30] Use of the Area for other activities, such as pipeline & cable laying and scientific research, unconnected with the exploitation of seabed mineral resources, do not fall within the competence of the ISA and therefore, can be freely carried out as part of the 'freedom of the high seas'.

It has such incidental powers consistent with the Convention, as are implicit in, and necessary for, the exercise of those powers and functions with respect to activities in the Area.

ISA is responsible for developing and overseeing regulations governing the issuance of prospecting, exploration and eventually, extraction licenses for minerals in the Area. The Authority has prepared the deep-seabed mining code as follows:

- Regulations on prospecting and exploration for polymetallic nodules in the Area[31]
- Regulations on prospecting and exploration for polymetallic sulphides in the Area[32]
- Regulations on prospecting and exploration for cobalt-rich crusts[33]

The current challenge though, is to develop regulations on the exploitation of these minerals. The powers and functions of the ISA are exercised through a number of organs, namely the Assembly,[34] the Council, and the Secretariat.[35] There are also subsidiary organs of the Council such as the Legal and Technical Commission.[36] Further, functions of the operational arm, the 'Enterprise' are presently being carried out by the Secretariat.[37] The mineral resources of the Area can only be explored and exploited in accordance with the rules, regulations, and procedures promulgated by the ISA. Otherwise, no claim, acquisition, or exercise of rights shall be recognized.[38]

The ISA Assembly has a number of specific powers and functions, including the consideration and the adoption of the regulations, rules, and procedures relating to prospecting, exploration, and exploitation of the resources of the Area upon the recommendation of the Council.[39] The Council is the executive organ of the ISA with exclusive power to approve applications for mining contracts or licenses submitted to it in the form of plans for exploration or exploitation.[40] The Legal and Technical Commission is the technical arm of the Council which makes recommendations to the Council on scientific and technical matters, and generally assists the Council in the administration of activities in the Area, including formulation of mining regulations.[41]

Procedures for Approval of Application

Exploration and exploitation of deep-sea minerals in the Area may only be carried out under a contract with ISA, and are subject to its rules, regulations, and procedures. Contracts may be issued to both public and private mining enterprises, provided they are sponsored by a State party to UNCLOS and meets certain standards of technological and financial capacity. The 1994 Agreement prescribes a special procedure for the approval of a plan of work for a contract by the Council. The plan of work is first reviewed by the Legal and Technical Commission in order to ascertain if the application has met the objective criteria set out in the Convention to qualify for a contract, and the required technical data and information set out in the regulations have been submitted. Once it is satisfied, the Commission, by a simple majority, recommends the approval of the plan of work (in the form of a contract) to the Council.[42]

The 1994 Agreement provides that the ISA Council would generally approve a plan of work for the exploration of deep-sea minerals on the recommendation from the Legal and Technical Commission. Nevertheless, the Council is also empowered to disapprove a plan of work if two-thirds majority of its members present and voting – including a majority of members present and voting in each of the chambers of the Council – vote against the approval of a plan of work.[43] If the Council does not take a decision on a recommendation for approval of a plan of work within a prescribed period, the recommendation shall be deemed to have been approved by the Council at the end of that period. The prescribed period shall normally be 60 days unless the Council decides to provide for a longer period. If the Commission recommends the disapproval of a plan of work or does not make a recommendation, the Council may nevertheless approve the plan of work in accordance with its rules of procedure for decision-making on questions of substance.'[44]

As on January 15, 2014, 14 contracts for exploration were in force – 12 for polymetallic nodules and two for polymetallic sulphides. Five plans of work for exploration had been approved by the Council, but have not yet been concluded in the form of contracts. Seven further applications were pending consideration before the Legal and Technical Commission. Table 12.2 shows the status of contracts for exploration of mineral resources, as on January 15, 2014.

Table 12.2: Status of Contracts for Exploration for Mineral Resources

A. Contracts for Exploration for Polymetallic Nodules				
Contractor	*Date of Entry of Contract*	*Sponsoring State*	*Location*	*Date of Expiry*
Inter-ocean metal Joint Organization, Poland	March 29, 2001	Bulgaria, Cuba, Czech Republic, Poland, Russian Federation & Slovakia	Clarion-Clipperton Fracture Zone (CCF Zone)	March 28, 2016
Yuzhmorgeologiya	March 29, 2001	Russian Federation	CCF Zone	March 28, 2016
Government of Republic of Korea	April 27, 2001	-	CCF Zone	April 26, 2016
COMRA	May 22, 2001	China	CCF Zone	May 21, 2016

Contractor	*Date of Entry of Contract*	*Sponsoring State*	*Location*	*Date of Expiry*
Deep Ocean Resources Development Co. Ltd.	June 20, 2001	Japan	CCF Zone	June 19, 2016
Institut français de Recherche pour l'Exploitation de la Mer	June 20, 2001	France	CCF Zone	June 19, 2016
Government of India	March 25, 2002	-	Central Indian Ocean Basin	March 24, 2017
Federal Institute for Geosciences & Natural Resources, Germany	July 19, 2006	Germany	CCF Zone	July 18, 2021
Nauru Ocean Resources Inc.	July 22, 2011	Nauru	CCF Zone	July 21, 2026
Tonga Offshore Mining Limited	January 11, 2012	Tonga	CC F Zone	January 10, 2027
Marawa Research & Exploration Ltd.	To be signed	Kiribati	CCF Zone	-
UK Seabed Resources Ltd.	February 8, 2013	UK	CCF Zone	February 7, 2028
G-TEC Sea Mineral Resources NV	January 14, 2013	Belgium	CCF Zone	January 13, 2028
UK Seabed Resources Ltd.	Applied on February 8, 2013	United Kingdom		
Ocean Mineral Singapore Pty Ltd.	Applied on April 19, 2013	Singapore		

B. Contracts for Exploration for Polymetallic Sulphides

Contractor	*Date of Entry of Contract*	*Sponsoring State*	*Location of Exploration Area*	*Date of Expiry*
COMRA	November 18, 2011	China	South-west Indian Ridge	November 17, 2026
Govt. of Russian Federation	October 29, 2012	-	Mid-Atlantic Ridge	October 28, 2027
Govt. of the Republic of Korea	To be signed	-	Central Indian Ocean	
Institut français de recherche pour l'exploitation de la mer	To be signed	France	Mid-Atlantic Ridge	
Government of India	Applied on March 26, 2013			

C. Contracts for Exploration for Cobalt-rich Ferromanganese Crusts

Contractor	*Date of Entry of Contract*	*Sponsoring State*	*Location of Exploration Area*	*Date of Expiry*
COMRA	April 29, 2014	China	Western Pacific Ocean	April 28, 2029
Japan Oil, Gas and Metals National Corporation	January 27, 2014	Japan	Western Pacific Ocean	January 26, 2029
Russian Federation	Applied on February 6, 2013			

Source: Compiled by author from selected decisions and documents of various sessions of ISA.

China's Quest for Deep-sea Minerals

The maritime domain is becoming increasingly important for China's national strategy, and is closely related to its sustainable economic development.[45] China attaches great importance to marine development and takes it as a critical component of its development strategy. Its ocean policy emphasizes the utilization of marine resources, and continuous exploration of the ocean for new resources, to enable sustainable development of its economy.[46] China aims to use the ocean to make the country more prosperous. President Xi Jingping has championed the efforts to build China into maritime power, saying his government will do everything possible to safeguard China's 'maritime rights and interests' and warning that 'in no way will country abandon its legitimate rights and interests'.[47]

China's efforts to establish a maritime development strategy experienced a breakthrough with the unveiling of the 12th Five-Year Plan (2011-2015) in March 2011. This Plan included a new chapter called 'Promote the Development of Marine Economy,' and clearly set out a policy guideline to develop and implement a marine development strategy, and improve marine development and control capabilities.[48] China unveiled its maritime power strategy in the 2012 report presented at the 18th Party Congress, by the then President Hu Jintao. While highlighting the major breakthrough in the development of a manned deep-sea submersible, the report emphasized on the need for enhancing capacity to exploit marine resources, resolutely safeguard China's maritime rights, and build China into a maritime power.[49]

China embarked on its quest for off-shore mineral resources by establishing the China Ocean Mineral Resources Research and Development Association (COMRA) in 1991. Since that time, COMRA has managed and supervised China's activities on exploration and development of resources in the international seabed area. Furthermore, China is in the process of preparing for specific legislation on subject.[50] China succeeded in taking a lead in deep-seabed mining when COMRA was registered as one of the seven pioneer investors for deep-seabed mining on March 5, 1991.[51] This played an important role in China's ratification of the UN CLOS on June 7, 1996. Since then, the Chinese government considered it to be helpful to maintain its substantive status as a 'pioneer investor' in deep-seabed resource development activities, and in fulfilling its long-term interests.[52]

On May 22, 2001, COMRA was granted a contract for prospecting and exploration of polymetallic nodules in the northern Pacific Ocean Area by the ISA. This was a major breakthrough in China's research and capacity building relating to deep-seabed exploration, accessing and extracting strategic mineral resources. It utilised this opportunity to initiate a long-term programme focusing on exploration, design, and development of a deep-seabed mining system, and of processing techniques. It conducted investigations to compare planning options and develop market projections for future supply and demand of metals. It also utilized this opportunity in accumulating data and experience concerning distribution of, and methods of exploration, for polymetallic sulphides and their environment. These experiences enabled COMRA to sign another contract with ISA for exploration of polymetallic sulphides in 10,000 sq km of the south-west Indian Ocean ridges in 2011.[53] Further, COMRA was granted a contract by ISA for exploration of the cobalt-rich ferromanganese crusts in the western Pacific Ocean on April 29, 2014.[54]

On August 27, 2010, China's achieved a new stride in the development of manned deep-sea submersible with the successful dive of *Jiaolong* submersible, to a depth 3,759 metres.[55] While this technological feat bolstered China's seabed mining capacity, the Chinese scientists used the opportunity to plant China's flag on the bottom of the seafloor (Figure 12.1).[56] This move resembles planting of the Russian flag on the seabed at the North Pole in 2007.[57] On July 27, 2011, *Jiaolong* submersible set a new record of diving 5,057 metres below the sea surface in the east Pacific Ocean. On June 30, 2012, the *Jiaolong* set a new national dive record after reaching 7,062 metres during its sixth trial dive in the Mariana Trench in the Pacific Ocean.[58] This marks a fresh breakthrough, and a giant leap in the development of China's deep-sea exploration technology. It has enabled China to conduct deep-sea scientific research and resources exploration in 99.8 per cent of the world's oceans, and to become one of the deep-sea faring countries.[59]

These developments propelled China towards acquiring the requisite skills, technology, capability, and experience to undertake deep-sea mining activities. China has now become a global leader in deep-sea mining and can leverage its capabilities to tap and exploit deep-sea strategic minerals and resources for its sustainable economic development.

Implications of China's Deep-sea Mining Capability

Over the last decade, China has made impressive progress in exploring the international seabed for strategic minerals, including achieving a Class A membership as a consumption country of mineral resources,[60] clinching contracts for exploration of mineral resources from ISA, and attaining a leading position in marine technology relating to manned deep-sea submersibles. China is the only country which has been granted contracts by the ISA for exploration of all three main mineral resources in the seabed beyond national jurisdictions,[61] under the deep-seabed mining regime established by the 1982 UNCLOS.

As with China's space program, it appears that an advancement in China's marine deep-sea exploration capabilities has been driven by three key factors, namely, national prestige, a sense of competition, and a desire to advance scientific progress, with a view to achieve maritime prowess. It is evident that China has utilized the opportunities in deep-seabed mining by not only strengthening its commercial interests, but also in expanding its strategic reach in the maritime domain, especially in the IOR.

The IOR is an important location in the contemporary maritime geopolitics. Inter-state competition over deep-sea strategic minerals is sharpening in the IOR. China is considered to be an extra-regional maritime power in the IOR. This has led China to subscribe to the 'string of pearls' strategy to secure its maritime interests – energy resources, SLOCs and deep-sea resources – in the IOR. By securing the exclusive rights for exploration of polymetallic sulphides in the southwestern Indian Ocean ridge, China has been able to increase its foothold in the Indian Ocean. China is likely to leverage it to stake further legitimacy as a strategic player in the IOR.

This means that enhanced Chinese deep-sea mining capabilities will have serious implications for geopolitics of the Indian Ocean, in particular, and the evolving architecture of maritime governance in general. Growing strategic reach of China in the IOR has been a major concern for littoral countries, especially India. This scenario poses new challenges for India as it strives to become a major maritime power with significant maritime interests and substantive naval capabilities.[62] To secure its own strategic ground in the IOR *vis-a-vis* China, India has undertaken important policy initiatives to develop its own deep-seabed mining capabilities with enhanced impetus.[63]

It is, thus, apparent that China's increasing deep-sea mining capabilities have empowered it to carve out a strategic niche in the maritime domain with Chinese characteristics. China is likely to leverage its monopoly in deep-sea mining to its advantage in the maritime domain. This is because of the fact that the marine development strategy is an important component of China's grand strategy to become a maritime power.

Conclusion

Growing global demand for mineral resources and recent technological developments have substantially increased the importance of deep-sea mining as a new frontier for strategic minerals. The imperative of finding alternatives to China-produced rare earth minerals has also driven the global resurrection of interest in deep-sea mining. This has led to the resurgence of deep-sea mining activities in the Area beyond national jurisdictions. Countries are making huge investments to compete with each other, in order to gain exclusive rights for exploration of local deep-sea mineral resources from the ISA.

Over the last decade, China has made great strides in exploring the international seabed for strategic minerals, by substantially enhancing its deep-sea mining capabilities. Its major achievements include getting contracts from ISA for the exploration of all three deep-sea mineral deposits, and technological breakthroughs for accessing almost 97 per cent of the deep-sea resources. Therefore, China's emergence as a leader in deep-sea mining has an increasing strategic dimension. It is thus, possible that China may use its increasing geopolitical influence in deep-sea mining as a political lever in the maritime domain. These developments will have serious geopolitical implications worldwide, especially so in the IOR.

NOTES

1. In 2013, the UK Prime Minister pledged to put Britain at the forefront of a new international seabed mining industry, which he claimed could be worth £40billion to the UK economy over the next 30 years. *The Guardian,* March 2013.
2. International Seabed Authority, 'Towards the development of a regulatory framework for polymetallic nodule Exploitation in the Area', Technical Study No. 11 (2013).
3. US, Japan and the European Union filed a complaint at the WTO against China's restrictions on rare earths exports in 2012.
4. Jim Hein, 'Prospects for Rare Earth Elements from Marine Mineral', ISA Briefing Paper, 02/12, May 2012.
5. J.L. Mero, *The Mineral Resources of the Sea, Oceanographic Series 1* (Amsterdam: Elsevier, 1965).
6. Statement of ISA Secretary-General during the launch of UK Seabed Resources Limited, the latest exploration contractor with the ISA, 14 March 2013
7. International Seabed Authority (ISA), A Geological Model of Polymetallic Nodule Deposits in the Clarion - Clipperton Fracture Zone, ISA Technical Study No. 6, 2010.
8. Global Ocean Commission, 'Strengthening Deep Seabed Mining Regulation', Policy Option Paper #5, November 2013.
9. 'United Nations Convention on the Law of the Sea, Montego Bay', 10 December 1982. In force since November 16, 1994. United Nations Treaty Series, vol. 1833, No. 1-31363, p. 397; 21 International Legal Materials 1261 (1982).
10. The area of the world's oceans totals approximately 361.1 million sq km, which represents 71 per cent of the Earth's surface. If all coastal States were to claim a 200-nm exclusive economic zone limit, the extent of ocean areas under national jurisdiction would be approximately 109.4 million sq km, making the size of the area beyond the limits of national jurisdiction (the 'Area') approximately 251.7 million sq km or 49 per cent of the Earth's surface. Three ocean areas in the 'Area' are considered as primary areas. The Clarion-Clipperton area is between the west coast of the continental United States and Hawaii, whose size is approximately 2.5 million sq km. The second area lies in the south-western Pacific basin. This area is about 1 million sq km. The third area in the central Indian Ocean basin, is about 500,000 sq km. The pioneer site awarded to India is in this area. These three areas account for about 2 per cent of the 'Area'.

11. UNCLOS Article 136.
12. Resources, when recovered from the Area, are referred to as 'minerals'. See UNCLOS, Article 133(b).
13. Part XI contains the legal framework governing 'activities in the Area'. It consists of five sections, which detail an extremely complicated but unique regime of the Area and its institutional framework Convention, UNCLOS Articles 133 to 191.
14. Agreement relating to the implementation of Part XI of the UNCLOS of December 10, 1982; in force simce July 28, 1994. UN General Assembly resolution 48/263; 33 International Legal Materials 1309 (1994); United Nations Treaty Series, vol. 1836, No. 1-31364, p. 42.
15. For detailed discussion of the deep seabed mining provisions of the Convention and the 1994 Agreement, see Myron H. Nordquist, Satya N. Nandan et al, Ed. United Nations Convention on the Law of the Sea, 1982: A Commentary, Vol. VI (Martinus Nijhoff Publications, Dordrecht, 2003).
16. UNCLOS Article 186.
17. UNCLOS Article 187.
18. Agreement, Annex, Section 2, paragraph 4.
19. Agreement, Annex, Section 5, Paragraphs 1 and 2.
20. Section 3 (2) of the Annex to the Agreement.
21. As on March 7, 2014, there are 166 States parties to UNCLOS. The United States is one of the last remaining countries that have not ratified UNCLOS, along with Iran, Libya, North Korea, Ethiopia and Burundi.
22. UNCLOS, Articles 156, 157.
23. Under the UNCLOS, the 'Enterprise' was given extensive powers to embark on seabed mining, transportation, processing and marketing of minerals recovered in the 'Area', either on its own or jointly with willing and qualified entities, including those from developing states. See Article 170 (1) of UNCLOS.
24. UNCLOS Article 139.
25. Section 2, Part XI of the UNCLOS.
26. The basic principles GA Res. 2749 (XXV) adopted by the UN General Assembly on December 17, 1970 became the basis for development of the regime for the 'Area' and its resources at the Third United Nations Conference on the Law of the Sea.
27. UNCLOS Articles 136, 137 and 141.
28. UNCLOS Article 137 (2).
29. UNCLOS Article 140(1).
30. Beyond its functions in the 'Area', the UNCLOS also gives the ISA certain powers and functions in relation to the continental shelf beyond 200 NM. Under Article 82 (4) of the UNCLOS, the ISA is to receive the payments or contributions from coastal states having extended continental shelf. Upon receipt of the payments or contributions, the ISA is required to distribute them among State Parties on the basis of equitable sharing criteria. This in essence gives the ISA a distributive role in respect of benefits derived from a maritime zone outside that of its field of primary competence, the 'Area'.
31. Regulations on prospecting and exploration for polymetallic nodules in the Area, adopted July 13, 2000. (ISBA/6/A/18 dated October 4, 2000). Decision of the Council of the International Seabed Authority relating to amendments to the 'Regulations on prospecting and exploration for polymetallic nodules in the Area' and related matters, ISBA/19/C/17(2013).
32. Regulations on prospecting and exploration for polymetallic sulphides in the Area, adopted May 7, 2010. (ISBA/16/A/12/Rev.1 dated 15 November 2010). Also reproduced in Selected Decisions 16, pp. 35-75.

33. Regulations on Prospecting and Exploration for Cobalt-rich Ferromanganese Crusts in the Area, adopted July 27, 2012 (ISBA/18/A/11 dated 22 October 2012).
34. The Assembly is the plenary organ of the ISA consisting of all the states parties to the UNCLOS and Agreement.
35. Article 158 (1), UNCLOS.
36. Section 1, para 4 of the Annex of the Agreement.
37. Section 2, para 1 of the Annex of the Agreement.
38. UNCLOS Articles 136 and 137.
39. UNCLOS Article 160; Agreement, Annex, Section 9, Paragraph 3.
40. Agreement, Annex, Section 3, Paragraph 11(a)
41. UNCLOS Article 165, Paragraph 2(f).
42. Convention, Annex III, Article 4.
43. Annex to the Agreement relating to the Implementation of Part XI of the UNCLOS 1982, Section 3: Decision-making, para. 11(a).
44. Annex, Section 3, Paragraph 11(a).
45. Masayuki Masuda, China's Maritime Strategy and Maritime Law Enforcement Agencies: Quest for a Maritime Power, in William Tow and Tomonori Yoshizaki, ed. *Beyond the Hub and Spokes* (Tokyo: National Institute of Defence Studies, 2014), pp. 59-80.
46. Intergovernmental Oceanographic Commission, White Paper on the Development of China's Marine Programmes, National Ocean Policy, Paris, UNESCO, 2007, p. 77.
47. Brahma Chellaney, 'Tackling new maritime challenges', *The Hindu*, November 5, 2013.
48. See Masayuki Masuda, supra note, p. 61.
49. see Masayuki Masuda, supra note; Chellaney, supra note ; Xinhua, Full text of Hu Jintao's report at 18th Party Congress, November 19, 2012 is available at http://english.peopledaily.com.cn/102774/8024786.html
50. Laws, regulations and administrative measures adopted by sponsoring States and other members of the International Seabed Authority with respect to the activities in the Area, ISBA/18/C/8, 2012 p.2.
51. ISBA/A/L.6, 15 August 1995; ISBA/7/C/4, June 22, 2001.
52. Hong Nong, *UNCLOS and Dispute Settlement: Law and Politics in South China Sea* (New York: Routledge, 2012), pp. 114-117.
53. Sunil Kr. Agarwal, 'China Moves in for 'Deep-sea mining' in the Southwest Indian Ocean', August 3, 2011, http://www.maritimeindia.org/Final%20Version%20of%20the%20Commentary%20on%20ISBA.Pdf (accessed February 25, 2014).
54. Wang Qian, 'Country gets OK to mine ocean floor', *Chinadaily.com.cn*, April 30, 2014, http://www. chinadaily.com.cn/china/2014-04/30/content_17475337.htm (accessed February 25, 2014).
55. Chen Xin, Submersible dives into ocean elite of nations, *China Daily*, August 27, 2010, http:// www.chinadaily.com.cn/china/2010-08/27/content_11210450.htm (accessed February 25, 2014).
56. Chen Xin ibid.
57. *International Business Times*, June 4, 2012.
58. 'Trial dives of China's manned submersible achieves great success', *Xinhua*, June 30, 2012, http:// news.xinhuanet.com/english/china/2012-06/30/c_131686816.htm, accessed February 25, 2014.
59. 'Trial dives of China's manned submersible achieves great success' *Xinhua*, ibid.
60. Yu Mincai, 'China and the U.N. Convention on the Law of the Sea', *Contemporary International Relations*, (November/December 2012), p. 61.

61. China was granted exclusive exploration rights for polymetallic nodules in the northern Pacific Ocean in 2001, for polymetallicsulphide deposits in south-western ridge in the Indian Ocean in 2011, and for cobalt-rich ferromanganese crusts in the western Pacific Ocean in 2014.
62. For detailed commentary on India's concern over Chinese rising maritime profile in IOR; see C. Raja Mohan, China Eyes the Indian Ocean, Samudra Manthan (Oxford University Press, New Delhi: 2013), Chapter 7, pp. 109-132.
63. Nuwan Peiris, 'China, India in race to exploit Indian Ocean seabed', *The Sunday Times*, (December 15, 2013).

Index

2010 CIA World Fact Book, 18
2012 PRC Defence White Paper, 10, 13
9/11 terrorist attacks, 136

A2AD strategy, 7, 12, 21
Active defence, 25
Admiral Alfred Thayer Mahan, 11
Admiral Jonathan Greenert, Chief of Naval Operations of the US Navy, 140
Admiral Zheng He, 6, 15
Air Defence Identification Zone (ADIZ), 42, 141
Antarctic Fishing Zones, 116
Antarctica, 114, 117
    Global Commons, 115-16
    Security Issues Concern, 119
Anti Ship Ballistic Missile (ASBM), 7, 78
Arctic Council, 44, 122-24, 126, 128-30
Arctic, 115, 117, 124, 127-28
    Dew Line, 121
    Ice Station Zebra, 121
    Security
        centres, 123
        in Context, 121
        issues concern, 120
ASBM-based Area Denial, 78
ASEAN Defence Minister's Meeting Plus (ADMM+), 28
ASEAN Regional Forum, 135
ASEAN-India partnership, 8

Ban Ki Moon, UN Secretary General, 26
Bangladesh, 57-58
    China supplier of military equipment, 57
    Military Imports by, 58
BCIM (Bangladesh China India and Myanmar), 57
Becoming a maritime power, 11
Blue water, 7, 12, 95, 108, 150
Border Control Department (BCD), 15, 91
Boxer rebellion, 4

Catapult-Assisted Take-Off but Arrested Recovery (CATOBAR), 110
China Communications Construction Company (CCCC), 93
    First Harbour Consultants Limited, 93
    Second Harbour Consultants Limited, 93
China Institute for Maritime Affairs (CIMA), 91
China Maritime Surveillance (CMS), 91, 146
China Ocean Mineral Resources Research and Development Association (COMRA), 94
China Ocean Shipping Company (COSCO), 14
China Shipbuilding Industry Corporation (CSIC), 93-94, 99
China State Shipbuilding Corporation (CSSC), 93, 99
China
    arms export, 53-54
    Blue Book, 70, 71
    first civilian manned undersea vehicle, 94
    fishing industry, 18
    GDP, 51
    geo-strategic frontiers, 71
    Growing Maritime Dimension of, 38-39
    growing relevance of maritime domain, 53
    huge civilian port infrastructure, 88
    Indian Ocean Strategy, 75-78
        Diversion to Counter US Rebalance, 76
        Naval Deployments, 78
        Naval Diplomacy, 76-77
        Naval Sustenance, 77-78
        Permanent Naval Presence, 76

Two-Ocean Navy, 75
influence in South Asian Littoral, 55-60
interpreting Grand Strategy in South Asian Littorals, 61-63
Malacca Dilemma, 40
Malacca dilemma, 9
maritime patrol vessels, 149
maritime rise, 3
merchant marine, 18
military-strategic, 73
National Security, 36
near seas, 11, 21
North and South Sea Fleet, 27
offshore areas, 36-37, 41
origin military hardware, 53
peripheral diplomacy, 37
primary area of maritime interest, 71
rise, 4
second largest economy, 51
silk routes, 65
strategy in distant seas, 43
China's Naval Shipbuilding
Capability, 106-7
Aircraft Carrier,100
Amphibious Ships, 109
Ballistic Missile Test-Bed Submarine,107
Carrier Aviation,110
Destroyer Program,108
Fast Attack Craft (FAC), 109
Frigates, 108-9
Non-nuclear Submarines, 107
Nuclear Submarines, 107
Location of Shipyards, 104-5
Role of Government, 103-4
Transformation of, 105
Ancillary Support,106
Commercial Vessel Design Capability, 105
Warship Design Capability, 106
Chinese
all under the heaven, 62
defence diplomacy, 66
defence exports, 53
geo-strategic, 47
maritime
anti-smuggling force, 146
economic trends, 50
outlet for continental China, 73
power, 11
research base, 90
strategy, 7
military
activity, 80
exports, 54
naval policies, 89
ports, 87
shipbuilding industry, 99
shipyards,
confrontation, 62
engagement, 62
participation, 62
shaping the environment, 62
strategic behaviour, 61
use CAD/CAM software, 105
strategic pillars, 62-63
DIME, 62
strategic vectors, 63
string of pearls strategy, 1, 48, 49, 66, 77
Chinese Central Military Commission (CMC), 26
Chinese Coast Guard (CCG), 16, 19, 145-51
Chinese Communist Party, 35-38, 42
Chinese Oceanographic Administration (COA), 145
Clarion Clipperton Zone (CCZ), 157
Cold Conflict, 139
Cold War, 21, 62, 135, 142
Colour revolutions, 39
Common Heritage of Mankind (CHM), 123, 154, 158-60
Comprehensive national power, 6
Consecutive Congressional Research Service (CRS), 30
Counter intervention, 12
CPC Central Committee Political Bureau, 25
Crimean peninsula, 4
Cultural Revolution, 5

Dalian Maritime University, 18
Dead Weight Tonnage (DWT), 53
Deep-sea Minerals, 162
China's Quest for, 165-66
Resources, 156
Cobalt-Rich Manganese Crusts, 157-58
Polymetallic Manganese Nodules, 156-57

Polymetallic Sulphides, 157
Deep-seabed
General Principles Governing, 159-60
mining, 154
Demand signal, 13
Deng Xiaoping, 5, 51
economic reforms, 7
Distant seas protection, 43
Distant Water Fishing (DWF), 18
fishing fleet, 19
Dong Feng-21 D anti-ship ballistic missile, 7

East China Sea, 2, 11-12, 30, 37, 42, 117, 141-43, 145-46, 148-49
European Union (EU), 136
Exclusive Economic Zone (EEZ), 19, 30, 94, 121, 123-24, 126, 136-37, 146, 157-58

Far seas, 12, 13, 20, 21
forces, 14
strategy, 25
First Aid Diplomacy, 29
First island chain, 7
Fisheries Law Enforcement Command (FLEC), 16, 91, 146
Flag of convenience, 18
Freedom of Navigation, 81

General Administration of Customs (GAC), 16, 91
General Liu Huaqing, 7
Geo-political, 73
Glazer, Bonnie S, 136
Global commons, 43
Global maritime economics, 50
Globalization, 4
Goldstein, Lyle, 90, 150
Great Leap Forward, 5
Great War, 3
Guided Missile Destroyers (DDG), 17
Gulf of Aden, 14, 43-44, 76
anti-piracy mission, 43
counter-piracy exercise, 28

Hinges
geo-political destiny, 2
Holmes, James, 150
Hu Jintao, Chinese President, 9, 24, 40, 42
Humanitarian Assistance and Disaster Relief (HADR), 13, 27, 32

Illegal, unreported, and unregulated (IUU), 19
India-China relations, 142
Indian Ocean Naval Symposium (IONS), 44, 75
Indian Ocean Region (IOR), 28, 29, 31, 36, 43, 44, 70-71, 77, 156, 167
Indo-China peninsula, 135
Indo-Japanese rapport, 8
Internally Displaced Persons (IDP) rehabilitation, 59
International Maritime Organization (IMO), 114, 128
International Seabed Authority (ISA), 156
Council, 163
Powers and Functions of, 161-62
International Shipping Lanes (ISL), 73
International Tribunal for the Law of the Sea (ITLOS), 158

J N Mero, 155
J-15 air wing, 13
Japan, 7, 16, 18, 38
Jiang Zemin, 39
Jiangkai II, 14
Jiaolong (Sea Dragon), 94-95

Kaplan, Robert, 9, 70
Knight, Shannon, 90
Kolkata to Kunming (K2K) Car Rally, 57
Kondratieff Waves, 47
Kunlunshan, 15
Kurile Islands, 7

Land Attack Cruise Missiles (LACM), 14, 21
Land-based Aircraft, 78
Landing Helicopter Assault (LHA), 15
Landing Platform Docks (LPDs), 15
Lee Teng-hui, President, 39
Li Keqiang, Prime Minister, 40-41
Liang Guanglie, Defence Minister, 39
Liaoning (CV-16), 13
Liquefied Natural Gas (LNG), 99
Long cycle school, 47
Look East policy, 8
Low-tension, long-term security, 42

MacDonalds syndrome, 4
Manchuria, 5
Margaret MacMillan, 3-4
Marine Design & Research Institute of China (MARIC), 105
Maritime Safety Administration (MSA), 16, 146
Maritime Silk Road (MSR), 1-2, 9, 41, 70, 75
MARPOL Convention, 129
Middle East, 6
Military Operations Other Than War (MOOTW), 25, 30, 32
    Activities, 26
    in Indian Ocean, 28
    W's Framework, 26
        What, 26
        Where, 27
        Whither, 30
        When, 31-32
Mineral Resources
    Status of Contracts for Exploration for, 163-64
Ming Dynasty, 6
Missile Proliferation, 80
Myanmar, 1, 3, 48, 55-57
    Military Imports by, 56
Myanmar's defence expenditure, 56

National Development and Reform Commission (NDRC), 90
National People's Congress (NPC), 91
NATO/US forces, 39
Naval Research Institute (NRI), 92
Near sea, 12
Neo-realism, 2
Nominal GDP, 51
Non-combatants evacuation operations (NEO), 13
Northern Sea Route (NSR), 120

Oceanographic Administration (SOA), 146
Office of Net Assessment (ONA), 48
Offshore
    active defense, 13
    defence, 25, 43
ONGC Videsh Ltd (OVL), 8
Opium Wars, 4, 6

Pakistan
Pakistan, 1, 3, 48, 55, 60, 77
    military expenditure, 60
    military imports by, 61
    PLA package, 60
    NORINCO package, 61
Panikkar, KM, 70
Paper tiger, 5
Peaceful development, 32
People's Liberation Army (PLA), 5, 10, 13, 15, 35, 40
    Second Artillery, 12
    aircraft carriers, 14
PLA Air Force, 12
PLA Navy (PLAN), 6-8, 11-13, 19, 24, 150
    Air Force, 12-13
    counter piracy operations, 14
    doctrine, 25
    far sea operations, 15
    frigate's, 43
    intent
        in Indian Ocean, 31
        in Pacific Ocean,30
    mission harmony 2011, 33
    modernization, 30
    nuclear-attack submarine, 44
    procedures, 25
    research organisations, 93
    ship visits Post Gulf of Aden Anti-Piracy Deployment, 29-30
    ships, 32
    strategy, 25
    surface combatants, 15
    tactics, 25
    tasks, 25-27
Polar Code, 129
Professor Geoffrey Till, 11
Purchasing Power Parity (PPP), 51

Qingdao Institute of Marine Geology (QIMG), 92

Rainwater, Shiloh, 123
RAND Report, 105
Real Term, 51
Rear Admiral Qiu Yanpeng, 33
Red Dog Mine, 118

Region of the Four Seas, 52
Regional Balance of Power, 79
Regional Stability and Security, 79
Republic of China (RoC), 89
Ro-Ro ships, 105

SAR Agreement, 129
Sea Line of Communications (SLOCs), 20, 26, 30, 65, 167
Sea Power, 11
Second island chain, 7
Seychelles, 1
Shanghai Merchant Ship Design & Research Institute (SDARI), 105
Sino-Bangladesh
  bilateral relations, 57
  defence linkages, 57
Sino-Myanmar relations
  energy sector, 55
  land infrastructure, 55
  maritime, 57
  rail, 55
Sino-Pak strategic relationship, 60
  Dry Port, 60
  Gwadar Port projects, 60
  Heavy Rebuild Factory (HRF), 60
  Kamra, 60
  Karakoram Highway, 60
  Pakistan Aeronautical Complex (PAC), 60
  Taxila, 60
Sino-Soviet split, 6
Sino-Sri Lankan
  strategic partnership, 59
Sino-US relations, 4
  cold confrontation, 142
Sino-Vietnam relations, 139
SIPRI trade register, 56
Sixth Counter-Piracy Task Group, 15
South Asian Association for Regional Corporation (SAARC), 44
South China Sea, 2, 8, 11-12, 37, 42, 48, 94, 105, 122, 134-43, 145, 148
  nervous neighbourhood, 137-39
South Korean Offshore Patrol Vessels (OPV), 58
Sri Lanka, 1, 48, 55, 59
  Military Imports by, 59
  military expenditure, 59
State Oceanic Administration (SOA), 15, 91
State Peace and Development Council (SPDC), 55
Surface Forces, 78
Surface to Air Missile (SAM), 14
SWOT, 71,
  Opportunities, 75
  Strengths, 74
  Threats, 75
  Weaknesses, 74

Tellis, Ashley, 82
The Economist, 17
The Guardian, 125
The New Silk Road, 65
Tianjin Institute for Water Transport Engineering (TIWTE), 87, 92-93
Tibet and Xinjiang
  Ethnic unrest in, 39
Tibetan Plateau, 9
Twenty-foot Equivalent Unit (TEU), 53

Ukraine
  quasi-civil war in, 4
UN Convention on the Law of the Sea (UNCLOS), 19, 115, 120, 126, 156, 158-62, 166
Unequal Treaties, 4
United Nations
  International Sea Bed Authority (ISBA), 94
United Nations Commission on Trade and Development's (UNCTAD), 50
Unmanned naval systems, 95
US Energy Information Administration (EIA), 135
US Geological Survey (USGS) report, 117
US, 5, 36, 38
  Air Force, 122
  Army War College monograph, 49
  Coast Guard, 16, 122, 148
  Congress, 30
  Department of Defence (DoD), 48, 121
  EEZ off Guam, 82
  in first Gulf War, 39
  influence in Pacific region, 30
  National Oceanographic and Atmospheric Administration (NOAA), 128

naval hegemony in the pacific, 30
naval vessels, 151
Navy 'Arctic Roadmap', 122
rebalance to Asia, 43

Vertical or Short Takeoff and Landing (VSTOL), 15
Victim mentality, 4
Vietnamese EEZ, 8

Weapons of Mass Destruction (WMD), 80-81
World Trade Organisation (WTO), 52
World War I, 3
World War II, 5, 88
Wright, David Curtis, 123

Xi Jinping, Chinese President, 1, 10, 19, 25-26, 37, 40, 41, 48, 165
China's Dream, 11